New Trends in the Use of Artificial Intelligence for the Industry 4.0

Edited by Luis Romeral Martínez, Roque A. Osornio Rios and Miguel Delgado Prieto

Published in London, United Kingdom

IntechOpen

Supporting open minds since 2005

New Trends in the Use of Artificial Intelligence for the Industry 4.0
http://dx.doi.org/10.5772/intechopen.86015
Edited by Luis Romeral Martínez, Roque A. Osornio Rios and Miguel Delgado Prieto

Contributors
Eva M. Urbano, Victor Martinez-Viol, Joaquim Minguella-Canela, Irene Buj Corral, Francisco Arellano Espitia, Lucia Ruiz Soto, Juan Jose Saucedo-Dorantes, Arturo Yosimar Jaen-Cuellar, David Alejandro Elvira-Ortiz, Xavier Domingo, Francesc Bonada, Lluis Echeverria Rovira, Gabriel Anzaldi, Cecilio Angulo, Alejandro Chacón, Pere Ponsa, Saeid Sadeghi Darvazeh, Iman Raeesi Vanaei, Farzaneh Mansouri Musolu, Germano Lambert-Torres, Erik Leandro Bonaldi, Levy Ely Oliveira, Vitor Almeida Bernardes, Luiz Eduardo Borges Da Silva, Jyri Rajamäki, Petra Tuppela, Alberto Cerezo-Narváez, Alejandro Javier Sánchez-Sotano, Jorge Salguero-Gómez, Andres Pastor-Fernandez, Francisco Abad-Fraga

First published in London, United Kingdom, 2020 by IntechOpen
IntechOpen is the global imprint of INTECHOPEN LIMITED, registered in England and Wales, registration number: 11086078, 7th floor, 10 Lower Thames Street, London, EC3R 6AF, United Kingdom
Printed in Croatia

British Library Cataloguing-in-Publication Data
A catalogue record for this book is available from the British Library

Additional hard and PDF copies can be obtained from orders@intechopen.com

New Trends in the Use of Artificial Intelligence for the Industry 4.0
Edited by Luis Romeral Martínez, Roque A. Osornio Rios and Miguel Delgado Prieto
p. cm.
Print ISBN 978-1-83880-141-0
Online ISBN 978-1-83880-142-7
eBook (PDF) ISBN 978-1-83880-466-4

An electronic version of this book is freely available, thanks to the support of libraries working with Knowledge Unlatched. KU is a collaborative initiative designed to make high quality books Open Access for the public good. More information about the initiative and links to the Open Access version can be found at www.knowledgeunlatched.org

For EU product safety concerns:
IN TECH d.o.o., Prolaz Marije Krucifikse Kozulić 3, 51000 Rijeka, Croatia, info@intechopen.com or visit our website at intechopen.com.

Meet the editors

Luis Romeral Martínez received his electrical engineering degree and a PhD from the Technical University of Catalonia (UPC), Barcelona, Spain, in 1985 and 1995 respectively. In 1988 he joined the Electronic Engineering Department of the UPC, where he is currently a professor. In 2001 he headed the foundation of Motion Control and Industrial Applications (MCIA) as a research group of the UPC. Since then, he occupies the Director's position. He is advisor of multiple theses and he has coauthored more than 350 peer-reviewed papers published in technical journals and conference proceedings. His research and technology transfer activity covers industrial maintenance, industrial electronics, energy efficiency and mechatronics.

Roque A. Osornio Rios received a PhD in Mechatronics from the Autonomous University of Queretaro, Queretaro, Mexico, in 2007. Dr. Osornio-Rios is a Level 3 National Researcher with the Mexican Council of Science and Technology (CONACYT). He is currently a head professor wit h the University of Queretaro, Mexico. He is advisor for more than 100 theses, and coauthor of more than 140 technical papers published in international journals and conferences. His fields of interest include hardware signal processing applied to mechatronics and power quality monitoring. Dr. Osornio-Rios is a fellow of the Mexican Academy of Engineering. He is also a member of the editorial board of the *Journal of Scientific and Industrial Research*.

M. Delgado Prieto received a PhD in Electronics Engineering from the Technical University of Catalonia, UPC, Barcelona, Spain, in 2012. Since 2008 he has worked as a researcher with the Motion Control and Industrial Applications Research Center (MCIA) and a teaching assistant in the Electronic Engineering Department at UPC. He is advisor of several theses and he has coauthored more than 75 peer-reviewed papers published in technical journals and conference proceedings. Currently, he is involved in technology transfer and project management activities around condition-based monitoring and the Internet of Things for the industry, energy and transport sectors.

Contents

Preface **XI**

Section 1
Cyber Physical Applications **1**

Chapter 1 **3**
Trends of Digital Transformation in the Shipbuilding Sector
by Alejandro Sánchez-Sotano, Alberto Cerezo-Narváez, Francisco Abad-Fraga, Andrés Pastor-Fernández and Jorge Salguero-Gómez

Chapter 2 **27**
Energy Infrastructure of the Factory as a Virtual Power Plant: Smart Energy Management
by Eva M. Urbano and Víctor Martínez Viol

Chapter 3 **49**
Novel Methods Based on Deep Learning Applied to Condition Monitoring in Smart Manufacturing Processes
by Francisco Arellano Espitia and Lucia Ruiz Soto

Chapter 4 **63**
Smart Monitoring Based on Novelty Detection and Artificial Intelligence Applied to the Condition Assessment of Rotating Machinery in the Industry 4.0
by Saucedo-Dorantes Juan Jose, Jaen-Cuellar Arturo Yosimar and Elvira-Ortiz David Alejandro

Section 2
AI Technologies and Tools **77**

Chapter 5 **79**
AI for Improving the Overall Equipment Efficiency in Manufacturing Industry
by Francesc Bonada, Lluís Echeverria, Xavier Domingo and Gabriel Anzaldi

Chapter 6 **101**
Decision Support Models for the Selection of Production Strategies in the Paradigm of Digital Manufacturing, Based on Technologies, Costs and Productivity Levels
by Joaquim Minguella-Canela and Irene Buj Corral

Chapter 7 127
Developing Cognitive Advisor Agents for Operators in Industry 4.0
by Alejandro Chacón, Cecilio Angulo and Pere Ponsa

Section 3
IIoT and Data Analytics 143

Chapter 8 145
Current Transducer for IoT Applications
by Erik Leandro Bonaldi, Levy Ely de Lacerda de Oliveira, Germano Lambert-Torres, Luiz Eduardo Borges da Silva and Vitor Almeida Bernardes

Chapter 9 165
How the Data Provided by IIoT Are Utilized in Enterprise Resource Planning: A Multiple-Case Study of Three Change Projects
by Jyri Rajamäki and Petra Tuppela

Chapter 10 175
Big Data Analytics and Its Applications in Supply Chain Management
by Saeid Sadeghi Darvazeh, Iman Raeesi Vanani and Farzaneh Mansouri Musolu

Preface

Industry 4.0 is based on the cyber-physical transformation of processes, systems and methods applied in the manufacturing sector, and on its autonomous and decentralized operation. Industry 4.0 reflects that the industrial world is at the beginning of the so-called Fourth Industrial Revolution, characterized by a massive interconnection of assets and the integration of human operators with the manufacturing environment, including supply chain, markets, other intelligent factories and logistics systems.

Indeed, information management, from data generation to decision-making, represents one of the main pillars to support a viable deployment of Industry 4.0. In this regard, data analytics and, specifically, artificial intelligence is the vehicular technology towards the next generation of smart factories.

By digitizing and interconnecting the industrial environment, it is possible to create virtual clones of the factory and its processes for the improvement of production and operational efficiency. Research and development of the techniques and methods associated with cyber-physical systems are based on the modelling and processing data collected by connected sensors and actuators. In particular, this data is integrated by software, artificial intelligence and big data–based algorithms for the development of advanced monitoring and control applications. This data is used to develop optimum decision-making, control, predictive maintenance and management algorithms for both industrial processes and assets.

This foreseen flexibility in production does not focus on a replacement for labour, but rather on a return to the people as the centre of production. In fact, automated production based on intelligent agents will impact in a new way on human intervention in the industry, increasingly oriented to knowledge and not to standardization and repetition independent of the complexity of the task. This evolution will promote the reconciliation of people with work, facilitating time management while increasing productivity.

In this regard, selected authors have been invited to contribute with their original research work as well as providing literature review articles that illustrate the current efforts that are taking place towards the related technologies, the artificial intelligence and the deployment of cyber-physical systems.

Thus, in this book, three sections are considered.

The first section includes current applications which reflect the increased demands over the cyber-physical technologies highly related with the digital transformation of industrial processes. Chapters cover design, organization, monitoring, optimization and control applications from different perspectives such as industrial sectors, specific industrial infrastructures and industrial machinery and processes.

The second section is focused on artificial intelligence technologies and tools enabling cyber-physical applications. Indeed, the machine learning and its supervised and unsupervised approaches for regression, classification and data mining represent the basis of the required data-driven methodologies and procedures. Chapters discuss smart manufacturing applications, predictive analytics procedures, decision support models and cognitive advisors, as well as their performance when applied to different industrial scenarios for a positive impact in characteristic key performance indicators.

Finally, the third section complements the use of artificial intelligence in Industry 1.0 from the deployment of the Industrial Internet of Things and related data analytics. Chapters consider the ubiquity of measurements through sensor networks and their integration with different data analytics procedures at different levels of computer-integrated manufacturing system in a industry.

The included chapters in this book show a diversity of current and new developments in the use of artificial intelligence on the industrial sector seen from the fourth industrial revolution point of view, namely, the cyber-physical applications, the artificial intelligence technologies and tools, Industrial Internet of Things and data analytics. This book contains high-quality chapters containing original research results and literature review of exceptional merit. Thus, it is in the aim of this book to contribute to the literature of the topic in this regard and let the readers know current and new trends in the use of artificial intelligence for the Industry 4.0.

Roque A. Osornio Rios, PhD
Faculty of Engineering,
Autonomous University of Querétaro,
San Juan del Río, Mexico

Luis Romeral Martínez, PhD and Miguel Delgado Prieto, PhD
Electronic Engineering Department,
Technical University of Catalonia,
Barcelona, Spain

Section 1

Cyber Physical Applications

Chapter 1

Trends of Digital Transformation in the Shipbuilding Sector

Alejandro Sánchez-Sotano, Alberto Cerezo-Narváez, Francisco Abad-Fraga, Andrés Pastor-Fernández and Jorge Salguero-Gómez

Abstract

The new paradigms of Industry 4.0 force all the industrial sectors to face a deep digital transformation in order to be on the edge in a competitive and globalized scenario. Following this trend, the shipbuilding industry has to establish its own path to adapt itself to the digital era. This chapter aims to explore this challenge and give an outlook on the multiple transformative technologies that are involved. For that reason, a case of study is presented as a starting point, in which the digital technologies that can be applied are easily recognized. A social network analysis (SNA) is developed among these key enabling technologies (KETs), in order to stress their correlations and links. As a result, artificial intelligence (AI) can be highlighted as a support to the other technologies, such as vertical integration of naval production systems (e.g., connectivity, Internet of things, collaborative robotics, etc.), horizontal integration of value networks (e.g., cybersecurity, diversification, etc.), and life cycle reengineering (e.g., drones, 3D printing (3DP), virtual and augmented reality, remote sensing networks, robotics, etc.).

Keywords: digital transformation, key enabling technologies, shipbuilding 4.0, Industry 4.0, artificial intelligence, complex projects

1. Introduction

In the twenty-first century, industrial organizations are expanding their business lines to offer maintenance, repair, and checkup services related to their products, as well as technical support, and are paying more and more attention to these services [1]. In this environment, shipyards nowadays comprise of designing, engineering and building, procurement and logistics, assembling and commissioning, as well as maintaining and repairing and transforming and advancement of vessels and marine equipment, among many others.

Ships, ferries, and offshore platforms are complex products with long service lives and high costs of construction, manning, operating, maintaining, and repairing [2]. In addition, these are usually built to order and involve complex production processes, with large-scale but short series production, high degree of customization, and intensive labor. In return, they provide high value-added but requiring large and fixed capital investments although they have long life cycles [3]. However, most of them do not always evolve in line with the development of the latest technology [4].

Due to the aforementioned context, productivity in shipbuilding sector is developing slower than other manufacturing industries. Many factors may be identified as the root causes for this lack of timing, as companies are focusing on their short-term profits, usually ignoring outside benchmarks. This creates a barrier to change, in addition of conservative regulations, that makes difficult the entry of disruptive innovations, causing a lack in terms of competitiveness [5].

This lack of productivity, which affects project-based industries (as shipbuilding), has been steadily discussed by both academics and practitioners [6–8], which have been suggesting and proposing measures to increase their performance. At an early stage, innovative working methods from better organization of the processes are involved [9], such as the promotion of a more efficient split of work in order to improve the coordination within and across companies involved through the supply chain [10]. Then, due to the introduction of the Industry 4.0 paradigm, emerging technological capacities, to design better products, improve the efficiency of their services, and offer new value-added processes, were applied. As a consequence, self-managed processes, people, machines, and systems are communicating and cooperating [11].

To achieve the Industry 4.0 paradigm, a number of key enabling technologies (KETs) are used. These technologies, both from real and virtual world, were first described by the Boston Consulting Group [12]. With the aim of transforming the current production system, technologies like autonomous robots, additive manufacturing, horizontal and vertical integration, Big Data, Internet of things, cybersecurity, cloud, augmented reality, and simulation were included.

In addition to the initial set of KETs, other technologies, such as autonomous guided vehicles [13], blockchain (BCH) [14], or artificial intelligence (AI) [15], own a great potential to be crucial in the digital transformation of industries. Particularly, a European Commission report [16] arises the AI as a transverse technology both to be applied in software-based systems (virtual world) and be embedded in hardware devices (real world). Using data gathered from the available sources, the integration of the AI with the other KETs will improve overall performance through better automatic decision-making based on analyzed data.

This chapter is structured as follows: Section 2 presents the objectives of the research. Section 3 develops the literature review. Section 4 relates the research method. Section 5 describes its implementation in a case study. Section 6 shows its findings, discussing the results obtained. Section 7 concludes the chapter, summarizing the contributions and proposing further research.

2. Objectives

The main purpose of this research is to explore the challenge of facing a deep digital transformation by the shipbuilding industry, in order to be on the edge in a competitive and globalized scenario. This chapter also aims to give an outlook on the multiple and transformative technologies that are involved, analyzing the importance of the digital transformation (digitalization, automation, exploitation, and integration) in complex projects and its application in the context of Industry 4.0, discussing the results of its potential implantation.

For that reason, a case of study is presented as a starting point, in which digital technologies applied are recognized. Afterwards, a social network analysis (SNA) is developed, in order to highlight the correlations and links between KETs, aiming to confirm the AI as a support to the others. Among those, vertical integration of production systems, horizontal integration of value networks, and life cycle reengineering are stressed. The research framework is summarized in **Figure 1**.

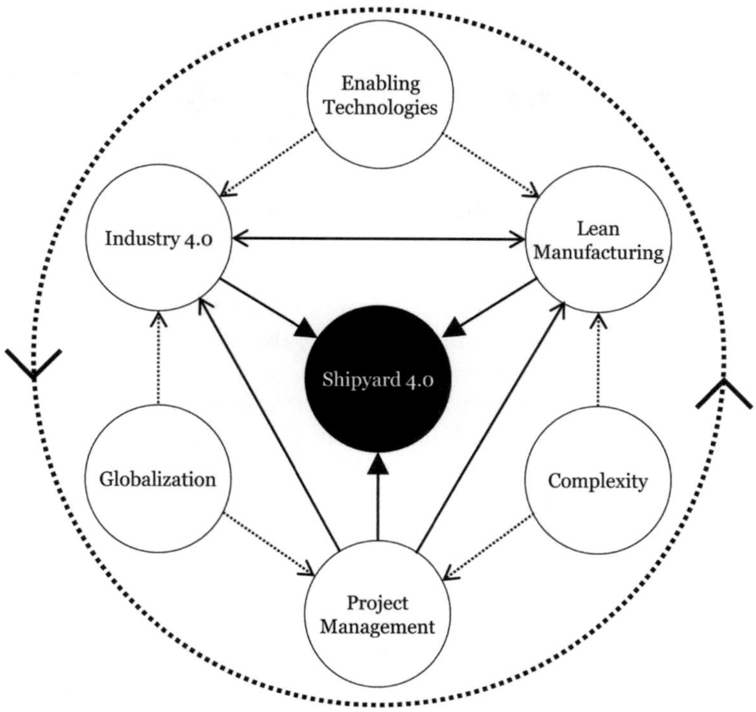

Figure 1.
Research framework.

3. Literature review

The shipbuilding sector is characterized by complex manufacturing processes, with a wide range of involved elements, low-volume serial production, and results of a high added value [17]. Faced with unpredictable conditions and intense competitors, the sector is forced to restructure its long-term objectives [18], as the most dynamic shipyards, which show a greater adaptation to the global market, get better results. In order to achieve this, they adopt research, development, and innovation (RDI) philosophies, launching bold business initiatives to counter these uncertainties using technology-driven practices that create infrastructure and empowerment, preparing them for the upcoming challenges [19].

3.1 Complexity in shipbuilding projects

Complexity is the property of projects that make them difficult to understand, foresee, and keep under control their overall behavior, even when given reasonably complete information about the system [20]. Every project has a degree of complexity, becoming one of the most important factors of their failure. Furthermore, project complexity presents additional challenges to achieve objectives, although some significant indicators can be chosen to measure and asses it [21], such as compliance and authorization, project organization, targets, resources, change orders, technology familiarity, and location, among others.

The two most common types of complexity within projects concern the organization and the technology [22]. Organizational complexity is caused by the engagement of several diverse and separate organizations for a limited period of time (both suppliers and consultants as well as temporary structures to manage the projects), depending on the hierarchical structures and organizational units [23].

In contrast, technological projects depend on the result produced, mainly due to the diversity of tasks [24]. Furthermore, although complexity is usually expressed by the means of cost, duration, or people involved, these criteria do not correlate well with how they are managed [25].

In summary, complex projects consist of ambiguity and uncertainty, interdependency, nonlinearity, unique local conditions, autonomy, emergent behaviors, and unfixed boundaries. According to these properties, projects can be classified as simple, complicated, chaotic, and complex [26]. On the other hand, complex projects are also influenced by significant external changes [27], from misaligned stakeholders' view of success, in which current tools and decision processes are unsuitable for analyze it. To respond positively to this complexity, it is necessary to imply both organizations and practitioners [28].

It can be noticed that complex projects undertaken by traditional methods, practices, and frameworks usually result inadequate in terms of scale, rate of change, heterogeneity, multiple pathways, and ambiguous objectives [29]. In this context, project management decouples and modularizes the complexity, freezing its components and controlling the variability associated [30]. In addition, the understanding of project complexity helps to identify problems, develop the business case and choice processes, and improve managerial capacities [31].

Increasing competitiveness on product quality, cost, and delivery while maintaining flexibility during the whole project (including design, engineering, and production) are a few of the challenges that many organizations currently encounter in the shipbuilding industry [32]. In settings of complex projects (as those from shipbuilding sector), the ability to make proper decisions when solving problems is essential in the production efficiency of the derived operations. In this context, shipyards must face these challenges from a combination of constraints, among which the technical level of their production facilities and the practices, techniques, and tools at the disposal of their staff stand out [33].

3.2 Lean manufacturing in the shipbuilding sector

Lean manufacturing has been the most remarkable methodology for improving the operational performance in manufacturing organizations in the last two decades [34], increasing their productivity and decreasing their costs [35]. Lean manufacturing helps industrial companies to transform themselves in order to add higher value, due to the use of a considerable set of tools, methodologies, and procedures focused on boost their performance [36], waste reduction, and better communication. This combination of information acquisition and management with new design and manufacturing techniques allows companies to redirect towards new trends that respond quickly to market changes [37]. If new features must be introduced to meet these demands, companies cannot compromise their efficiency. In fact, they will try to improve it despite these challenges [38].

There are different points of view in the literature related to how lean manufacturing and Industry 4.0 interact together to influence the performance of processes involved. Some studies suggest that lean manufacturing is a mediator of their relationship [39, 40], while other suggests that Industry 4.0 is a moderator [41]. Others investigate their supportive effects without hypothesizing which of the two is the moderator [42, 43], and even other studies emphasized the interaction between them in many contexts, depending on industry and company size [44].

If shipbuilding manufacturers want to operate with lean production principles, they must establish the shipbuilding project management plan based on optimized production and overall resource balance, decomposing product tasks according to zone, stage, and type and clarifying the relationship between tasks and resources [45]. In this context, Industry 4.0 opportunities are used as a methodological and strategic tool to accelerate the engagement of shipbuilding suppliers. In these cases, lean tools mostly aim to introduce and motivate the implementation of these concepts into practice through the entire supply chain, whereby the objectives are needed to be fully understood and cross-functional teams are expected to be active in the value stream creation [46]. However, other requirements are needed, as design and assembly building methods [47].

If arbitrariness and uncertainty (affecting quality, production, operation, and logistics) are not faced, low productivity and management efficiency are the most probable result. To successfully address these challenges, shipbuilding companies must enhance their technology and management innovation, as well as actively adopt advanced production systems, for improving their efficiency [48].

3.3 Industry 4.0 in the shipbuilding sector

Industry 4.0 is a vital evolution for the survival of any industrial organization. Particularly those which target global markets, pursue a strategic distinction that supports the necessary excellence in their deliverables [49]. This implies a top-down transformation that applies to a wide range of methods, tools, and techniques involved in production management, improved processes and workplaces, and developing staff's skills [50]. Industry 4.0 modernizes the organizational processes and makes them more efficient. This involves the entire company, from operational to strategic management. In this competitive context, industrial companies need to redesign their strategies, enabling not only better resource allocation but also infrastructure investment and quality systems [51].

Industrial companies aiming to reach flexible manufacturing, with very low waste and high quality in their deliverables, are constantly evolving, in order to set them apart from their competitors. In that sense, they try to get higher levels of efficiency and productivity, associating new technologies within their processes. This use of disruptive methodologies helps them to create value, connecting and sharing information between companies and customers [52] and increasing also their applied innovation to offer complete solutions [53].

Among the Industry 4.0's main points of interest for the shipbuilding industry are artificial intelligence (pattern recognition, process automation, simulation, etc.), compatibility systems and task reassignment (occupational health and safety, decision-making, etc.), virtual and augmented reality, additive manufacturing and Internet of things, and more, specifically, the automatic generation of timelines, the creation of mathematical analysis models and evaluation of production processes, the integration of high-quality algorithms with computer-aided design (CAD) and with product life cycle management systems (PLM). In this context, the digital transformation of the shipbuilding industry optimizes the production and the operational efficiency, through the analysis and integration of storing, connecting, and organizing the information generated by different sources [17, 54].

This necessary transformation has led the shipbuilding sector to adopt the concept of Industry 4.0. The concept of "Shipyard 4.0" [55] is described as the result of the application of the Industry 4.0 to this sector. The Shipyard 4.0 involves deep changes in the shipyard production system including facilities, advanced product design, management changes, and the implementation of the digital technologies. Therefore, the Shipyard 4.0 initiative has to be the response of the shipbuilding sector to the digital transformation.

4. Case study

This research has opted for a case study since there is almost no previous research on the topic and the empirical observations are insufficient to turn it into a quantitative study. Probably, this is expected mainly due to confidentiality and competitive reasons. Companies do not tend to share the information that would be required for a more extensive analysis. In fact, when there is only limited theoretical knowledge, an inductive strategy leads to an emerging theory from a case study which can be a good starting point [56].

Building a theory from a case study is a research strategy that involves using the case to create theoretical constructions, propositions, and/or empirical evidence of midrange theory [57]. If a theoretical sampling of a single case is chosen, they must be unusually revelatory and extremely exemplar or represent unique opportunities to acquire research insights [58].

The case company is Navantia, a Spanish state-owned (and worldwide as well) reference in the design, construction, and integration of high technology military and civilian naval platforms [19]. Navantia is an ETO manufacturer that offers design, engineering, manufacturing, and project management of products (e.g., frigates, aircraft carriers, submarines, patrol vessels, logistic ships, defense systems, and wind power) and services (e.g. life support, repairs, maintenance, modernization, training, and simulation) [59]. Navantia has facilities in Spain and Australia. It also has offices in Brazil, India, Norway, Saudi Arabia, Turkey, and the USA.

The organization model applied by the company is mostly a line organization, in which department leaders are part of the project team and allocate tasks to their own staff on a periodic basis type with only a few people allocated specifically per each project. However, this type of organization is not usually associated with engineering to order contexts, where large and complex project environments have already been usually adopted [60].

Navantia is immersed in a major transformation process directed towards to increase the company sustainability in the twenty-first century market, in which technological innovation and digitalization are essential to change, encompassing all areas of the organization. The key to transformation lies not only in the implementation of innovative solutions but also in the transformation of processes and people themselves: a more agile organization, an interactive management culture, and a renewed talent management, both internally and externally, are fundamental to success [61]. Since 2015, Navantia has been striving to shape digitalization in the shipbuilding sector. This new concept of the connected Industry 4.0 emphasizes the exploitation of the potential of new technologies based on product and service innovation, client-centric approach, data value, and operational excellence.

Navantia's Shipyard 4.0 concept includes processes and products, which are integrated to operate ecologically, efficiently, and flexibly, and has an advantage over traditional systems, which are based on [62]:

- Vertical integration of the shipbuilding production processes (connectivity, additive manufacturing, Internet of things (IoT), radiofrequency, collaborative robotics, etc.), to guarantee production that is safe, fast, and adapted to the context, with a better price-performance ratio, operates online, consumes less energy, and better protects the environment

- Horizontal integration of value creation networks (cybersecurity, innovation, diversification, etc.), to attend to the needs of the interested parties in an integrated way, responding individually to them

- Reengineering of the value chain (drones, 3D/4D printing, artificial intelligence (AI), virtual and augmented reality (VAR), remote sensing networks, robotics, etc.), introducing changes that affect the lifecycle

Navantia's transformation involves an improvement in its tools and processes throughout the value chain and renewing its production centers, fully integrating them in a new digital ecosystem: the Shipyard 4.0. This change to smart factories is carried out focusing on equipment and products, applications, the company itself, and people as the main field of action [61]. At the moment, Navantia consider 13 KETs, as shown in **Figure 2**. Through these technologies, which are described below, the company is facing the digital transformation in different areas of the system and manufacturing process, regardless of whether new emerging technologies can also be introduced in the future.

4.1 Navantia key enabling technologies

4.1.1 3D printing (3DP)

3D printing is a new manufacturing process which is also known as additive manufacturing. It consists on the manufacturing of a part adding material layer by layer. This technology is getting a lot of attention nowadays, and it is expected

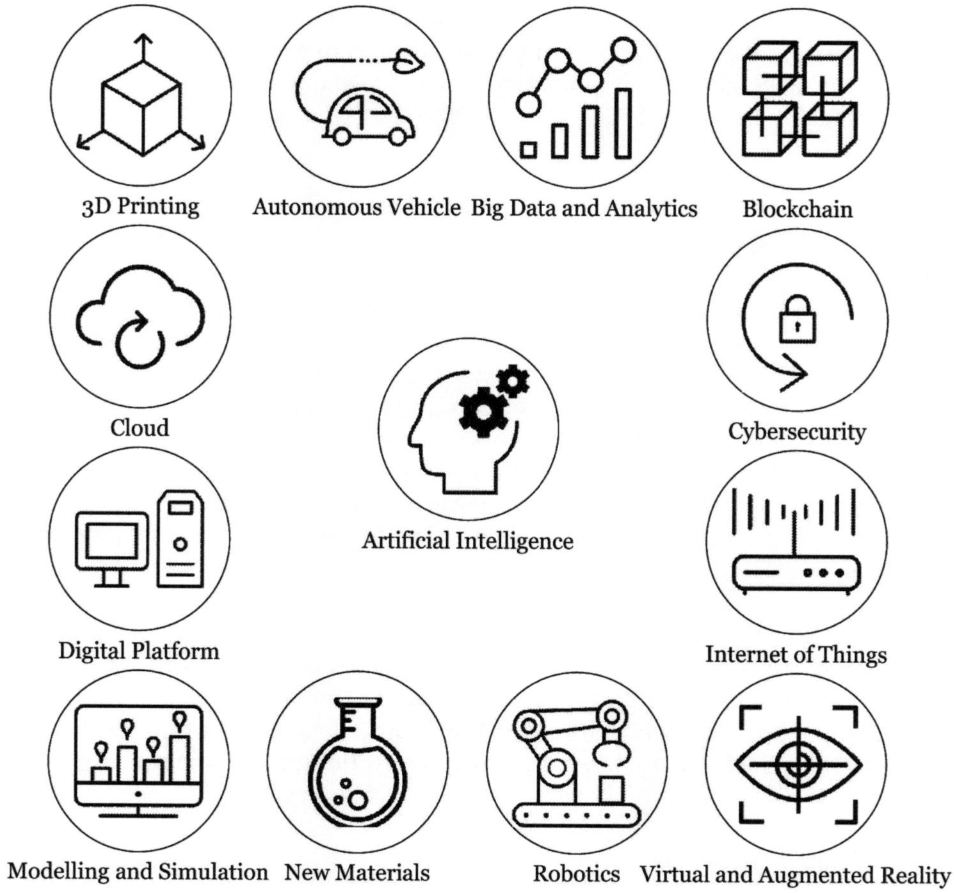

Figure 2.
Key enabling technologies by Navantia. Based on [61].

to become a major revolution in different industrial sectors. Particularly, in the shipbuilding industry, there are recent studies in which they use a polymeric-based additive manufacturing technology [63]. This technology is being used to make large, nonstructural parts, reducing the overall manufacturing costs, which also reduces the manufacturing time.

On the other hand, wire arc additive manufacturing (WAAM) technology is also under research. In this case, the polymer is replaced by a metal wire melt due to the heat produced by an electric arc [64]. This technology has the potential to replace components of the vessels which still needs to be made of metal, reducing the manufacturing costs. This assumption leads to the inevitable redesign of the ship to evaluate which parts are able to change its manufacturing technology. Therefore, it is clear that this technology still needs other changes to have the impact it is supposed to have.

4.1.2 Autonomous guided vehicles (AGV)

Autonomous guided vehicles are used for processing and transporting goods inside a factory environment [65]. They are considered smart due to their capability onboard of making decentralized decision to avoid collisions and stablish the best path planning possible to reach its destination.

Therefore, the technology of the autonomous guided vehicles makes the smart factory possible due to the flexible logistic and transport of materials within the workshop. Its application mainly affects the internal supply chain, with the aim of delivering components just in time, which has implications with the lean manufacturing system and a direct impact on the overall performance. The use of these technologies, along with simulation and artificial intelligence [13], makes the decision-making more reliable.

4.1.3 Big Data analytics (BDA)

The growing expansion of the information available due to the evolution of systems, digital products, and the development of the IoT has introduced the concept of Big Data. These are technologies which allow the capture, aggregation, and processing of the amount of the ever-growing data received by the different systems [66]. This volume of data is increasing at higher speed than the previous technologies which were capable of processing and getting valuable information of it. For that reason, the Big Data analytics is needed.

Big Data analytics is the set of techniques that make the vast amount of information generated by the other KETs manageable. At the same time, it models the data in order to get knowledge, supporting the decision-making process and even generating new solutions [66].

This amount of data, mainly gathered by sensors and the IoT, is usually storage and can be analyzed in the cloud (in real time or later) [67], which makes a very close relationship between these three technologies. Moreover, Big Data analytics has implications with other KETs too, such as additive manufacturing [68], AI [69], or simulation [70], which make the Big Data analytics one of the core driver technologies of the Industry 4.0, having also connections in the shipbuilding industry [71].

4.1.4 Blockchain (BCH)

Blockchain is a technology that can be used in any digital transaction that ends up taking place in the future Shipyard 4.0. As it is a decentralized data base in which all data are checked and confirmed by different actors before adding new information ("blocks") to the data chain, this technology improves tracking and reliability of the information due to the impossibility to change isolated information [72].

Blockchain has capabilities to promote resilience, scalability, security, autonomy, and trustworthiness [14] to every information exchange. Therefore, applications in the supply chain operation can take advantage of this technology through the smart contracts, increasing the automation and avoiding the use of intermediaries [73].

4.1.5 Cloud

The cloud is essentially a network infrastructure that supports the interconnection of Industry 4.0 through servers and cloud computing technologies [74]. It allows large data applications such as storage space, computing capacity, and resource sharing, among others. It also provides worldwide access to the information accordingly with specific access type and service provided, which can be split in different layers, named as infrastructure as a service (IaaS), platform as a service (PaaS), and software as a service (SaaS), granting different kinds of access to the cloud [75].

As the industry becomes increasingly digital in manufacturing environments, the cloud computing concept has evolved into cloud manufacturing, in which users can request services during the whole lifecycle of the product. This is a change of mind-set for industrial companies as the approach differs from the previous production-oriented to the newly service-oriented concept of manufacturing, increasing flexibility during the design process [75].

Due to the remote access to the information and the application of cyber-physical systems in distributed manufacturing systems, the concept of collaborative cloud manufacturing is possible. This means that organizations with different production units connected through a collaborative network are able to synchronize themselves, multiplying the overall capacities without further investment [76]. According to this, the cloud has a fundamental role in the smart factory concept for the shipbuilding industry, in which complex projects that are undertaken in long-term can reduce the overall production time to meet on-demand expectations.

4.1.6 Cybersecurity (CS)

The huge amount of information that is sent from different devices to the cloud and backwards creates new opportunities and vulnerabilities to the industrial companies. This scenario compromises confidential information due to the banishment of the physical boundaries [77]. For this reason, the evolution of security towards the virtual world is needed, giving birth to the cybersecurity, which aims to increase the security levels in IoT environments.

The cybersecurity, by definition, is a process consisting three objectives: to protect, detect, and respond to cyber-attacks [78]. Particularly, the two main objectives are the ones that rely on data protection and are given more attention since Internet of things networks have to be built in a safe environment that allows a safe interoperability between the facilities. But not only the information is at risk. As the manufacturing units are connected to the network, they can also be shut down, change its normal behavior, or even modify the product design. All of these factors lead to an enormous economic loss and should therefore be avoided [79].

In summary, this technology needs to be addressed and takes an important role in the context of any enterprise, which aims to carry a deep digital transformation out. To achieve a successful smart factory, the concept of "security by design" is mandatory in which both, data and cyber-physical systems, are adequately protected [77].

4.1.7 Digital platform (DP)

The digital platform is the answer that Navantia has given to the horizontal and vertical integration. Horizontal and vertical integrations involve every stakeholder that takes part in the production process, including marketing, supply chain operations, or engineering, among others. Referring to each integration to the intercompany or intracompany, respectively, the global output is a real-time data sharing among every part implied in the process [75].

To make this integration possible, a digital platform, aided by cloud computing, is the perfect answer to gather all the agents, both from the supplier or the client, as it can be accessed remotely from different geographical areas to collaborate in the process, updating the information needed in real time and resulting in a fully updated system, which can give further information according to all the data received. Therefore, Big Data analytics and cybersecurity are also connected with the digital platform.

4.1.8 Internet of things (IoT)

The IoT refers to the connectivity of every device within a network that is able to generate data from sensors or embedded electronic devices, which are sent afterwards to the cloud through a transmission system [80]. As every "thing" is generating data, the connection between IoT and Big Data analytics is clear. This technology also includes the concept of cyber-physical systems, being the gateway to fuse the real world with the virtual world, bringing physical objects into the network.

In the industrial sector, the application of the IoT is known as the industrial Internet of things, having particular implications and principles that must be fulfilled [81]. These principles include, among others, interoperability, wireless communication, decentralization, real-time feedback, or system-wide security to avoid outsider's intromission, which can put all the data on risk. In this way, cybersecurity technology acquires an important role in protecting the industrial environment.

A study on the implications this technology can handle in complex engineering projects, namely, the ones carried out in the shipbuilding industry, is also under investigation [82]. This research concludes that it is possible to create a "digital construction site" for shipbuilding, in which the IoT plays a strategic role as it is being used in specific applications.

4.1.9 Modeling and simulation (M&S)

By definition, a simulation is the imitation of the operation of a real-world process or system over time. Simulation involves the generation of an artificial history of the system and the observation of that artificial history to draw inferences concerning the operating characteristics of the real system that is represented [83]. Therefore, almost any real world can be modeled into the virtual one, in order to study and predict its behavior after developing and applying specific events. In this way, many kinds of simulations appear, each regarding one different area of study [84].

Although Industry 4.0 represents a new paradigm, this can be also accomplished by simulation. Due to high levels of digitization and the increased integration of the whole product lifecycle, the traditional stand-alone simulations are not able to fulfill those new requirements.

In this challenging scenario, the concept of digital twin appears, which consists of the digital representation of an asset that can alter its properties and behavior by information and data [85]. This is the result of adopting a system design approach, which allows to train on a virtual machine and to identify potential issues with the real machine if it is combined with a model predictive analysis, deep learning, and AI. Besides, this enables to optimize its own performance, because it will be able to predict faults and coordinate with other machines, thanks to machine-to-machine interaction.

These technologies are being applied also in the shipbuilding industry, in which CAD/CAM/CAE solutions are already in use; meanwhile, discrete event simulation as the previous step of the digital twin is under development. Moreover, the application of finite element methods for new materials is also a technology with a huge potential to advance them.

4.1.10 New materials (NM)

The development of new materials, such as those based on composite carbon fiber- and fiber-reinforced plastic, polymers, or new metal alloys [86], facilitates to redesign the shipbuilding sector's product to add or replace several components. The use of these materials can offer a weight reduction, leading to a decrease in fuel consumption, which would end up making the vessels eco-friendlier.

The advantages of introducing these materials can also strengthen the corrosion resistance [87]. This can be achieved thanks to the use of new materials which are resistant to the corrosive action of salt water, leading to an increase in the added value of the ships provided.

4.1.11 Robotics (robot)

The robotics is one of those technologies from the third industrial revolution that holds a paradigm change with this new industrial revolution. In that sense, the manufacturing paradigm, from mass production towards customized production, makes the robots need to be more flexible and autonomous [75]. On the other hand, the use of advanced sensors makes the integration between robot and operator possible, resulting in collaborative robots or cobots [88].

Despite this technology is mostly used to undertake very easy repetitive actions, like in a production line, advanced shipyards have achieved to introduce this technology within its manufacturing system, increasing drastically its performance [89]. Furthermore, new advances have been managed to develop robots for specific shipbuilding tasks, such as pipe inspection or hull cleaning. In the case study, Navantia has also researched regarding robotic welding [90].

4.1.12 Virtual and augmented reality (VAR)

The VAR could be englobed within modeling and simulation technologies [84]. However, as this technology involves partial or complete human immersion, as well as pursues a different aim, the VAR has been treated separately.

On the one hand, the virtual reality implies a full immersion of the human being within a virtual world using a special device connected with a simulation. In this virtual world, the user can interact with virtual elements in order to train and improve the operator knowledge significantly. It has also applications in product testing and validation of complex products [91].

On the other hand, the augmented reality converges the real world with the virtual one through a device, adding data from the virtual system (or digital twin), exactly where needed. This technology is useful not only in the manufacturing processes but also in maintenance tasks. Using augmented reality also offers applications in assuring quality control, location of products and tools, warehouse management, and support for the visualization of hidden areas [92], among others.

In the shipbuilding industry, both technologies are already being used in small applications for training and part positioning.

4.1.13 Artificial intelligence (AI)

The AI is one of the Industry 4.0 driver technologies. According to the European Commission, AI refers to "systems that display intelligent behavior by analyzing their environment and taking actions (with some degree of autonomy) to achieve specific goals" [16]. Its application in the industrial sector has resulted in the "intelligent manufacturing" concept [93], which, along with the other recent emerging Industry 4.0 KETs, will allow more flexible and efficient operations in the smart factory [15]. In order to achieve a good implantation of this technology, the industrial AI framework is also proposed with a clear structure, methodology, and ecosystem [15].

In the shipbuilding industry, there are already some applications in terms of design vessels for optimizing the overall performance [94]. The applications of AI are mainly related with the development of other technologies, acting as an enabler to impulse the potential of each one of the other KETs [95]. This is shown in the interaction between AI and the particular effect it deploys.

4.2 Social network analysis (SNA)

Due to the existing correlation between the KETs selected in this case study, it is possible to develop a social network in order to confirm the links among them. A social network is defined as a finite set of actors (such as people, organizations, or technologies) and the relationship among them [96]. The social network perspective focuses on these relations as an important addition to the standard social research, which is mainly concerned in the attributes of the social units. The social network analysis (SNA) is similar to the mind map technique, which allows to represent the ideas and their relationships. This method has already been used to the study the Industry 4.0 enablers [97]. The SNA is an innovative technique and research tool that has already been successfully used to find the relationship between different technologies and resources relative to the Industry 4.0 [80].

The MoSCoW method is used [98] to establish the network of Navantia's KETs. This method stands for "Must, Should, Could and Won't Have" criteria, and it is mainly used to stablish a priority list. In this case, a variant of the method is considered to weight the different interaction possibilities:

- Must have. Numeric value 3: The technology studied needs the crossed technology one mandatory.

- Should have. Numeric value 2: The technology studied can have major connection with the crossed technology.

	3DP	AuV	BD	BCH	Cloud	CybS	AI	DP	IoT	M&S	NM	Robot	VAR
3DP	0	0	1	1	1	1	2	1	1	3	2	1	0
AuV	1	0	1	1	2	2	2	0	2	1	0	0	1
BD	0	0	0	2	3	2	2	1	3	0	0	0	0
BCH	0	0	0	0	1	2	2	0	0	0	0	0	0
Cloud	0	0	1	1	0	2	2	1	1	0	0	0	0
CybS	0	0	1	2	1	0	2	1	0	0	0	0	0
AI	0	0	2	1	2	2	0	1	2	1	0	0	0
DP	0	0	1	1	3	1	1	0	1	0	0	0	0
IoT	0	0	2	1	3	1	2	1	0	1	0	0	0
M&S	0	0	1	0	1	0	2	1	1	0	0	0	1
NM	2	0	2	0	0	0	2	0	0	2	0	0	0
Robot	1	1	2	1	1	1	2	0	2	2	1	0	1
VAR	0	0	2	1	2	1	2	1	1	3	0	0	0

Table 1.
Relationship among Navantia's key enabling technologies.

- Could have. Numeric value 1: The technology studied can have minor connection with the crossed technology.

- Won't have. Numeric value 0: The technology studied does not need the crossed technology.

In the first place, a nonsymmetric matrix is created, in which the nonlinear dependencies between the KETs are shown. Each row shows the dependency of a KET with the others. For example, VAR is dependent of M&S, but it is not the same in the other way around. These binary and paired comparison assessments were completed by the expert committee of Navantia, as summarized in **Table 1**. Once the data is ready, it is introduced in the software UNICET (version 6.675) [99], which will return the analyzed data (from the social network) and graphic representation.

5. Results

Once the data is analyzed, the results give information regarding the relationship between KETs, as betweenness, centrality, closeness, or density. However, the measures of centrality and betweenness are the ones to be taken into account. Centrality is the grade of each actor which is linked with the others. In a nonsymmetric matrix, the difference between ins and outs means the necessity of other technologies have of the chosen one (ins) and the necessity of the chosen technologies have of the others (outs). In addition, betweenness is the possibility that an actor has to intermediate the communications between pairs of actors. These are also known as bridge actors. The grade of centrality and betweenness is summarized in **Table 2**, where the main results are shown in bold.

These results show that both the AI and the cloud are the most demanded technologies among the other KETs (more than 0.55 relatively), while the individual

	Outdeg	Indeg	nOutdeg	nIndeg	Betweenness	nBetweenness
3DP	14.000	4.000	0.389	0.111	5.667	4.293
AuV	13.000	1.000	0.361	0.028	0.000	0.000
BDA	13.000	16.000	0.361	0.444	2.250	1.705
BCH	5.000	12.000	0.139	0.333	0.000	0.000
Cloud	8.000	**20.000**	0.222	**0.556**	2.000	1.515
CybS	7.000	15.000	0.194	0.417	0.917	0.694
AI	11.000	**23.000**	0.306	**0.639**	**10.417**	**7.891**
DP	8.000	8.000	0.222	0.222	0.583	0.442
IoT	11.000	14.000	0.306	0.389	3.583	2.715
M&S	7.000	13.000	0.194	0.361	**9.500**	**7.197**
NM	8.000	3.000	0.222	0.083	0.000	0.000
Robot	15.000	1.000	0.417	0.028	2.500	1.894
VAR	13.000	3.000	0.361	0.083	0.583	0.442

Table 2.
Centrality and betweenness grade of Navantia's KETs.

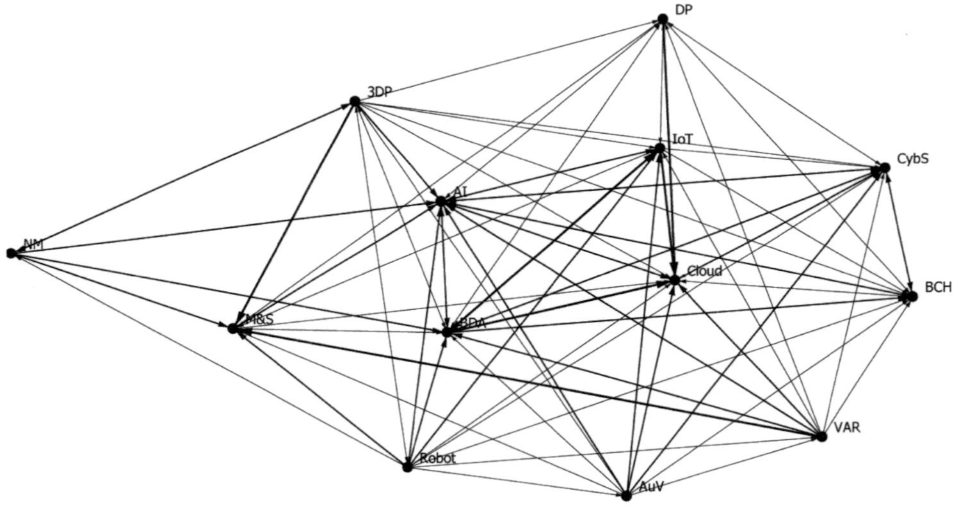

Figure 3.
Social network among Navantia's key enabling technologies.

dependency of each KET on the others is not too high, being robotics the most dependent. In terms of betweenness, the AI stands out again, followed closely by modeling and simulation. These are the two technologies with more capacity to stablish interactions between other technologies, which is an important added value to consider. The social network result is drawn in **Figure 3**, in which the connections between the technologies are represented.

The network shows the four main technologies on which the rest of the technologies revolve: artificial intelligence (AI), cloud, Big Data analytics (BDA), and Internet of things (IoT). This is consistent with the principles of the digital transformation and with the implications that the use of AI has to achieve a further development of the other KETs either due to direct integration or as an enabler linker for other technologies. These results also show the importance each of the technology has in the shipbuilding industry. This could be used to stablish a criterion, in order to support one technology over another.

6. Conclusions

In this book chapter, a state of the art of the shipbuilding industry is carried out. This includes a literature review in shipbuilding complex projects, lean manufacturing implications in shipbuilding, and the introduction of the fourth industrial revolution into this industrial sector, and there is a need to overcome the difficult situation that it is currently facing. To go further in this research, a study case is presented. The Spanish state-owned shipyard Navantia is chosen to study how a shipyard is challenging the digital transformation and introducing KETs in its production system. Afterwards, a revision of the advances and the integration of these technologies in the shipbuilding industry are presented.

Moreover, due to the relationship that exists among the KETs, a SNA is performed. This analysis has confirmed the main technologies that the Industry 4.0 has to prioritize during its implementation. From the nine original technologies, Big Data analytics, Internet of things, and cloud are highlighted. On top of those, artificial intelligence appears to join the cloud as the technology that will have the biggest impact in the Industry 4.0, due to its potential to increase the benefits of the other key enabling technologies.

Acknowledgements

This work is part of the advances of an industrial doctoral thesis within the framework of the "Agreement between the University of Cadiz and Navantia S.A., S.M.E. for collaboration in the promotion of the training of research staff for the completion of doctoral theses in companies," acknowledging both entities to enable, finance, and facilitate its development.

Conflict of interest

The authors declare no conflict of interest.

Author details

Alejandro Sánchez-Sotano[1*], Alberto Cerezo-Narváez[1], Francisco Abad-Fraga[2], Andrés Pastor-Fernández[1] and Jorge Salguero-Gómez[1]

1 Department of Mechanical Engineering and Industrial Design, University of Cadiz, Spain

2 Navantia S.A. S.M.E. Bahía de Cádiz Shipyard, Spain

*Address all correspondence to: alejandrojavier.sanchez@uca.es

References

[1] Herterich MM, Uebernickel F, Brenner W. The impact of cyber-physical systems on industrial services in manufacturing. Procedia CIRP. 2015;**30**:323-328

[2] Favi C, Campi F, Germani M, Manieri S. Using design information to create a data framework and tool for life cycle analysis of complex maritime vessels. Journal of Cleaner Production. 2018;**192**:887-905

[3] Baginski L, Pitassi C, Barbosa JGP. Technological capability in the Brazilian naval industry: A metric for offshore support vessels. RAI—Revista de Administração e Inovação. 2017;**14**(2):109-118

[4] Kolić D, Fafandjel N, Zamarin A. Lean manufacturing methodology for shipyards. Shipbuilding. 2012;**63**(1):18-29

[5] Eriksson T, Vahlo J, Rissanen T, Koponen A. Management myopia and project management. Insiders vs outsiders. In: ISPIM Innovation Symposium. Fukuoka, Japan: The International Society for Professional Innovation Management (ISPIM); 2018. pp. 1-9

[6] Vrijhoef R, Koskela L. The four roles of supply chain management in construction. European Journal of Purchasing & Supply Management. 2000;**6**(3-4):169-178

[7] Ng ST, Rose TM, Mak M, Chen SE. Problematic issues associated with project partnering—The contractor perspective. International Journal of Project Management. 2002;**20**(6):437-449

[8] Xue X, Wang Y, Shen Q, Yu X. Coordination mechanisms for construction supply chain management in the Internet environment. International Journal of Project Management. 2007;**25**(2):150-157

[9] Hansen MJ, Vaagen H. Collective intelligence in project groups: Reflections from the field. Procedia Computer Science. 2016;**100**(1877):840-847

[10] Aloini D, Dulmin R, Mininno V, Ponticelli S. Key antecedents and practices for Supply Chain Management adoption in project contexts. International Journal of Project Management. 2015;**33**(6):1301-1316

[11] Iordache O. Implementing Polytope Projects for Smart Systems, Studies in Systems, Decision and Control. 1st ed. Vol. 92. Cham: Springer; 2017. p. 197

[12] Lorenz M, Rüßmann M, Strack R, Lueth K, Bolle M. Industry 4.0. The Future of Productivity and Growth in Manufacturing Industries. Boston, USA; 2015

[13] Yao F, Keller A, Ahmad M, Ahmad B, Harrison R, Colombo AW. Optimizing the scheduling of autonomous guided vehicle in a manufacturing process. In: 16th International Conference on Industrial Informatics (INDIN). Porto, Portugal: IEEE; 2018. pp. 264-269

[14] Viriyasitavat W, Da Xu L, Bi Z, Sapsomboon A. Blockchain-based business process management (BPM) framework for service composition in industry 4.0. Journal of Intelligent Manufacturing. 2018:1-12. (In press)

[15] Lee J, Davari H, Singh J, Pandhare V. Industrial Artificial Intelligence for industry 4.0-based manufacturing systems. Manufacturing Letters. 2018;**18**:20-23

[16] European Commission. Artificial Intelligence for Europe. Brussels, Belgium: Digital Single Market; 2018

[17] Rouco Couzo M, Quiroga Pazos M, Cebral Fernández M, Morgade Abeal R, García del Valle A, Morgade Abeal D. El Astillero 4.0: Modelado y Simulación del Astillero de Navantia-Ferrol. In: 56° Congreso de Ingeniería Naval e Industria Marítima. Madrid: Asociación de Ingenieros Navales y Oceánicos de España (AINE); 2017. pp. 1-15

[18] Cagalj A, Veza I, Markovina R. Interactive networked company in shipbuilding industry. Strojarstvo. 2009;**51**(1):15-26

[19] Ramsay S. A case for a new warship-building strategy. Maritime Affairs: Journal of the National Maritime Foundation of India. 2012;**8**(1):150-156

[20] Vidal LA, Marle F, Bocquet JC. Measuring project complexity using the Analytic Hierarchy Process. International Journal of Project Management. 2011;**29**(6):718-727

[21] Dao BP. Exploring and Measuring Project Complexity. College Station, TX, US: Texas A&M University; 2016

[22] Wiskerke J, Veeke H, Pruijn J, Groen C, Hopman H. Knowledge framework on the execution of complex projects. The development of a functional framework using a systems approach. In: International Conference on Information and Knowledge Engineering (IKE). Athens, Greece: The Steering Committee of The World Congress in Computer Science, Computer Engineering and Applied Computing (WorldComp); 2016. pp. 73-78

[23] Hall DJ, Saias MA. Strategy follows structure! Strategic Management Journal. 1980;**1**(2):149-163

[24] Baccarini D. The concept of project complexity: A review. International Journal of Project Management. 1996;**14**(4):201-204

[25] Duncan J. The structure of cognition: Attentional episodes in mind and brain. Neuron. 2013;**80**(1):35-50

[26] Bakhshi J, Ireland V, Gorod A. Clarifying the project complexity construct: Past, present and future. International Journal of Project Management. 2016;**34**(7):1199-1213

[27] Hayes S, Bennett D. Managing projects with high complexity. In: Cooke-Davies T, Crawford L, Patton JR, Stevens C, Williams TM, editors. Aspects of Complexity: Managing Projects in a Complex World. Newtown Square: Project Management Institute; 2011. pp. 17-27

[28] Cooke-Davies T. Complexity in project management and the management of complex crojects. In: Cooke-Davies T, Crawford L, Patton JR, Stevens C, Williams TM, editors. Aspects of Complexity: Managing Projects in a Complex World. Newtown Square: Project Management Institute; 2011. pp. 1-13

[29] Sistemas y Tecnología de IBM. Watson-Un sistema Diseñado para Respuestas. El futuro del diseño de sistemas optimizados de cargas de trabajo. Madrid; 2011

[30] Loch C, Payne FC. Strategic management: Developing policies and strategies. In: Cooke-Davies T, Crawford L, Patton JR, Stevens C, Williams TM, editors. Aspects of Complexity: Managing Projects in a Complex World. Newtown Square: Project Management Institute; 2011. pp. 41-55

[31] Geraldi J, Maylor H, Williams T. Now, let's make it really complex (complicated). International Journal of Operations & Production Management. 2011;**31**(9):966-990

[32] Kjersem K, Jünge GH. Improving planning process for

ETO-projects: A case study. In: Nääs I, Vendrametto O, Mendes Reis J, Gonçalves RF, Silva MT, von Cieminski G, et al., editors. Advances in Production Management Systems, APMS 2016, IFIP Advances in Information and Communication Technology. Vol. 488. Cham: Springer International Publishing; 2016. pp. 927-934

[33] Hellgren S. The Bayesian Model for Cruise Shipbuilding: A Process for Production efficiency and Organization. Vol. 240. Helsinki, Finland: Aalto University; 2016

[34] Found P, Bicheno J. The Routledge companion to lean management. In: Netland TH, Powell DJ, editors. The Routledge Companion to Lean Management. New York, NY: Routledge; 2016. pp. 23-33

[35] Sanders A, Elangeswaran C, Wulfsberg J. Industry 4.0 implies lean manufacturing: Research activities in industry 4.0 function as enablers for lean manufacturing. Journal of Industrial Engineering and Management. 2016;**9**(3):811

[36] NG T, Ghobakhloo M. What derives lean manufacturing effectiveness: An interpretive structural mode. International Journal of Advances in Applied Sciences. 2017;**4**(8):104-111

[37] Ghobakhloo M, Azar A. Business excellence via advanced manufacturing technology and lean-agile manufacturing. Journal of Manufacturing Technology Management. 2018;**29**(1):2-24

[38] Sartal A, Vázquez XH. Implementing information technologies and operational excellence: Planning, emergence and randomness in the survival of adaptive manufacturing systems. Journal of Manufacturing Systems. 2017;**45**:1-16

[39] Tortorella G, Miorando R, Caiado R, Nascimento D, Portioli Staudacher A. The mediating effect of employees' involvement on the relationship between Industry 4.0 and operational performance improvement. Total Quality Management and Business Excellence. 2018:1-15. (In press)

[40] Kamble S, Gunasekaran A, Dhone NC. Industry 4.0 and lean manufacturing practices for sustainable organisational performance in Indian manufacturing companies. International Journal of Production Research. 2019:1-19. (In press)

[41] Tortorella GL, Giglio R, van Dun DH. Industry 4.0 as a moderator on the relationship between lean and operational performance. In: 25th International Annual EurOMA Conference: To Serve, to Produce and to Servitize in the Era of Networks, Big Data and Analytics. Budapest, Hungary: University of Twente; 2018. pp. 1-10

[42] Tortorella GL, Fettermann D. Implementation of Industry 4.0 and lean production in Brazilian manufacturing companies. International Journal of Production Research. 2018;**56**(8):2975-2987

[43] Rossini M, Costa F, Tortorella GL, Portioli-Staudacher A. The interrelation between Industry 4.0 and lean production: An empirical study on European manufacturers. International Journal of Advanced Manufacturing Technology. 2019;**102**(9-12):3963-3976

[44] Pinho C, Mendes L. IT in lean-based manufacturing industries: Systematic literature review and research issues. International Journal of Production Research. 2017;**55**(24):7524-7540

[45] Jiang G, Feng D, Zhu W. Toward efficient merchant shipbuilding based on the lean production methodology. Journal of Ship Production and Design. 2016;**32**(4):245-257

[46] Beifert A, Gerlitz L, Prause G. Industry 4.0—For sustainable development of lean manufacturing companies in the shipbuilding sector. In: Kabashkin I, Yatskiv I, Prentkovskis O, editors, Lecture Notes in Networks and Systems. Vol. 36. Cham: Springer International Publishing; 2018. pp. 563-573

[47] Jiang G, Feng D, Zhu W. Lean shipbuilding for project-based manufacturing. In: Industrial and Systems Engineering Research Conference. Nashville, USA: Institute of Industrial and Systems Engineers (IISE); 2015. pp. 1730-1739

[48] Buer S-V, Strandhagen JO, Chan FTS. The link between Industry 4.0 and lean manufacturing: Mapping current research and establishing a research agenda. International Journal of Production Research. 2018;**56**(8):2924-2940

[49] Agrawal A, Schaefer S, Funke T. Incorporating Industry 4.0 in corporate strategy. In: Analyzing the Impacts of Industry 40 in Modern Business Environments. Hershey, USA: IGI Global; 2018. pp. 161-176

[50] Ragulina YV, Shkodinsky SV, Mishchenko VV, Romanova YA. Scenarios of development of Industry 4.0 in the conditions of knowledge economy's formation and their consequences for modern economic systems. In: Studies in Systems, Decision and Control. Cham, Switzerland: Springer; 2019. pp. 227-234

[51] Paranitharan KP, Babu R, Pandi PA, Jeyathilagar D. An empirical validation of integrated manufacturing business excellence model. International Journal of Advanced Manufacturing Technology. 2017;**92**(5-8):2569-2591

[52] Gunasekaran A, Papadopoulos T, Dubey R, Wamba SF, Childe SJ, Hazen B, et al. Big data and predictive analytics for supply chain and organizational performance. Journal of Business Research. 2017;**70**:308-317

[53] Costa N, Patrício L, Morelli N, Magee CL. Bringing service design to manufacturing companies: Integrating PSS and service design approaches. Design Studies. 2018;**55**:112-145

[54] Hmeshah K, Erbach N, Bronsart R. Impact of production requirements on high-quality ship product data models. Journal of Engineering for the Maritime Environment. 2016;**230**(3):508-522

[55] Recamán RÁ. Navantia's Shipyard 4.0 model overview. Cienc y Tecnol buques. 2018;**11**(22):77

[56] Siggelkow N. Persuasion with case studies. The Academy of Management Journal. 2007;**50**(1):20-24

[57] Eisenhardt KM. Building theories from case study research. The Academy of Management Review. 1989;**14**(4):532

[58] Yin RK. Case Study Research: Design and Methods. 3rd ed. SAGE: Thousand Oaks; 2003. p. 183

[59] Navantia. Products and Services [Internet]. 2018. Available from: https://www.navantia.es/en/products-and-services/

[60] Gosling J, Naim MM. Engineer-to-order supply chain management: A literature review and research agenda. International Journal of Production Economics. 2009;**122**(2):741-754

[61] Navantia. Shipyard 4.0. 2018 [Internet]. 2018. Available from: https://www.navantia.es/en/navantia-4-0/shipyard-4-0/

[62] Fraga LP. Enabling Technologies and Cyber-Physical Systems for Mission-Critical Scenarios. Universidade da Coruña; 2017

[63] Moreno Nieto D, Casal López V, Molina SI. Large-format polymeric pellet-based additive manufacturing for the naval industry. Additive Manufacturing. 2018;**23**:79-85

[64] Knezović N, Topić A. Wire and arc additive manufacturing (WAAM)—A new advance in manufacturing. In: Karabegović I, editor. New Technologies, Development and Application, Lecture Notes in Networks and Systems. Cham, Switzerland: Springer International Publishing; 2019. pp. 65-71

[65] Mehami J, Nawi M, Zhong RY. Smart automated guided vehicles for manufacturing in the context of Industry 4.0. Procedia Manufacturing. 2018;**26**:1077-1086

[66] Bi Z, Cochran D. Big data analytics with applications. Journal of Management Analytics. 2014;**1**(4):249-265

[67] Jun C, Lee JY, Kim BH. Cloud-based big data analytics platform using algorithm templates for the manufacturing industry. International Journal of Computer Integrated Manufacturing. 2019;**32**(8):723-738

[68] Majeed A, Lv J, Peng T. A framework for big data driven process analysis and optimization for additive manufacturing. Rapid Prototyping Journal. 2019;**25**(2):308-321

[69] Tao F, Qi Q, Wang L, Nee AYC. Digital twins and cyber–physical systems toward smart manufacturing and Industry 4.0: Correlation and comparison. Engineering. 2019;**5**(4):653-661

[70] Taylor SJE. Distributed simulation: State-of-the-art and potential for operational research. European Journal of Operational Research. 2019;**273**(1):1-19

[71] Bao J, Zheng X, Zhang J, Ji X, Zhang J. Data-driven process planning for shipbuilding. Artificial Intelligence for Engineering Design Analysis and Manufacturing AIEDAM. 2018;**32**(1):122-130

[72] Lin C, He D, Huang X, Choo K-KR, Vasilakos AV. BSeIn: A blockchain-based secure mutual authentication with fine-grained access control system for industry 4.0. Journal of Network and Computer Applications. 2018;**116**(March):42-52

[73] Chang SE, Chen Y-C, Lu M-F. Supply chain re-engineering using blockchain technology: A case of smart contract based tracking process. Technological Forecasting and Social Change. 2019;**144**:1-11

[74] Wang S, Wan J, Li D, Zhang C. Implementing smart factory of Industrie 4.0: An outlook. International Journal of Sensor Networks. 2016;**12**(1):3159805

[75] Alcácer V, Cruz-Machado V. Scanning the Industry 4.0: A literature review on technologies for manufacturing systems. Engineering Science and Technology, an International Journal. 2019;**22**(3):899-919

[76] Rauch E, Seidenstricker S, Dallasega P, Hämmerl R. Collaborative cloud manufacturing: Design of business model innovations enabled by cyberphysical systems in distributed manufacturing systems. Journal of Engineering. 2016;**2016**:1-12

[77] He H, Maple C, Watson T, Tiwari A, Mehnen J, Jin Y, et al. The security challenges in the IoT enabled cyber-physical systems and opportunities for evolutionary computing & other computational intelligence. In: 2016 IEEE Congress on Evolutionary Computation (CEC). Vancouver, BC, Canada: IEEE; 2016. pp. 1015-1021

[78] Piedrahita AFM, Gaur V, Giraldo J, Cardenas AA, Rueda SJ. Virtual incident response functions in control systems. Computer Networks. 2018;**135**:147-159

[79] Tsuchiya A, Fraile F, Koshijima I, Ortiz A, Poler R. Software defined networking firewall for industry 4.0 manufacturing systems. Journal of Industrial Engineering and Management. 2018;**11**(2):318

[80] Da Costa MB, Dos Santos LMAL, Schaefer JL, Baierle IC, Nara EOB. Industry 4.0 technologies basic network identification. Scientometrics. 2019;**121**(2):977-994

[81] ur Rehman MH, Yaqoob I, Salah K, Imran M, Jayaraman PP, Perera C. The role of big data analytics in industrial Internet of Things. Future Generation Computer Systems. 2019;**99**:247-259

[82] Lopes Miranda Junior H, Albuquerque Bezerra NR, Soares Bezerra MJ, Rodrigues Farias Filho J. The internet of things sensors technologies and their applications for complex engineering projects: A digital construction site framework. Brazilian Journal of Operations & Production Management. 2017;**14**(4):567-576

[83] Banks J, Carson JS II, Nelson BL, Nicol DM. Discrete-Event System Simulation. Prentice Hall: Upper Saddle River, USA; 2010. p. 564

[84] Mourtzis D, Doukas M, Bernidaki D. Simulation in manufacturing: Review and challenges. Procedia CIRP. 2014;**25**(C):213-229

[85] Rodič B. Industry 4.0 and the new simulation modelling paradigm. Organizacija. 2017;**50**(3):193-207

[86] Cavendish Group. The challenges of using new materials in shipbuilding [Internet]. Marine & Offshore Technology. 2017. Available from: http://www.marineoffshoretechnology.net/features-news/challenges-using-new-materials-shipbuilding

[87] Ferraris S, Volpone LM. Aluminum alloys in third millennium shipbuilding: Materials, technologies, persepectives. In: 5th International Forum of Aluminum Ships. Tokyo, Japan. 2005. pp. 1-10

[88] Koch PJ, van Amstel MK, Dębska P, Thormann MA, Tetzlaff AJ, Bøgh S, et al. A skill-based robot co-worker for industrial maintenance tasks. Procedia Manufacturing. 2017;**11**(June):83-90

[89] Samsung. The Future of the Global Shipbuilding and Offshore Industries [Internet]. Samsung Heavy Industries. 2017. Available from: http://www.samsungshi.com/eng/deFaulT.aspx

[90] Galindo PL, Morgado-Estévez A, Aparicio JL, Bárcena G, Soto-Núñez JA, Chavera P, et al. Development of a customized interface for a robotic welding application at navantia shipbuilding company. In: Third Iberian Robotics Conference (ROBOT 2017), Advances in Intelligent Systems and Computing. Vol. 694. Cham, Switzerland: Springer International Publishing; 2018. pp. 43-52

[91] Roldán JJ, Crespo E, Martín-Barrio A, Peña-Tapia E, Barrientos A. A training system for Industry 4.0 operators in complex assemblies based on virtual reality and process mining. Robotics and Computer-Integrated Manufacturing. 2019;**59**(May):305-316

[92] Fraga-Lamas P, Fernandez-Carames TM, Blanco-Novoa O, Vilar-Montesinos MA. A review on industrial augmented reality systems for the Industry 4.0 shipyard. IEEE Access. 2018;**6**:13358-13375

[93] Yao X, Zhou J, Lin Y, Li Y, Yu H, Liu Y. Smart manufacturing based on cyber-physical systems and beyond. Journal of Intelligent Manufacturing. 2019;**30**(8):2805-2817

[94] Abramowski T. Application of artificial intelligence methods to preliminary design of ships and ship performance optimization. Naval Engineers Journal. 2013;**125**(3):101-112

[95] Dopico M, Gomez A, De la Fuente D, García N, Rosillo R, Puche J. A vision of industry 4.0 from an artificial intelligence point of view. In: International Conference on Artificial Intelligence (ICAI 2016—WORLDCOMP 2016). Las Vegas, USA: CSREA Press; 2016. pp. 407-413

[96] Wasserman S, Faust K. Social Network Analysis: Methods and Applications. New York, USA: Cambridge University Press; 1994. p. 857

[97] Havle CA, Ucler C. Enablers for Industry 4.0. In: 2nd International Symposium on Multidisciplinary Studies and Innovative Technologies (ISMSIT). Ankara, Turkey: IEEE; 2018. pp. 1-6

[98] Agile Business Consortium. Chapter 10: MoSCoW Prioritisation [Internet]. DSDM Agile Project Framework Handbook. 2014. Available from: https://www.agilebusiness.org/page/ProjectFramework_10_MoSCoWPrioritisation

[99] Borgatti SP, Everett MG, Freeman LC. UCINET 6 for Windows: Software for Social Network Analysis. Cambridge, USA: Harvard Analytic Technologies; 2002

Chapter 2

Energy Infrastructure of the Factory as a Virtual Power Plant: Smart Energy Management

Eva M. Urbano and Víctor Martínez Viol

Abstract

Smart energy factories are crucial for the development of upcoming energy markets in which emissions, energy use and network congestions are to be decreased. The virtual power plant (VPP) can be implemented in an industrial site with the aim of minimizing costs, emissions and total energy usage. A VPP considers the future situation forecasting and the situation of all energy assets, including renewable energy generation units and energy storage systems, to optimize the total cost of the plant, considering the possibility to trade with the energy market. For a VPP to be constructed, a proper communication system is essential. The energy management system (EMS) enables the monitoring, management and control of the different energy devices and permits the transference of the decisions made by the VPP to the different energy assets. VPP concept is explained together with the methods used for forecasting the future situation and the energy flow inside the facility. To reach its benefits, the optimization of the VPP is assessed. After that, the communication technologies that enable the VPP implementation are also introduced, and the advantages/disadvantages regarding their deployment are stated. With the tools introduced, the VPP can face the challenges of energy markets efficiently.

Keywords: virtual power plant, smart grid, energy hub, ANFIS, communication technologies, energy management system

1. Introduction

Industry 4.0 is normally understood as smart factories where automation, digitalization, Internet of Things (IoT), cognitive computing and others are used. However, this does not stand without the use of energy. There is a settled relationship between energy consumption, energy prices and economic growth in different countries. For industries, the access to reliable and affordable energy is crucial to create greater economic and social prosperity. In the industry that is emerging nowadays, the physical processes are studied, modeled and monitored, and physical systems communicate and cooperate in a real-time scenario in order to optimize the behavior of the plant. The same can be done with energy. To reach the best efficiency of a manufacturing plant, the energy consumption processes have to be studied, modeled and monitored; the communication of the energy flows between equipment has to be known, and future situation prediction and real-time decisions have to be taken regarding energy purchasing, energy trading, generation and consumption.

There are several reasons for why the development of energy-smart factories is interesting. Policy is making an effort in order to achieve a reduction of greenhouse gas emissions, an increase in the share of renewable energy and an improvement in the energy efficiency. As an example, in Europe, the energy usage in the industrial sector accounts for more than 25% of total energy consumption, process heating having the most significant use with 66% followed by electricity with 26%. If energy efficiency measures are developed and incorporated in the industrial sector, the potential savings can be of more than 20% as shown in [1]. Regarding the increase in the share of renewable energies, it will be possible with the integration of smart energy systems. Some renewable energy sources such as solar and wind power generation are characterized by an intermittent nature. One of the fundamental properties of the electric grid is that the supply (generation) and the demand (consumption) must always be balanced. With the increase in the share of renewable power sources, the energy may not be generated in the best suited moment and with the exact amount of power dealing to grid instability and not assuring a security of supply. By defining, integrating and controlling the energy flow in order to optimize the consumption of energy hubs (EH) and, from there, exploit it in virtual power plants (VPP), the industrial sector the electricity usage can be optimized, allowing a greater efficiency and flexibility, improving the capacity factor of the installed renewable energy sources. Up to date, the EH concept has been presented by several studies in the industrial field, and its expansion into a VPP is a new research field in which the focus is the possibility of energy trading with the grid, as can be seen in [2, 3].

The constant monitoring of the energy flow combined with the integration of different energy generation sources will require management technologies capable of recognizing, predicting and acting in a way to guarantee quality, sustainability and efficiency, including costs, in energy consumption. Therefore, modern energy management systems should be able to monitor and exploit large volumes of data collected by various types of meters transmitted by digital channels mainly based on the IoT. The application of artificial intelligence techniques related with machine learning and big data will require thousands of meters collecting data at high resolution and high frequency (gigabytes per day), and, in order to assure the reliability and quality of this data, some aspects must be addressed such as the data model, the integration of information coming from several inputs or the data security.

The optimization of energy use will produce a direct reduction of costs and pollutants as the total energy consumption will be less. By increasing the share of renewable energy sources in the grid, the merit order will change. The merit order ranks the available energy sources from its operational cost, the cheaper ones being the first to meet the demand. Solar power generation and wind power generation are of the cheapest energy generation technologies, so if they are able to provide power, the operational cost of the last active power plant in order to meet demand will be less, allowing a more economic purchase of energy.

The path to reach a smart energy grid in the Industry 4.0 has already started. Development has been observed in the area of energy technologies, improving the efficiency of isolated systems. However, the overall energy efficiency can be greatly improved if multi-energy assets are analyzed and utilized in a more unified way. Energy assets can be interconnected physically in a plant, improving the energy usage in the plant and creating an EH. There is also the possibility to aggregate different plants physically or virtually, creating a digital entity of active prosumers that will be presented to the grid as a unique system that will be able to both consume and generate electricity.

This chapter is structured as follows. In Section 2, the VPP concept and tools are explained. First of all, its definition is exposed. This definition broadens the concept of EH and its functionality, creating a new entity able to perform an optimization considering internal and external factors. Secondly, the forecasting tools for predicting the situation at a stated horizon are presented. These tools include the forecast of renewable energy sources and demand and energy price from the grid. Third, the EH concept and method are developed for a general industry. Then, the optimization of the system is assessed, and resolution methods are proposed for obtaining high-quality results. In Section 3, some aspects related to the automation pyramid and the communication requirements of its levels are presented. Then some of the communication technologies and protocols are briefly introduced. Last of all, conclusions are drawn in Section 4.

2. Industry as a virtual power plant

One of the most important characteristics of the electrical grid is the constant balance between generation and consumption. With the rise of intermittent renewable energies, a degree of uncertainty is introduced. The discontinuity of this type of generation should not affect the fulfillment of the demand at every instant. With a proper management of energy assets and energy storage systems, renewable energy sources can be satisfactorily introduced without compromising the stability of the system. Once the balance between supply and demand is assured, there is leeway to generate an economic benefit from the energy transferred and stored inside a facility, such as a VPP. The VPP would be a power prosumer, meeting the local demand, and profit its own energy assets to trade energy with the external grid. Nowadays, the smart microgrid and prosumer concepts are being developed and tested in the tertiary sector, as can be seen in [4, 5]. Although the advancements are done, the presented ideas need further investigation. The prosumer smart grid approach can also be implemented in the industry, creating an energy-smart entity that will deal with the challenges and demands of the coming energy markets and will produce a profit from the exploitation of its own equipment against the external primary energy grids.

2.1 Virtual power plant concept

A VPP is a network of decentralized, medium-scale power-generating units as well as flexible power consumers and batteries. A VPP can be implemented in an industrial site, composed by all the controllable energy assets and the renewable energy generation units in the factory.

The VPP operates its energy assets efficiently taking into account the forecast of internal and external factors with the aim of maximizing the efficiency of the system in economic and environmental terms. As an example, internal factors can comprise coefficient of performance (COP) and efficiencies of energy equipment, energy storage capacity, energy generation at a given moment, cost of the different subsystems and reschedulable loads (both electrical and thermal). External factors may be constituted by electricity, natural gas and waste prices.

In **Figure 1** an example of a VPP is shown. It can be appreciated that the communication with the electrical grid is bidirectional, allowing to buy and sell electricity depending on the forecasted conditions. The working behavior lays in an energetic, economic and environmental evaluation that considers the forecasted input energy price, the forecast of available energy inside the VPP and the forecasted demand.

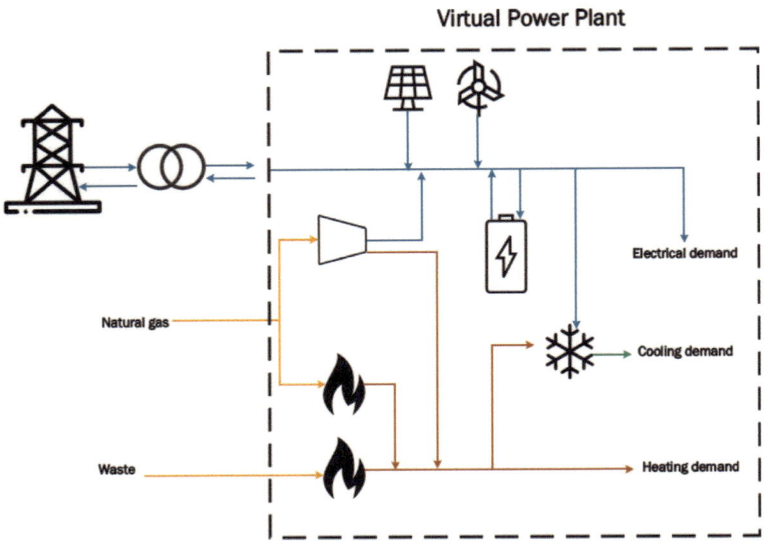

Figure 1.
Example schematic of a VPP where renewable energy sources (solar and wind) are present together with cogeneration system, boilers, absorption cooling and energy storage systems.

The benefits of implementing a VPP affect not only the industrial site itself but also the electrical grid through demand response (DR). The creation of a VPP out of an industrial facility will lead to:

- Integration of intermittent renewable energy, not only in the VPP but also in other points of the grid due to the electricity price response of the VPP. Also, expensive investments to expand the distribution network can be avoided if the generation is locally available.

- Integration of small electricity producers into the distribution network. The VPP itself is seen by the grid as a small electricity producer when the electricity cost is high, and thus there is a need to increase the generation at that moment.

- Optimization of energy use inside the VPP. The demand is analyzed, modeled and predicted using artificial intelligence method, and the optimal operation point of energy providers is computed.

- Optimization of the integration of electric vehicles (EV) for vehicle to grid (V2G) and grid to vehicle (G2V). The storage systems managing the surplus energy at the VPP can be combined with the EV batteries, which will work then as a part of the system. In this way not only the energy storage systems are improved, but also the EV-grid integration is made easier.

- Reduction of emissions. By integrating renewable energy sources and increasing the efficiency of the energy used, the emissions are directly reduced.

- Exploitation of energy assets. The systems present in a facility are nowadays not used in all its potential. With the implementation of a VPP, its working periods will be optimized according to internal and external factors and allowing an exploitation and efficient use of all energy carriers present in a system.

- Market opening. There are several facilities that will allow the creation of a VPP. However, their owners and operators are not aware of the possibilities and benefits it will produce. The introduction of a VPP in an industrial site will lead to a market opening that will encourage other similar facilities to take the same role, and thus the previous benefits will be amplified to the whole electrical grid.

- Autonomy and strong position of the owner of the facility in front of the operators of the electricity market that will allow a greater competitiveness market.

To implement the VPP features, the future energy status of the system should be continuously computed, which includes demand, generation of renewable sources and energy prices. This information leads to VPP operation including energy conversion and storage, which drives the EH, a crucial part of the VPP as it optimizes the path from energy input to demand. Once the forecast of the future situation and the model of the EH is obtained, the VPP is formed. The objective of the VPP is to fulfill local demand while, at the same time, exploiting its own energy assets to be able to trade electricity with the grid. During the modeling and the optimization of the VPP, the electricity exchange with the grid, the energy transfer with the energy storage system, the dispatch factors between the present transformers and the destination of power from the PV system are computed to assure an optimal operation from the economical, energetic and environmental points of view.

2.2 Future situation forecasting

Forecasting is the process of making predictions of the future based on past and present data analyzing the trends that appear. Forecasting can be qualitative or quantitative. For the application to a VPP, quantitative methods are more suitable, as they are based on past data to estimate future states and do not lay on subjective opinions. This approach extracts patterns of the available data and assumes that these are expected to continue in the future and are applied usually to short- and medium-term forecasts. There are several models used for forecast, and its suitability depends on the nature of the problem that is being studied. Examples of them are time series, causal and econometric forecasting and artificial intelligence. The forecast of several variables is needed to optimize the VPP. The demand, generation from renewable energy sources and electricity price from the grid are used in order to compute the optimal operation point of the VPP.

2.2.1 Renewable energy

The prediction of the renewable energy that is generated depends directly on the climatic conditions and the characteristics of the equipment. The prediction of weather conditions, i.e. sun irradiation and wind speed, can be obtained from the meteorology databases. Two types of renewable energy systems will be shown in this section: photovoltaics (PV) and wind power (WP) generation.

On the one hand, for a PV system, the most important factor in estimating its performance is solar radiation. The uncertainty in solar radiation is the largest source of error in the computation of the energy provided, as shown in [6]. The solar radiation depends on the orientation and the inclination of the area studied. Once this value is obtained, the theoretical energy output can be computed. However, the result should be corrected by adding a performance ratio that is influenced by factors such as shadows, dust, dirt, frost, snow, reflectance of the module surface, conversion efficiency, sunlight spectrum and temperature. As an example, in **Figure 2**, extracted from [7], the performance of different chemistries along temperature is shown. The value of the performance ratio (η) can be obtained statistically, and then the output power of the PV system will be:

$$P = P_{nom}\frac{G}{1000}\eta \tag{1}$$

where G is the received solar irradiance in W/m^2 and P_{nom} the peak power in kW.

On the other hand, for the case of wind turbines, there is a direct relationship between wind speed and energy output [8]. The extra parameter that has to be considered is air density, which can be computed using temperature and pressure and obtained from a meteorological database as with the wind speed. The output power can be computed with the data specified by using the wind turbine power curves provided by the manufacturer. These curves are obtained by the manufacturer by means of theoretical and statistical analysis of the performance of the turbine.

The previous methods are useful for a first assessment of the energy generated by the renewable sources. However, after the renewable energy sources equipment are installed and working on an industrial environment, the generation forecast can be improved by modeling specifically its behavior. A correlation of meteorological data with PV and WP output should be performed to assure high model accuracy and obtain the real efficiency and performance of the equipment. According to [9, 10], artificial neural networks (ANN) and support vector machine (SVM)-based forecasting methods are suitable for the modeling and prediction of the behavior of PV generation systems, while ANN, adaptive neuro-fuzzy inference systems (ANFIS) and autoregressive moving average (ARMA) perform well for WP generation.

2.2.2 Demand

The demand is the amount of load that the system has and the energy that is required to be fulfilled. Inside a VPP, this demand can be divided into two types: manageable and non-manageable. Non-manageable loads are those which run continuously or that cannot be controlled. Inside a VPP, the owner or end user can

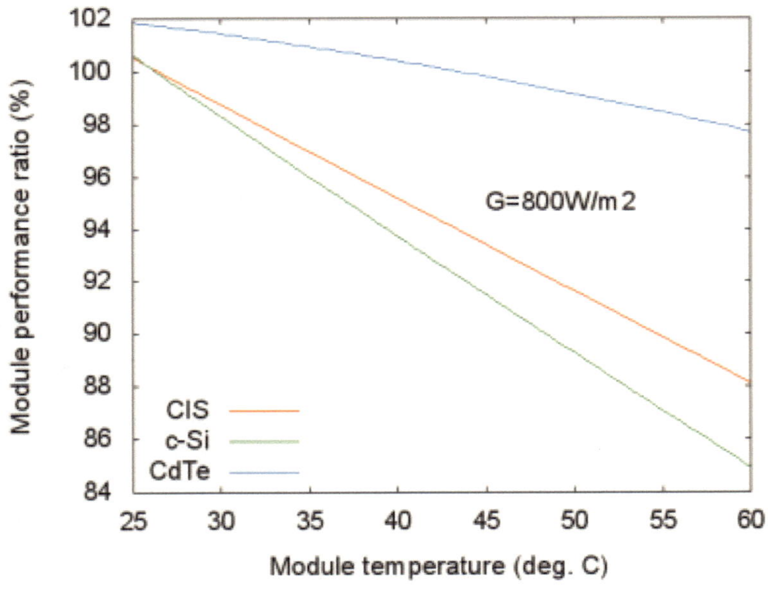

Figure 2.
Performance of PV modules with a solar radiation of 800 W/m².

decide which loads are manageable and which are not according to the business objective criteria. Manageable loads can be further divided into shiftable, interruptible and heating, ventilation and air conditioning (HVAC) loads. The forecasting of both types of demands follows a different way and will be now assessed.

2.2.2.1 Non-manageable loads

Classically, energy loads can be either electrical or thermal. The behavior of both types of demand lies in the same principles, so the prediction of them can be done using the same method. In recent times, the artificial intelligence methods that have been used for load forecasting (LF) include mainly neural networks, expert systems and support vector machines. Nowadays, the focus lays in the development of hybrid methods, combining different forecasting methodologies. For example, in [11] a LF method based on self-organized map and support vector machine is developed. The method is tested for prediction of the power consumption of a whole city. However, its suitability for an industrial site application has not been proven. In [12] an extreme learning machine with the Levenberg-Marquardt method is proposed, and in [13] the possibility to use artificial neural network to create a hybrid method with other techniques such as backpropagation, fuzzy logic, genetic algorithm and particle swarm optimization is shown. The industry is a sector where the demand can have an irregular and infrequent behavior depending on several conditions, and it is constantly under improvement processes. For this reason, a method that enables periodically auto-adjustment and high accuracy results is searched. ANFIS aim at mapping input to output for highly nonlinear processes such as energy management field. ANFIS was first introduced in [14] as a combination of two soft computing methods: artificial neural network and fuzzy logic. The ANFIS architecture is an adaptive network that uses supervised learning on learning algorithm, which has a function similar to the model of Takagi-Sugeno FIS [15]. This architecture is shown in **Figure 3**, extracted from [16].

In the first layer, the fuzzification of the inputs takes place. This is done by a membership function which can be a Gaussian membership function, a generalized bell membership function or other types of membership function. The parameters of this layer that define the membership function are called premise parameters. In the second layer, the fire strength of the rule is calculated. The output is the result of multiplying the signals coming into the node. In the third layer, a calculation of the ratio between the *i*th rule firing strength and the sum of all rules firing strength is

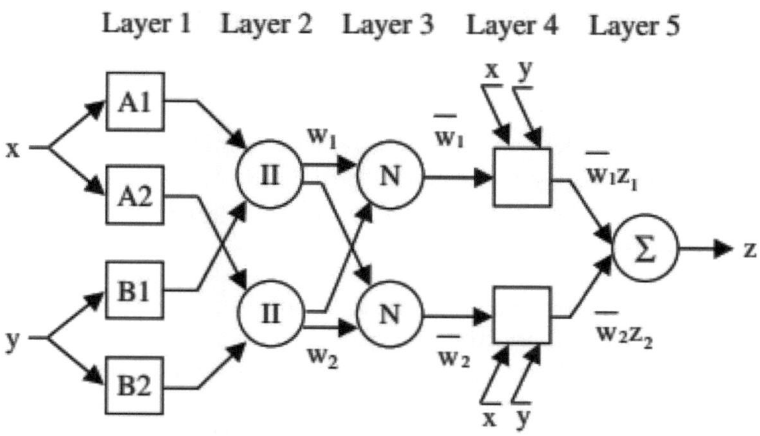

Figure 3.
ANFIS architecture.

done. The output is named the normalized firing strength. The fourth layer executes the Takagi-Sugeno fuzzy reasoning method. The parameters that appear here are the consequent parameters. Finally, in the last layer, the computation of the overall output as the summation of all incoming signals from previous nodes is done. It can be seen that the parameters that need to be trained are the premise and consequent parameters, present in layers 1 and 4. They can be obtained in the learning process by using the forward path and the backward path. During the forward path, the premise parameters are specified, while the consequent parameters change using a recursive least square estimation, and, during the backward path, the consequent parameters obtained remain fixed, while the error propagates to the first layer updating the premise parameter in a gradient descent way.

2.2.2.2 Manageable loads

According to [17], manageable loads can be divided into:

- Shiftable: Loads with predefined working cycles and load profiles. These loads appear between certain time limits which are specified by the end user. In an industry, these can be formed by noncritical processes with a variant energy consumption profile which can be rearranged on time depending on the production goals for the specific time interval.

- Interruptible: These loads are defined by its state, which can be either on or off. When its state is on the consumption remains constant. An example of a load of constant consumption is a water heater. The heating of water can be interrupted and restarted according to the time specification by the end user and the thermal inertia of the system.

- HVAC: Air conditioning and heating devices. Its consumption depends on parameters such as ambient conditions and comfort level specified by the end user.

The consumption of these loads depends on the situation on different factors regarding the state of the EH, the forecast of renewable energy input, the forecast of non-manageable demand and the price of energy from the distribution grids. The consumption of manageable loads is not forecasted but optimized inside a VPP according to restrictions specified by the end user with the objective of minimizing a utility function, which will be presented in the energy optimization section.

2.2.3 Energy price from the grid

In a future situation, demand side management (DSM) will be broadly implemented in the energy grids, specifically in the electrical grid. The price of the electricity is specified in the wholesale market with an anticipation of 24 h for each hour of consumption. In a situation where a VPP wants to interact with the market and obtain benefits from the exploitation of its energy assets, it is important to predict the price of the electricity in order to be able to optimize its energy carriers and offer or demand electricity from the grid.

In [18], two methods to predict next-day electricity demand and price daily curve are proposed given past curves: robust functional principal component analysis and nonparametric models with functional response and covariate. In [19], a hybrid methodology is proposed, combining autoregressive integrated moving average (ARIMA) with adaptive dynamic corrector lazy learning algorithm.

Although these methods were studied, due to the integration of renewable energies in the electricity market and the changes in the structure of the pricing that it supposes, during the last years, ANN have been the focus to forecast electricity prices. ANN models for short-term electricity modeling perform better than time series models such as ARIMA models, as shown in [20]. It is also verified that the performance of ANN depends on appropriate input parameters; clustering and data selection algorithms of k-nearest neighbor algorithm and mutual information methods were used. The problem of this model is the need to remove trend and seasonal components. In the electricity market, there are strong seasonal effects and other nonlinear patterns that harm ANN forecasting performance. In [21] a robust method to solve the seasonal problem with ANN is proposed and verified. The method is seasonal autoregressive neural network (SAR-NN) defined as a dynamic feedforward artificial neural network. In [16] a hybrid approach based on the combination of particle swarm optimization and ANFIS is proposed and demonstrated in a case study in Spain. The study shows that soft computing techniques such as neural networks can be much more efficient computationally and accurate if correct inputs are considered. To select the most suitable inputs, several methods can be used, and genetic algorithm (GA) is one of them. The combination of ANFIS with GA has been proved to solve market price prediction and other economic parameters, as shown in [22, 23].

2.3 Energy hub model

The energy conversion equipment of the VPP forms the EH. In order to develop the model and the optimization of the system to create a VPP, the EH should be modeled. An EH is a multi-carrier energy system consisting of multiple energy conversion, storage and/or network technologies and characterized by some degree of control. In **Figure 4** an example of a schematic of an EH can be seen. In the figure, it is possible to appreciate that the EH in this case is composed by the energy conversion equipment, excluding the storage system. The EH is nowadays understood as the set of energy drivers that allow energy management. However, with the implementation of the VPP concept, the energy management possibilities are expanded and can take place in a level above the EH. Thus, although in most cases energy storage is included inside the EH, when a VPP is implemented, the trading

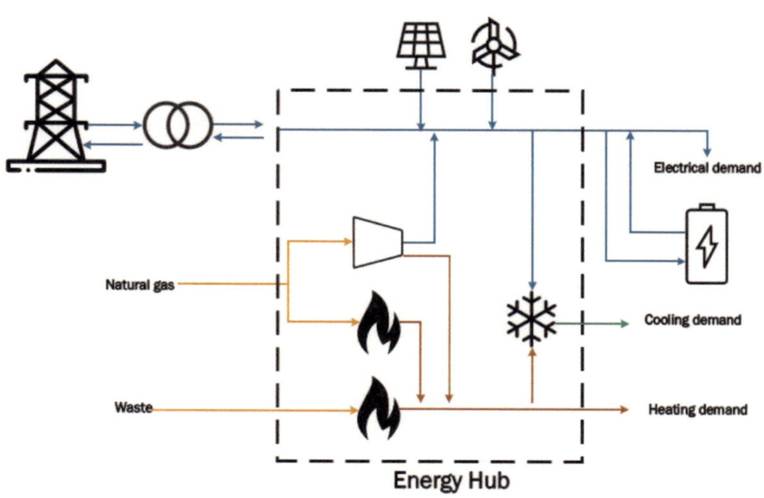

Figure 4.
Example schematic of an EH.

relationships are placed outside the EH, so it becomes coherent to also place the energy storage system outside the EH but inside the VPP.

In this section the formulation of an EH will be established from a generic perspective. According to [24], the relationship between input power and output power inside and EH is:

$$\begin{bmatrix} L_\alpha \\ L_\beta \\ \dots \\ L_\gamma \end{bmatrix} = \begin{bmatrix} \eta_{\alpha\alpha} & \eta_{\alpha\beta} & \dots & \eta_{\alpha\gamma} \\ \eta_{\beta\alpha} & \eta_{\beta\beta} & \dots & \eta_{\beta\gamma} \\ \dots & \dots & \dots & \dots \\ \eta_{\gamma\alpha} & \eta_{\gamma\beta} & \dots & \eta_{\gamma\gamma} \end{bmatrix} \begin{bmatrix} P_\alpha \\ P_\beta \\ \dots \\ P_\gamma \end{bmatrix} \tag{2}$$

where L represents the demand, P the power input and η the coupling matrix. It has to be observed that according to the example proposed, the energy coming from the electrical grid and the energy coming from the battery can be placed both in the demand and in the generation side.

The determination of the coupling matrix needs to be assessed taking into account the amount, characteristics and interconnections of the energy equipment. In the following paragraphs, an outline of relationships depending on different situations is carried out. These basic rules form the information needed to develop the model for more complex systems. With these, it will be possible to establish the coupling matrix that represents the EH and which relates the generation side with the demand side.

2.3.1 Energy converter with one input and one output

In this case an energy converter β with an input energy P_α has one only output: L_β. The power relationship between input and output is represented by:

$$L_\beta = P_\alpha \eta_{\beta\alpha} \tag{3}$$

where $\eta_{\beta\alpha}$ is the performance indicator of the converter, which can be the COP or the efficiency depending on the equipment considered. The COP can be constant or can be dependent on different parameters such as temperature or operating point.

2.3.2 Energy converter in series

This case represents the situation where all the output from one energy converter goes directly to another energy converter. This is called multistage energy conversion. The power output at the end of the last energy converted is computed by multiplying all the COPs in the chain. For the case with two energy converters:

$$L_\theta = P_\alpha \eta_{\beta\alpha} \eta_{\theta\beta} \tag{4}$$

2.3.3 Available energy in a converter

The power provided by an energy converter or energy source can be supplied to several energy converter or demand points. Power can be given to these systems simultaneously as long as there is energy available in the energy converter or generator. This can be represented mathematically as:

$$\sum_{i=1}^{n} P_{\alpha i} \leq P_{\alpha} \tag{5}$$

where:

$$P_{\alpha i} = P_{\alpha i} v_i \tag{6}$$

v_i being the dispatch factor to the different demands connected to the same source.

2.3.4 Upper and lower production limits

Every energy conversion equipment has a range within which it is possible to generate or convert electricity. It has to be assured that the energy that passes through the equipment falls between the specified thresholds. Mathematically it is expressed as:

$$lb_{\gamma} \leq P_{\alpha} \eta_{\gamma\alpha} \leq ub_{\gamma} \tag{7}$$

where lb_{γ} and ub_{γ} are the lower and upper limits, respectively.

The basic rules for the proper development of the coupling matrix have been explained. Their logic can be applied to any system composed by interconnected energy assets to develop the mathematical model of an EH.

2.4 Energy optimization

The optimization is an essential step for the successful implementation of a VPP. Once the model of the system has been developed, an evaluation of the state of the plant at a specified number of time instants has to be carried out to achieve all the benefits mentioned in this chapter. The optimization will allow to reach the best efficiency in the use of resources from an economical and environmental perspective as well as facilitate to the grid the integration of active prosumers, demand side management (DSM) and renewable energy sources.

An optimization is the selection of the best solution for a specified problem. The simplest optimization problems deal with the maximization or minimization of a variable. In mathematics, conventional optimization problems are usually stated in terms of minimization. A general manner to represent one of these is:

$$\text{Given}: f : A \rightarrow \Re$$
$$\text{Find}: x_0 \in A \text{ such that } f(x_0) \leq f(x) \text{ for all } x \in A$$

For the purpose here assessed, f can be considered as the energy of the system that is being considered, the operational and maintenance cost, the environmental impact or any other aspect related to the exploitation of energy assets. The function f is the *objective function* that wants to be minimized. A is a subset of the real space that is understood as a set of constraints that needs to be achieved or fulfilled. It is represented as group of equalities and inequalities that the solution should meet to be valid. In the energy frame, these equations deal with factors such as meeting the demand and comply with the operational bounds of the system. The domain A of f is called the *search space,* and the elements x in A are called *candidate solutions*. There are several types of optimization problems and possible solutions depending on the nature of the situation that is being studied. For a system where several energy assets are present and a time optimization has to be carried out, multi-period mixed-integer problems are the ones that represent the most of its operation, as can be seen in [25].

There are different purposes that lead to the decision of building a VPP, as, for example, total energy use, energy cost, production scheduling and emissions. All these factors have to be reflected in the objective function. The most used method to handle multi-criteria decisions is the weighted global criterion method. This method allows the interested party to adjust the preferences of the system. The objective function is obtained as:

$$f = \sum_{j=1}^{N} f_j^{trans} w_j \tag{8}$$

where f_j^{trans} is a normalized value of a single objective function and w_j the relative weight assigned to that objective function. f_j^{trans} is created in order to obtain the same range for the different objectives contemplated and has to be calculated as:

$$f_j^{trans} = \frac{f_j(x,y) - f_j^{\min}}{f_j^{max} - f_j^{\min}} \tag{9}$$

where f_j^{max} and $f_j^{\min}$ are maximum and minimum values of the objective function in question, respectively.

In order to obtain the optimal operation point of the VPP, the optimization process should be performed in two stages. The first stage deals with the decision of where to introduce or extract energy from the battery, decision of selling or buying energy from the electrical grid and the scheduling of manageable loads. The scheduling horizon of this optimization is normally one day, as this is the time interval at which the electricity price from the market is known. The scheduling horizon is divided into time slots; usually there are 96 time slots per day, one every 15 minutes. As shown in [17], the objective function in this optimization case is formed by three terms: energy cost, scheduling preferences and climatic comfort. For the case of the energy cost, it can be expressed as:

$$f_1^1 = B\sum_t P_{BE}C_{BE} + A\sum_t P_{CB}C_{CB} + (1-B)\sum_t P_{SE}C_{SE} + (1-A)\sum_t P_{DB}C_{DB} \tag{10}$$

where A and B are Booleans that designate if the VPP if selling/buying electricity from the grid and charging/discharging the battery. The other parameters refer to the following:

- P_{BE}: energy bought from the electrical grid
- C_{BE}: cost of the energy bought from the electrical grid
- P_{CB}: energy inserted in the battery
- C_{CB}: cost for inserting energy in the battery
- P_{SE}: energy sold to the electrical grid
- C_{SE}: cost of energy sold to the electrical grid. It has to be noted that this value is negative

- P_{DB}: energy extracted from the battery
- C_{DB}: cost of the energy extracted from the battery

The objective function related to the scheduling is expressed as:

$$f_2^1 = \frac{\sum_{SL} \sum_t \gamma}{N_{SL}} \tag{11}$$

where γ is a scheduling preference parameter and N_{SL} is the number of scheduling loads. Last of all, the objective function for the comfort is:

$$f_3^1 = g^{max} + \frac{\sum_{SL} \sum_t g_r}{RT} \tag{12}$$

where g^{max} is the maximum temperature gap allowable, g_r is the real temperature gap, R are the rooms considered and T are the time slots. For this first optimization stage, the restrictions should contain the fulfillment of non-manageable loads, the characteristics of manageable load (working cycles, minimum number of consecutive ON slots, maximum number of consecutive slots OFF, etc.) and power restriction on the energy input.

Once the energy input and output from the grid, batteries and loads are obtained, the second stage deals with the optimization of the energy flow inside the EH. In this case the objective functions are related to maximizing the efficiency and minimizing the energy cost and the total emissions. The function that represents the total energy use can be represented as:

$$f_1^2 = \sum_{\alpha} \sum_{t} P_t^{\alpha} \tag{13}$$

where P_t^{α} represents the energy generated or converted by α at the time instant t. It can also represent the energy input to the VPP such as the electricity from the grid and the natural gas. For the case of the cost of the system, the objective function is:

$$f_2^2 = \sum_{\alpha} \sum_{t} P_t^{\alpha} \lambda^{\alpha} \tag{14}$$

where λ^{α} represents the cost of the energy for a converter or energy input α. Last of all, for considering the emissions of the system:

$$f_3^2 = \sum_{\alpha} \sum_{t} P_t^{\alpha} e^{\alpha} \tag{15}$$

where parameter e^{α} represents the emission factor of the energy provided by α. For this stage, the restrictions should include the fulfillment of the demand and the power limitation of the different energy converters inside the EH.

3. Communication architecture and data management

As it has been mentioned in the previous section, forecasting techniques based on data-driven models are widely used when dealing with energy-related variables. This kind of models usually needs huge amounts of information to properly train or tune their inner structures, and once the models are generated, the central controller must be capable of sending the forecasted schedule decisions to each system's local controller. To do so, not only a sensor network has to be deployed in the facility, but also an efficient data communication system is needed.

Therefore, one of the key elements of the VPP concept is the communication systems. The existence of reliable, accurate, efficient and safe data exchange is crucial for a bidirectional, near real-time information flow. In addition, the current trend in the field is to make use of a service-oriented architecture (SOA), enabling an easy integration of the plant data in systems that can analyze and optimize not only the operation of the facility itself but also the global operation of the whole energy grid. To this extent, the cloud computing platforms such as Amazon Web Services, Microsoft Azure or Google Cloud.

The cost of implementing a communication system can be high, so it is vital to select a suitable data communication technology. There are several wired and wireless technologies available that can provide the required communication infrastructure. The selection of one (or more) of these communication technologies will depend on the quality of service (QoS), data range, reliability, latency, economic viability, etc. The capabilities offered by these technologies are also strongly related to the VPP grid structure. Looking it from the prosumer point of view, the main automation system is the energy management system (EMS) which is responsible for the management and optimization of the energy assets supervised in the VPP.

3.1 Energy management systems

The term energy management system (EMS) refers to an integrated system that enables the monitoring, management and control of several devices providing the necessary support for an effective operation of electrical generation and transmission facilities.

At a high level, the architecture of an EMS is divided into three layers which are management, automation and field levels [26] as depicted in **Figure 5**. The management (or supervisory) level comprises the human interface with the system by means of human machine interfaces (HMI) or SCADA-like software systems and contains most of the system logic and modules related with data analysis. The automation (or local) level provides the primary control devices connected via networked controllers and usually operating via BACnet, ZigBee, etc. protocols. The field (or plant) level represents the physical devices like energy meters, sensors and actuators installed to the plant equipment. These devices should be connected to local controllers by means of field-bus communications to allow control functionalities.

VPP supervision and control systems can be centralized or decentralized [27]. In the centralized control, all the knowledge about the devices in the VPP and the energy market is located in the central controller. Although this is a simple solution in most of the cases, when dealing with a large number of devices, the optimization of the control strategy can become computationally expensive for the central controller. In a distributed or decentralized control, the complexity is divided vertically within the VPP. Local controllers supervise and define the control strategy, and a higher-level controller coordinates their decisions in order to reach a global optimum state.

3.2 Communication requirements

The architecture defined above is organized in three hierarchical levels. Each of these communication layers has its requirements in terms of bandwidth, latency or cyber security. For example, at the field level, to have a large bandwidth is not a

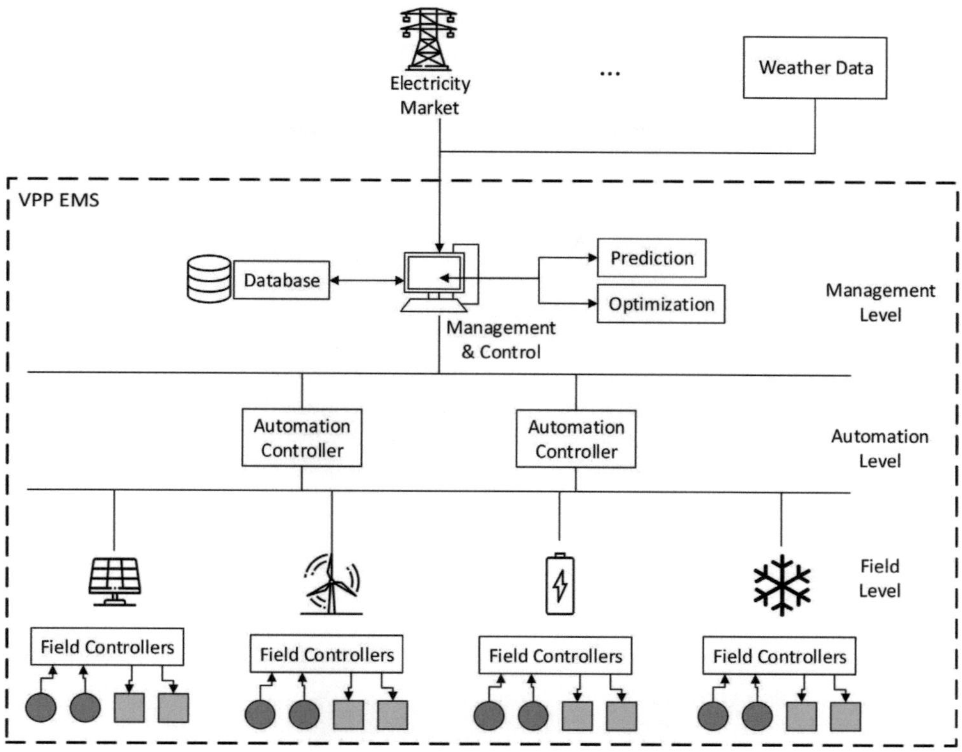

Figure 5.
EMS three-level architecture.

common requirement, but a short latency is mandatory given the near real-time control performed at this level.

3.2.1 Field level requirements

The total amount of data sent per node per transmission is typically less than a hundred bytes. That being the case, the communication bandwidth at this level is well within 100 kbps [28]. The sampling and transmission frequency are commonly between a range of 5 and 15 min. A simulation carried out in [29] showed that larger data collection frequencies fail at detecting short-term voltage anomalies. Besides, a time synchronization service is required to refer all the data gathered in the plant with respect to the UTC. A general-purpose time synchronization service like the network time protocol (NTP) is used given that the accuracy required does not exceed the order of seconds.

Typically, the sensors manage analogical data that is then is handled to an analog to digital converter (ADC) followed by an interface to a process control computer. The sensors can also have a digital communication module and contain embedded digital electronic processing systems. Actuators work in a reverse sense, converting electrical signals to the appropriate physical variable. However, as they have to amplify the energy level to produce the change in the real variables, actuators are high-power devices, while sensors are not.

3.2.2 Automation level requirements

At the automation level, the data from several local controllers is received; typically, the order of system it aggregates is in the order of tens. Hence, a bandwidth of more or less 1 Mbps is enough to fulfill its requirements [28]. The time synchronization and latency are also limited like in the field level.

The automation level is in charge of several tasks such as the monitoring of the variables to check the system or component failure, the management of the set points for the important process variables and the control reconfiguration and tuning of the control loops.

3.2.3 Management level requirements

The management level shares a large part of the requirements of the automation level. Typically, in this layer, the main limits for its requirements are represented by the capabilities of the already existing communication infrastructure.

Here, the information arrives as time series type of data; this data is characterized by having a timestamp associated with each value. In the management level, this data is collected and analyzed to perform some actions like process scheduling or maintenance management.

3.3 Communication technologies and protocols

When a message is transmitted onto a bus, it has to contain information like the identifier of the sending device, the message or data to transmit, the destination device address and some additional information (e.g. for error checking). After that, when the message reaches the destination device, this one has to know not only the message codification but also how to handle its reception using procedures to avoid collisions and prioritization.

These rules about connectivity and communication are defined by the communication system protocol. These protocols for VPP system must adhere to several criteria: efficient and reliable communication, interoperability with other systems and integration into the power system. For easier integration, it is usually desirable that the VPP system supports the communication protocols already in use by any other equipment. In addition to standardized protocols, there are many proprietary protocols like C-Bus or PROFIBUS.

Both wired and wireless technologies have been specified through standards. The advantages of wired technologies over wireless ones are the higher data transmission rate, security and reliability but at the expense of high installation cost. On the other hand, wireless technologies have fewer installation costs and can be easily deployed, but they exhibit low data transmission rates and signal interference problems. With the advent of ICT and IoT, more and more sensors and meters are needed to be integrated, monitored and controlled. In this situation, the lower deployment cost and better scalability of wireless technologies make them better candidates. In the below sections, some of the widely used communication technologies for metering and sensory purpose will be covered.

3.3.1 Power line carriers

In terms of wired technologies, PLC is the most widely used technology [30]. Power line carriers (PLCs) consist of introducing a modulated carrier signal over the existing electricity grid. No additional wiring is required; therefore, PCL can be considered as a cost-effective and straightforward solution. PLC can be classified into two major categories: narrowband PLC and broadband PLC.

The operating rate of the narrowband PLC is in a range of 3–500 kHz. It can be further classified as low data rate and high data rate narrowband PLC. The former is a single carrier technology with data rate up to 10 kbps and works on the recommendations of standards like LonWorks or KNX. The high data rate narrow-band is a multi-carrier technology with a data rate below 1 Mbps. The broadband PLC technology has an operating range of 2–250 MHz with a data rate of hundreds of Mbps.

PLC technologies have been used since a long time ago for electric energy-related services in industrial automation like remote meter reading and remote load management. PCLs can be applied in any point of the VPP environment, and its main advantage is the low running costs, and that can be installed using current infrastructure. The security issues are solved like in the ZigBee technology, using the 128-bit AES encryption.

3.3.2 GSM and GPRS

Global System for Mobile Communications (GSM) is known as the world's most deployed cellular technology. It operates on the 1800 MHz and 900 MHz bands, and its data rate is up to 270 kbps. General Packet Radio Service (GPRS) data rate is much larger than GSM. Its main drawback is the reliability of Short Message Service (SMS) in case of network congestion.

The main application of GPRS and GSM is in smart metering solutions for remote billing and power consumption monitoring, usually applied in smart grids covering from the generation stage to the consumption one, including both the transmission and distribution.

3.3.3 WiFi

Wireless sensing technology has been gaining popularity in the last years given the fact that wireless sensors are easy to install and cheaper in price and, among all the wireless sensing technologies, WiFi is the most popular. Developed under the IEEE 802.11 standards family, it provides a robust performance even in noisy channels and supports a wide range of data rates. The local security issues are tackled by the WPA2 protocol based on the 128 bit AES encryption technique, and to ensure secure communication through public Internet access, virtual private networks (VPNs) are typically used [31].

WiFi is the most dominant wireless technology for the high speed it can offer but is more expensive than other technologies because of its higher consumption and device price. WiFi is mostly used for building automation, remote control, meter reading, etc. in the tertiary sector and has been used as a proxy for human occupancy in some HVAC actuation models.

3.3.4 Ethernet

Ethernet is a low-cost communication method and is widely used for communication between PLCs and SCADA systems. Ethernet is available like optical fiber, shielded twisted pairs or coaxial cables. Among these, optical fiber is more secure and popular due to the absence of electromagnetic interference and electrical current. Ethernet uses carrier-sense multiple access with collision detection (CSMA-CD) methods for sensing data. Ethernet is not suitable for real-time application because the a priori estimation of the data packet maximum transmission time is impossible.

The main disadvantage of Ethernet is its wired nature and the need of deploying a new cable network. However, it is robust and does not have running costs. The most common implementation of Ethernet in today's industrial automation field is to use an Ethernet/IP network, applying the capabilities of traditional Ethernet to connect different facilities in the same network via the Internet.

3.3.5 Modbus

Introduced by Modicon Corporation, it is widely used due to its simplicity and reliability. It includes a remote terminal unit (RTU), transmission control protocol (TCP) and ASCII mode of transmission and supports RS-232, R-422, RS-485 and Ethernet-based equipment. Because of its simplicity and open-source availability, it is popular for local communication building and also has become the standard for industrial SCADA systems.

The security issues are not addressed in Modbus. It does not support authentication nor encryption; thus, it is less secure and more vulnerable to cyberattacks.

3.3.6 OPC UA

The OPC UA is a machine-to-machine communication protocol for industrial automation developed by the OPC Foundation. It is the next generation of the original OPC which is applied in different technologies like building automation or process control. OPC UA was developed to tackle the emerging needs of industrial automation.

OPC UA was designed to be fully scalable and enable both the horizontal and vertical communications across all the layers. In addition, it uses a service-oriented architecture, and two transport protocols are defined: an optimized TCP for high performance and a HTTP/HTTPS web service with binary or XML-coded messages.

Table 1 shows a summary of the main characteristics of each of the communication technologies reviewed.

3.4 Selection of sensing solution

According to [32], the factors that influence the selection of sensing and metering solutions are the following:

- Accuracy: In Europe, the accuracy of meters is defined by directives such as the Measuring Instruments Directive (MID). A common feature in this kind of directives is to classify the meters by their percentage accuracy.

- Ease of deployment: The ease of deployment refers to the different installation and networking challenges that must be tackled. For example, wireless sensors have reduced installation costs and provide better flexibility than their wired counterpart. Other factors to consider are the interoperability, installation in an accessible location or safety regulations.

- Communication protocol: As it has been seen in the previous section, there is a wide range of communication technologies each with its advantages and disadvantages.

- Resolution: The resolution determines the possible level of analysis that can be performed. As aforementioned the typical data collection rate is within a range between 5 and 15 minutes.

- Cost: The cost of the equipment is always a driver when deciding the metering equipment. Both initial costs and operating costs must be considered. Usually,

Technology	Type of technology	Characteristics
PLC	Wired	• Low installation costs (no additional wiring is required) • Cost-effective, widely used solution • Narrowband PLC: up to 500 MHz with a data rate below 1 Mbps • Broadband PLC: up to 250 MHz with a data rate of hundreds of Mbps
GSM/GPRS	Wireless	• World's most deployed wireless technology • Operates on 900 and 1800 MHz bands • Rate up to 270 kbps • Low reliability in congested networks
WiFi	Wireless	• Most popular wireless technology • Robust even in noisy channels • Security issues tackled by the WPA2 protocol
Ethernet	Wired	• Low-cost solution • Not suitable for real-time sensing • Needs a new cable network
Modbus	Comm. protocol	• Simple and reliable • Open-source • Standard for SCADA systems • Vulnerable to cyberattacks
OPC UA	Comm. protocol	• Robustness • Scalable and platform independent • Standard transport and encoding protocols (TCP and HTTP)

Table 1.
Summary of characteristics of the technologies and protocols reviewed.

the number of sensors is limited to the minimum to provide adequate control and ensure compliance with regulations.

- Availability: The geographical availability of a particular manufacturer's sensing solution. It will affect to the delivery time and provisioning of technical support.

4. Conclusions

In this chapter the concept of VPP has been explained as the solution for the challenges of upcoming energy markets. The forecasting of future energy situation regarding demand, energy prices and renewable generation has been assessed, reaching the conclusion that artificial intelligence methods are best suited for the stated purpose. The internal energy assets have been modeled by means of an EH. By adding these factors, the VPP is constructed, and its optimization can be carried out. The optimal operation point is obtained by considering current and future energy prices from the market, renewable energy generation, manageable and non-manageable demands and costs and operation constraints of energy equipment. For it to be possible, the EMS and the communication technologies of the plant have to be studied and adapted. The high-level structure and requirements of the EMS have been explained together with the more common communication technologies and protocols. Its advantages and drawbacks have been presented and the important factors for the selection of the sensing technologies described. By incorporating all the exposed factors in an industrial plant, a VPP can be created which will satisfactorily help the energy grid to evolve and will also produce a benefit for the exploitation of its own energy equipment.

Author details

Eva M. Urbano and Víctor Martínez Viol*
MCIA Research Centre, Polytechnic University of Catalonia, Barcelona, Spain

*Address all correspondence to: victor.martinez.viol@upc.edu

References

[1] Chan Y, Kantamaneni R. Study on energy efficiency and energy saving potential in industry and on possible policy mechanisms. 2015; 1-461

[2] Davatgaran V, Saniei M, Mortazavi SS. Optimal bidding strategy for an energy hub in energy market. Energy. 2018;**148**:482-493

[3] Choi S, Min SW. Optimal scheduling and operation of the ESS for prosumer market environment in grid-connected industrial complex. In: 2017 IEEE Ind Appl Soc Annu Meet IAS 2017 2017. 2017. pp. 1-7

[4] Mengelkamp E, Gärttner J, Rock K, et al. Designing microgrid energy markets: A case study: The Brooklyn microgrid. Appl Energy. 2018;**210**: 870-880

[5] Barzegkar-ntovom GA, Kontis EO, Kryonidis GC, et al. Performance assessment of electrical storage on Prosumers via pilot case studies. In: 2019 1st Int Conf Energy Transit Mediterr Area (SyNERGY MED). 2019. pp. 1-6

[6] Huld T. Estimating solar radiation and photovoltaic system performance, the PVGIS approach. In: AFRETEP 1ST Reg Work; Kampala. 2011. pp. 1-84

[7] European Commission. Photovoltaic Geographical Information System (PVGIS). Available from: http://re.jrc.ec.europa.eu/pvgis.html [Accessed: 12 March 2019]

[8] Vestas Wind Systems A/S. General Specification V90–3.0 MW 60 Hz Variable Speed Turbine General Specification for V90–3.0 MW. 2004. pp. 1–31

[9] Chen Q, Folly KA. Wind power forecasting. IFAC-PapersOnLine. 2018; **51**:414-419

[10] Das UK, Tey KS, Seyedmahmoudian M, et al. Forecasting of photovoltaic power generation and model optimization: A review. Renewable and Sustainable Energy Reviews. 2018;**81**:912-928

[11] Shu F, Luonan C. Short-term load forecasting based on an adaptive hybrid method. IEEE Transactions on Power Apparatus and Systems. 2006;**21**: 392-401

[12] Li S, Wang P, Goel L. A novel wavelet-based ensemble method for short-term load forecasting with hybrid neural networks and feature selection. IEEE Transactions on Power Apparatus and Systems. 2016;**31**:1788-1798

[13] Baliyan A, Gaurav K, Kumar Mishra S. A review of short term load forecasting using artificial neural network models. Procedia Computer Science. 2015;**48**:121-125

[14] Jang JR. ANFIS: Adaptive-network-based fuzzy inference system. 1993;**23**. DOI: 10.1109/21.256541. [Epub ahead of print]

[15] Takagi T, Sugeno M. Derivation of fuzzy control rules from human operator's control actions. IFAC Proceedings. 1983;**16**:55-60

[16] Pousinho HMI, Mendes VMF, Catalão JPS. Short-term electricity prices forecasting in a competitive market by a hybrid PSO-ANFIS approach. International Journal of Electrical Power & Energy Systems. 2012;**39**:29-35

[17] Agnetis A, De Pascale G, Detti P, et al. Load scheduling for household energy consumption optimization. IEEE Transactions on Smart Grid. 2013;**4**: 2364-2373

[18] Aneiros G, Vilar J, Raña P. Short-term forecast of daily curves of electricity demand and price. International Journal of Electrical Power & Energy Systems. 2016;**80**:96-108

[19] Vaccaro A, El-Fouly THM, Canizares CA, et al. Local learning-ARIMA adaptive hybrid architecture for hourly electricity price forecasting. In: 2015 IEEE Eindhoven PowerTech, PowerTech 2015. 2015. DOI: 10.1109/PTC.2015.7232253. [Epub ahead of print]

[20] Keles D, Scelle J, Paraschiv F, et al. Extended forecast methods for day-ahead electricity spot prices applying artificial neural networks. Applied Energy. 2016;**162**:218-230

[21] Saâdaoui F. A seasonal feedforward neural network to forecast electricity prices. Neural Computing & Applications. 2017;**28**:835-847

[22] Svalina I, Galzina V, Lujić R, et al. An adaptive network-based fuzzy inference system (ANFIS) for the forecasting: The case of close price indices. Expert Systems with Applications. 2013;**40**:6055-6063

[23] Wei LY. A hybrid model based on ANFIS and adaptive expectation genetic algorithm to forecast TAIEX. Economic Modelling. 2013;**33**:893-899

[24] Kampouropoulos K, Andrade F, Sala E, et al. Multiobjective optimization of multi-carrier energy system using a combination of ANFIS and genetic algorithms. IEEE Transactions on Smart Grid. 2018;**9**:2276-2283

[25] Kampouropoulos K. Multi-Objective Optimization of an Energy Hub Using Artificial Intelligence. Universitat Politècnica de Catalunya; 2018

[26] Brooks DJ, Coole M, Haskell-Dowland P, et al. Building Automation & Control Systems: An Investigation into Vulnerabilities, Current Practice & Security Management Best Practice. Perth; 2017. Available from: https://goo.gl/RM7ukP

[27] Zia MF, Elbouchikhi E, Benbouzid M. Microgrids energy management systems: A critical review on methods, solutions, and prospects. Applied Energy. 2018;**222**:1033-1055

[28] Pasetti M, Rinaldi S, Manerba D. A virtual power plant architecture for the demand-side management of smart prosumers. Applied Sciences. 2018;**8**:432

[29] Wan Yen S, Morris S, Ezra MAG, et al. Effect of smart meter data collection frequency in an early detection of shorter-duration voltage anomalies in smart grids. International Journal of Electrical Power & Energy Systems. 2019;**109**:1-8

[30] Erlinghagen S, Lichtensteiger B, Markard J. Smart meter communication standards in Europe—A comparison. Renewable and Sustainable Energy Reviews. 2015;**43**:1249-1262

[31] Kolenc M, Nemček P, Gutschi C, et al. Performance evaluation of a virtual power plant communication system providing ancillary services. Electric Power Systems Research. 2017;**149**:46-54

[32] Ahmad MW, Mourshed M, Mundow D, et al. Building energy metering and environmental monitoring—A state-of-the-art review and directions for future research. Energy and Buildings. 2016;**120**:85-102

Chapter 3

Novel Methods Based on Deep Learning Applied to Condition Monitoring in Smart Manufacturing Processes

Francisco Arellano Espitia and Lucia Ruiz Soto

Abstract

The Industry 4.0 is the recent trend of automation and the rotating machinery takes a role of great relevance when it comes to meet the demands and challenges of smart manufacturing. Condition-based monitoring (CBM) schemes are the most prominent tool to cover the task of predictive diagnosis. With the current demand of the industry and the increasing complexity of the systems, it is vital to incorporate CBM methodologies that are capable of facing the variability and complexity of manufacturing processes. In recent years, various deep learning techniques have been applied successfully in different areas of research, such as image recognition, robotics, and the detection of abnormalities in clinical studies; some of these techniques have been approaching to the diagnosis of the condition in rotating machinery, promising great results in the Industry 4.0 era. In this chapter, some of the deep learning techniques that promise to make important advances in the field of intelligent fault diagnosis in industrial electromechanical systems will be addressed.

Keywords: Industry 4.0, condition-based monitoring, deep learning

1. Introduction

In recent years within the industrial sector, there is a trend toward the evolution to the Industry 4.0 paradigm, which implies the integration of multiple technologies for the start-up of intelligent factories capable of adapting to the needs and production processes. In these intelligent manufacturing systems, the diagnosis of the condition of the machine is of great importance to prevent failures and avoid monetary losses caused by work stoppages in production. The condition-based monitoring (CBM) schemes are the most accepted to carry out this task. However, one of the main challenges within CBM schemes is the construction of models capable of adapting to highly complex manufacturing systems, which are also subject to high variability of their operating conditions and under the presence of high noise.

Meanwhile, deep learning (DL), or also known as deep neural networks (DNN), has become an analytical tool that has attracted more and more attention from researchers in different areas of research in recent years. The main skill DNN has the ability to learn and extract useful patterns from the data. Therefore, there is currently a tendency to make use of this ability of DNNs to extract significant features from complex manufacturing systems, in order to find the characteristic patterns of faults and thus be able to diagnose anomalies in a timely manner.

As a branch of machine learning, the DL appears from the learning capacity of the artificial neural networks (ANNs); however, the learning capacity of the ANN is limited and presents problems when making the adjustment of weights through error correction (backpropagation). Therefore, different DL architectures have been developed based on stacking multiple layers of ANN, such as auto-encoders, convolutional neural networks, or restricted Boltzmann machine. These architectures seek to obtain hierarchical representations and intrinsic relationships of the data.

The main reason for the application of techniques based on DL in the study of the condition of electromechanical systems is due to the limitation presented by the basic analysis schemes. A traditional diagnostic scheme consists in the extraction and selection of feature engineering from the acquisition data, followed by the application of a dimensionality reduction process and the training of a prediction model based on machine learning which includes support vector machines (SVM), simple neural networks (NN), or regression algorithms.

The main limitation of these traditional diagnostic models is the low capacity to adapt to complex electromechanical systems, and therefore, they have difficulties to adequately characterize all the variability of operation and the different condition states including faults. Unlike traditional schemes based on machine learning, DL schemes are not limited to characterizing systems with only a set of pre-established features, but, through the construction of structures based on neural networks, they are able to extract hierarchical representations of the data. These representations or extracted features have a greater representative capacity because the schemes for their extraction are through non-linear algorithms; with this, a structure based on deep learning is able to learn the adjacent non-linearities of faults and multiple operating conditions of modern manufacturing processes that integrate rotary systems among their components.

The purpose of this literature is to review the emerging research papers of DL focused on condition monitoring. After the brief summary of the DL tools, the main applications of deep learning are about the monitoring of the condition of electromechanical systems.

2. Deep neural networks

To solve binary classification problems, one of the algorithms inspired by the learning process of biological neural networks was called perceptron [1]. The perceptron consists of an input unit directly connected to an output node; the pattern learning process is performed through an operation called activation function. To solve more complex problems, multi-layer perceptron called artificial neural networks (ANN) are used. The training process of these ANNs is performed by executing multiple iterations each time a new measurement is presented, and the weights and biases are adjusted by following a training and error correction algorithm called backpropagation [2].

By adding more hidden layers to the network, it is possible to create a deep structure capable of extracting more complex patterns and finding more hidden data relationships. These deep architectures with multiple hidden layers are known as deep neural networks (DNN). However, a trivial problem, which arises in the training of DNN as more hidden layers are added to the network, is that the correction of the error does not propagate toward the first layer of the network, generating a problem of vanishing of the gradient, hindering the learning process.

2.1 Convolutional neural network

One of the main DNN-based architectures for feature extraction is convolutional neural networks (CNNs). A convolution neural network is a kind artificial neural network designed specifically for identifying patterns of the data [3]. This type of architecture uses a multi-channel input, such as an image or multiple combined signals. The central idea behind CNN is the mathematical operation of convolution, which is a specialized type of linear operation. Each CNN layer performs a transform domain, where the parameters to perform the transformation are organized as a set of filters that connect to the input and thus produce an output layer. The output of a CNN layer is a 3D tensor, which consists of a stack of arrays called feature maps; these features can be used as an input to a next layer of the CNN scheme. A simple CNN architecture is shown in **Figure 1**.

CNN has three main states: convolution, pooling, and fully connected. Convolution puts the input signal through a set of convolutional operators or filters, each of which activates certain features from the data. Pooling minimizes the output through performing a decrease in non-linear sampling, reducing the number of parameters that the network needs to learn. The last layer is a fully connected layer that produces a vector of *N* dimensions, where *N* is the number of classes that the network can predict. This vector contains the probabilities for each class any of the data considered. Finally, the output of a convolutional network is connected to a classification stage, in order to obtain a diagnosis.

2.2 Auto encoders

The auto-encoder is a type of symmetrical neural network that tries to learn the features in a semi-supervised manner by minimizing reconstruction error. A typically structure of an auto-encoder is show in **Figure 2**. This has three layers: input layer, hidden layer, and output layer. The learning procedure of AE consists in two stages: encoder and decoder stages. Input layer and the hidden layer are regarded as an encoder, and the hidden layer and the output layer are regarded as a decoder.

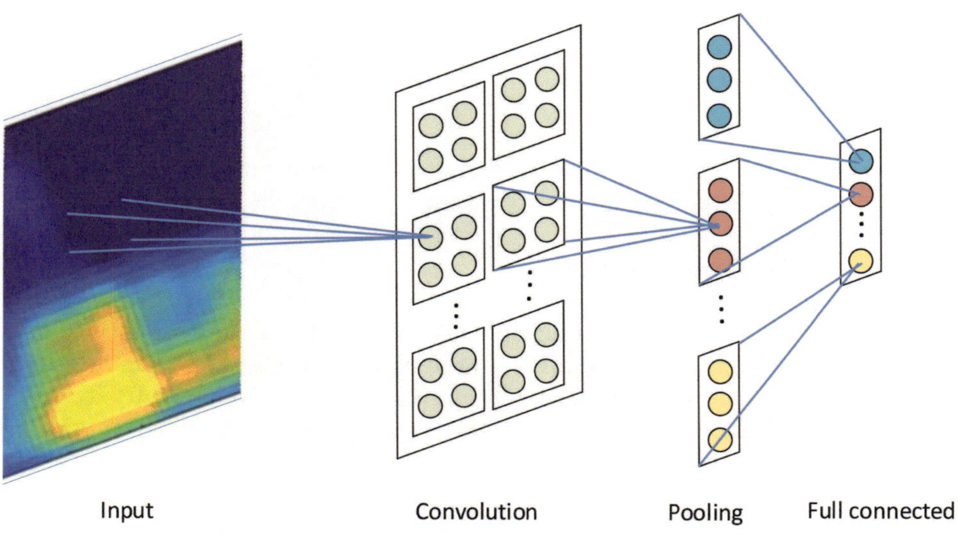

Figure 1.
Architecture of a CNN comprising commonly used layers as convolution and pooling.

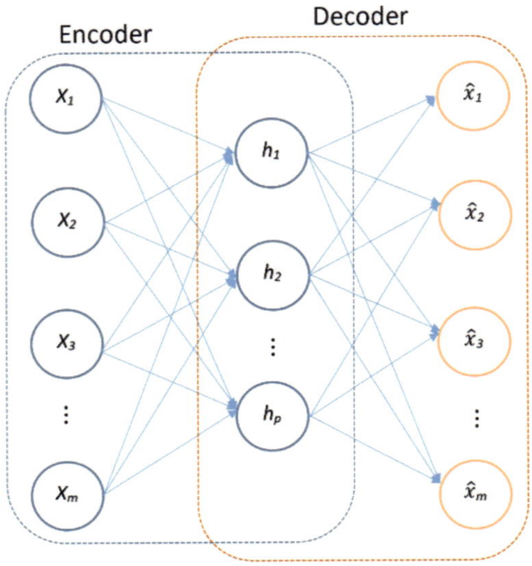

Figure 2.
Architecture of an auto-encoder.

The encoder process is described by $f_{\{W^1,b^1\}}(x) = s_f(W^{(1)}x + b^{(1)})$, and the decoder process is $g_{\{W^2,b^2\}}(x) = s_g(W^{(2)}x + b^{(2)})$, where s_f and s_g are the activation functions of the encoder and decoder, respectively, W is the weight vector between these different layers, and b is the bias. W and b are the trainable parameters of encoder and decoder stages. Furthermore, the sigmoid function is chosen as an activation function to the network. For any sample x^m from input data set $\{x^m\}_{M_{m=1}}$, where M is the number of samples, the encoder stage computing an encode vector $a^m = f_{\{W^1,b^1\}}(x^m)$. Also, a^m can be regarded as a feature representation that the encoder process learning from the input data.

To improve the performance of the traditional auto-encoder, a sparse restriction term is introduced, generating a variant known as sparse auto-encoder (SAE) [4–6]. The sparse restriction term works on the hidden layer to control the number of "active" neurons. In the network, if the output of a neuron is close to 1, the neuron is considered to be "active," otherwise it is "inactive." With the sparse restriction, SAE can obtain proper parameter sets by minimizing the cost function

$$J_{sparse}(W,b) = \frac{1}{M}\sum_{m=1}^{M} L(x^m,\hat{x}^m) + \lambda \cdot ||W||_2^2 + \beta \cdot \sum_{j=1}^{n} KL(\rho||\hat{p_j}) \quad (1)$$

where $L(x^m,\hat{x}^m) = ||x - \hat{x}^m||$ is the average sum of squares error term, λ is the weight decay parameter, β is the sparsity penalty parameter, and ρ is the sparsity parameter.

2.3 Restricted Boltzmann machine

A restricted Boltzmann machine (RBM) is a type of neural network formed by two layers that consist of two groups of units including visible units v and hidden units h with the constraint that there only exists a symmetric connection between visible units and hidden units, and there are no connections between nodes with a same group, as shown in **Figure 3**. These networks are modeled by using stochastic units, habitually Gaussian.

The learning procedure includes several stages known as Gibbs sampling, which gradually modifies the weights to minimize the reconstruction error. These type of NNs is commonly used to model probabilistic relationships between variables.

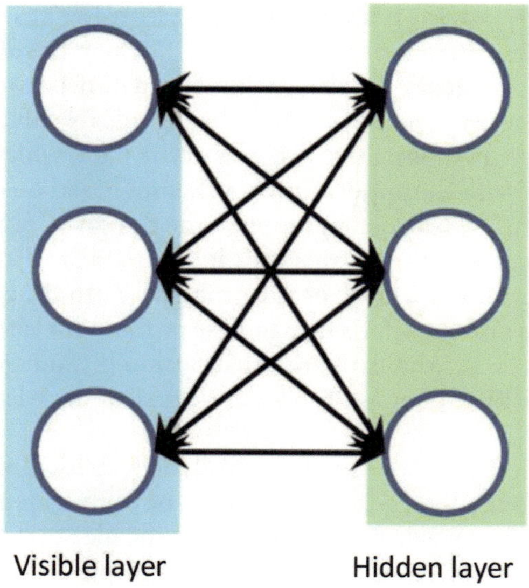

Figure 3.
Schematic illustration of restricted Boltzmann machine.

The most used algorithm to perform the training of an RBM is the contrastive divergence (CD) method [7]. Contrastive divergence is a type of unsupervised learning algorithm; it consists of two stages that can be called positive and negative stages. During the positive stage, the network parameters are modified to replicate the training set, while during the negative stage, it attempts to recreate the data based on the current network configuration.

Restricted Boltzmann machines can be used in deep learning networks in order to extract characteristic patterns from the data. For example, deep belief networks can be designed by stacking various RBM and performing a fine-tuning the resulting deep network with gradient descent and backpropagation. Like the CNN network, a classification stage is connected to the deep network output.

3. Applications of deep learning in condition-based monitoring

For several years, the best tools for monitoring electromechanical systems were data-driven schemes [8]. However, with the increase in the complexity of the systems, the increase in case studies, and the need to incorporate new operating conditions, traditional machine-based schemes are insufficient to characterize such complexity because their discriminative capacity is decreasing. Consequently, the study of the condition of the machine has been moving toward the incorporation of techniques based on deep learning.

Applications such as feature extraction, dimensionality reduction, novelty detection, and transfer learning are some of the tasks that can be carried out through the three deep learning techniques mentioned above: CNN, AE, and RBM.

3.1 Feature extraction

The schemes that are able to extract features effectively and have the ability to handle large data dimensions are needed. Automation of feature engineering has become an emerging topic of research in academia; in recent years, it have emerged deep learning (DL) techniques capable of dealing with the complexity presented in many cases of study. DL is a branch of machine learning based on multi-layer neural networks or deep neural networks (DNNs), where the objective of each layer or level is to learn to transform your input data into a non-linear and more abstract representation. The transformation learned through DNN can contain information that preserves the discriminative features of the data, which helps distinguish the different classes. With the application of schemes based on deep learning, it has been possible to reduce the dependence on the design of functions and limit the manual selection of features; in this way, it is possible to dispense with human experience or great prior knowledge of the problem. With the emergence of deep learning, many fields of research have made use of these tools to facilitate the processing of massive data. In applications such as vision [9], image recognition [10], medical analysis [11], and other applications, the use of deep learning has obtained valuable results.

An example of application of schemes based on deep learning applied to industrial machines is presented in [12]; in this study, they implemented a structure of deep learning known as a stacked denoising auto-encoder to extract data characteristics from five data sets. Another application example is the approach proposed in [13]; in this study, they used a fully connected winner-take-all auto-encoder for the diagnosis of bearing faults, and the model is applied directly on temporary vibration signals without any time-consuming feature engineering process. The results indicate that the implemented method can learn from sparse features from input signals. In [5], they performed an unsupervised learning procedure for the automatic features extraction for the identification of bearing failures. First, they performed a non-linear projection to compress the information through a technique called compressed sensing, followed by the automatic feature extraction in transform domain using a DNN based on sparse stacked auto-encoders. The proposed approach highlights the effectiveness of extracting features automatically through the deep neural network, which demonstrate that they contain relevant information that helps the diagnostic process and thereby helps to reduce human labor. Another investigation in which CNN is applied for the diagnosis of faults in spindle bearings is presented in [14]. In this approach, the image is used as input for CNN to learn the complex characteristics of the system. Finally, the output is processed by a multi-class classifier. This method demonstrated a good classification efficiency regardless of the load fluctuation.

3.2 Dimensionality reduction

Deep learning has attracted attention in several fields of study because it allows the extraction of features from complex signals and the processing of large data. Although the application of deep learning in the diagnosis of faults in industrial machines has concentrated on the automatic extraction of features, the utility of these tools goes further; a clear example is the application of DNN structures for the compression or reduction of dimensionality of data. As we have seen above, structures based on DNN are able to learn intrinsic relationships of the data; however, during this learning process, it is possible to generate a reduced representation of the data. A structure based on DNN capable of learning a coded and reduced representation is the so-called auto-encoder. Unlike linear dimensional reduction techniques, such as principal component analysis (PCA) and linear discriminant analysis (LDA), a structure of stacked auto-encoders can provide a non-linear representation that was learned from the data provided. Therefore, a reduction of dimensionality based on the auto-encoder can provide a better representation that helps to discriminate between the conditions of the machine. An example of the difference between the application of a linear technique for the reduction of dimensionality and one based on the auto-encoder is shown in **Figure 4(a)** and **(b)**, correspondingly.

The management of large data dimensions represents a problem and a challenge in different studies. This is reported in [15], where the generation of big data constitutes a challenge in schemes for protection against cyber-attacks. Therefore, they propose a methodology based on DNN for dimensionality reduction and feature extraction. The method is compared with other dimensionality reduction techniques. The results show that this approach is promising in terms of accuracy for real-world intrusion detection.

A research applied in monitoring the condition for diagnosis of rolling bearing is shown in [16]. In this study, they propose two structures of auto-encoder, a sparse auto-encoder (SAE) and denoising auto-encoder (DAE) for the dimensionality reduction and for the extraction of characteristics, correspondingly. The results show that the applied methodology can effectively improve the performance of fault diagnosis of rolling bearings.

3.3 Novelty detection

To avoid the incorrect evaluation of the health of the machinery, it is necessary to incorporate the current CBM schemes, the ability to classify data from novel scenarios or in test cases, where there is not enough information to describe anomalies. In this regard, research has been carried out to deal with the appearance of unknown scenarios in monitoring schemes. Novelty detection is the method used to recognize test data that differ in some aspects of the data available during training [17]. The study scenarios in which novelty detection schemes have been implemented include detection and medical diagnoses, damage detection in structures and buildings, image and video processing, robotics, and text data mining.

Recent contributions to novelty detection in CBM schemes have managed to combine the classic approaches of multi-faults detection and the ability to detect new operating modes [18]. This study has two main aspects; first, a new signal measurement is examined by a novelty detection model by one-class support vector machine (OC-SVM) method. If the measurement is cataloged as novel, the system is considered to be working under a new operation condition or a new fault. If the measurement is cataloged as known, the system is working under healthy or faulty condition, previously trained.

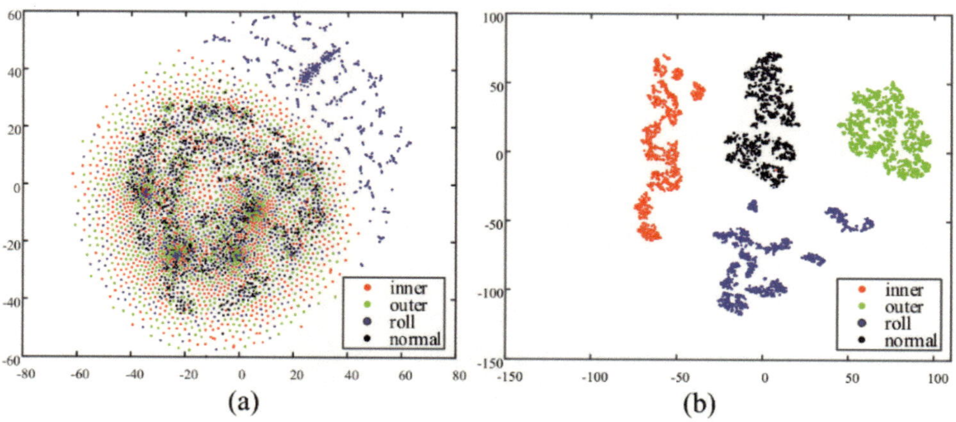

Figure 4.
Resulting two-dimensional by applying: (a) linear technique and (b) DNN architecture.

The task of novelty detection to recognize test data other than the data available during training depends on the method used. The novelty detection process consists of testing the data patterns that were not seen before and comparing them with the normality model, and this may result in a novelty score. The score, which may or may not be probabilistic, is generally compared to a decision threshold, and the test data is considered new if the threshold is exceeded. In applications that use dimensionality reduction to represent the patterns of the data in novelty detection schemes, it is common to find the projections of the data of the normal operation mode delimited by a region or frontier. In these studies, the samples that are outside that delimitation are considered as abnormalities. A representation of a space delimited by two characteristics is shown in **Figure 5**.

Detecting new events is an important need of any data classification scheme. Since we can never train a learning system under all conditions and with all possible objects with the data that the system is likely to find, it is important that it has the ability to differentiate between information from known and unknown events during testing. Many studies have faced in practice the challenging task involved in novelty detection. In this sense, several novelty detection models have been implemented, demonstrating that they work well in different data. Models to novelty detection include both Frequentist and Bayesian methods, information theory, extreme value statistics, support vector methods, other kernel methods, and neural networks.

On the other hand, although the use of DL-based techniques to carry out novelty detection tasks related to the study of the condition of electromechanical systems has not been reported in the literature, in other fields such as automatic driving, it has been proposed to use the reconstruction skills of the AE to carry out this task [19]. For this, the ability of the reconstruction of AE of the input data is used; if the error measurement is low, it is intuited that the input data correspond to known data, whereas if the error loss is high, they are considered unknown data and, therefore, they are data with which the system has not been trained. It is, therefore, believed that DL-based tools can represent a powerful analysis for the study of novelty detection in CBM schemes applied to electromechanical systems.

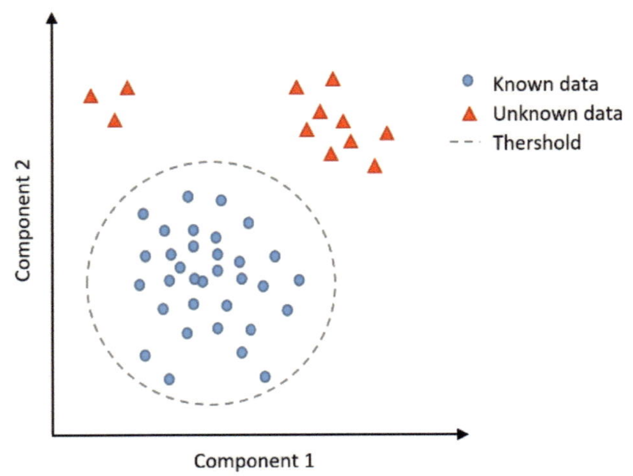

Figure 5.
Delimitation of a boundary by a novelty detection model.

3.4 Transfer learning

Some disadvantages that still prevails in many tasks of classification, regression, and grouping is that the approach that addresses this problem is made under the assumption that all data must be in the same working conditions and have the same distribution of data and space of characteristics to carry out those tasks. However, this assumption in the real world does not happen. This problem occurs because sometimes only a few training data are available for a domain of interest or working condition that is different or similar to that of the planned classification task. For these cases, knowledge transfer would help to improve the performance of the learning process, avoiding strenuous retraining work and the effort of data labeling. In this sense, various applications have begun to explore innovative techniques to address this problem, resulting in schemes based on transfer learning, domain adaptation, and various machine learning techniques.

As seen in the literature, schemes based on deep learning (DL) can learn complex and discriminative relationships from the data. Therefore, it has begun to use structures based on DL with the aim of transferring knowledge from a source task to a target task.

Traditional machine learning algorithms have made great strides in data-based fault diagnosis. They perform the diagnosis on test data using models that are trained on previously collected labeled or unlabeled training data. However, most of them assume that the data must be in the same working conditions and that the distributions of the data for each class considered are the same. The use of transfer learning schemes, in contrast, allows domains (operating conditions), tasks (failure classification), and distributions (number of samples) used in training and testing to be different.

Research on transfer learning has attracted more and more attention; as a result of which, one of the first learning techniques related to knowledge transfer is the multi-task learning framework, which tries to learn several tasks at the same time, even when they are different. In this scheme, transfer learning obtains knowledge of one or several source tasks and applies that knowledge to a target task, being the source task and target task symmetric in many ways. Unlike the learning of multiple tasks, the objective of transfer learning is the target task and not to learn all the source tasks and target tasks at the same time. The roles of the tasks of source and target are no longer the same, but they are similar in the transfer of knowledge.

Figure 6 shows the difference between the learning processes of traditional learning techniques and transfer learning. As we can see, traditional machine learning techniques try to learn each task from scratch, whereas transfer learning techniques try to transfer the knowledge of some previous tasks to a target task when the latter has differences, but also similarities with the source task.

One of the investigations related to transfer learning applied to the diagnosis of faults in industrial systems is the one presented in [20]. In this study, they use the skills of deep learning schemes to extract features with hierarchical representation samples in frequency domain and combine it with a transfer learning process to consider a target task different from the source task. The results obtained show a considerable performance; however, the proposed scheme still considers that the samples of the source domain and the target domain are equal.

Another work related to transfer learning is the one proposed in [21], for the diagnosis of bearing failures. Their proposal analyzed different operating conditions for the source task and the target task. The knowledge transfer process is done through a structure based on neural network, where it first learns the characteristics of a source task, followed, that structure is partially modified to adapt to a new

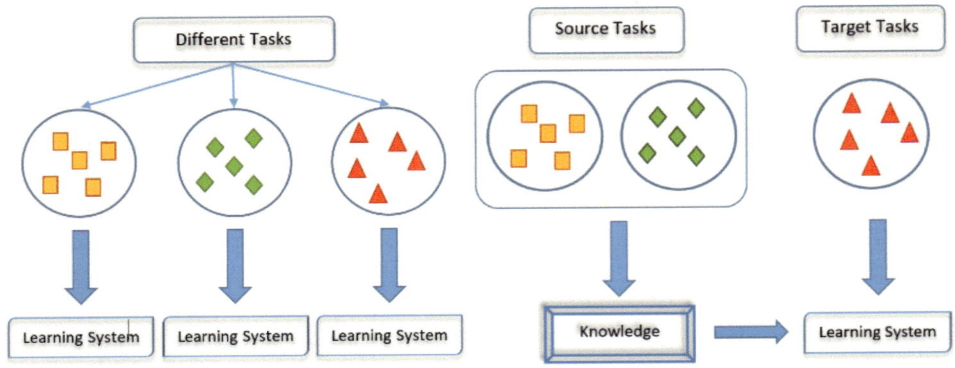

Figure 6.
Multi-task learning framework process and transfer learning process.

target task; however, it conserves part of the weights with which the homework network was trained. The obtained results showed that in some occasions, using a method with knowledge transfer improves the diagnostic performance. However, this performance is affected when the differences between the source task and the target task are increased. With the incorporation of schemes based on transfer learning, we can allow us to adapt different structures based on DL to transfer the experience learned in a diagnostic task and improve performance in a similar but different task.

4. Experimental case of deep learning in CBM

As a case study, the comparison of three different approaches to carry out the process of dimensional reduction in a diagnostic analysis of multi-faults in an electromechanical system is presented, by applying two linear techniques: principal component analysis (PCA) and linear discriminant analysis (LDA), and a technique based on deep learning: an auto-encoder.

The proposed case study to evaluate the performance of multiple fault diagnostic detection in an electromechanical system under the three different schemes is presented in **Figure 7**. First, signal conditioning and acquisition is carried out over vibration signals. Second, the estimation of the 15 statistical-time-based features, such as rms, skewness, mean, kurtosis, impulse factor, etc., is done over each signal. Third, the study of three high-dimensional feature reduction methods, that is, principal component analysis and linear discriminant analysis and sparse auto-encoder, is carried out. Finally, fourth, an NN-based classification structure is performed, where the fault diagnosis and corresponding probability value are obtained. The resulting performance of the considered scheme is analyzed in terms of classification in front to different high-dimensional feature reduction schemes. In addition, it is worth mentioning the resulting projections into a two-dimensional space with an accumulated variance of 95 between the two axes, in the case of PCA analysis. While under an AE study, the effectiveness is measured through the calculation of the MSE reconstruction error, which after 1200 epochs for each of the hidden layers is approximately 0.06.

The goal of the proposed approach is to evaluate the information extraction and dimensionality reduction capabilities of a non-linear technique such as auto-encoder. For this, a methodology based on the study of the condition using vibration signals is implemented. For different condition, they have been considered to be evaluated in terms of the induction motor: healthy condition (He), bearing fault

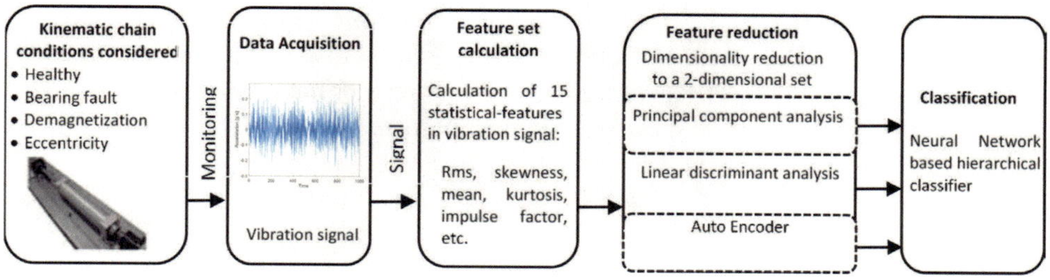

Figure 7.
Proposed scheme for multiple faults diagnosis.

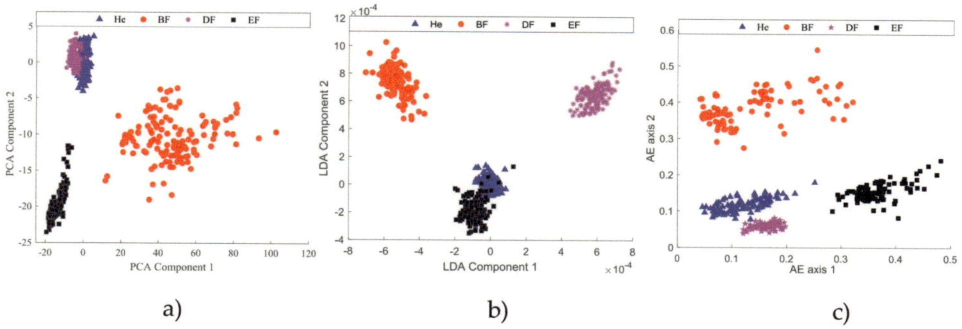

Figure 8.
Evaluation of resulting projections into a two-dimensional space. (a) PCA. (b) LDA. (c) Auto-encoder.

(BF), demagnetized fault (DF), and eccentricity fault (EF). In order to numerically characterize the acquired physical magnitudes, a 1-s segmentation is proposed. For each segment, a set of statistical-time features is calculated. To verify the effectiveness of a non-linear dimensionality reduction technique, the projections resulting from the process of reduction of the three techniques are shown in **Figure 8**.

Finally, the classification stage with the NN-based classifier has been configured with five neurons in the hidden layer, besides a logistic sigmoid function has been used as output activation function and 100 epochs are considered for training using the backpropagation rule. The classification ratios for the test sets are approximately 95% for PCA, 98% for LDA, and 99% for auto-encoder.

Two important things can be concluded from this study: first, highlight the capabilities of an SAE-based approach to automatic learning of the most significant characteristics (those that provide more discriminative information) and that this translates into an increase in performance. Second, in regard with the dimensionality reduction, the auto-encoder-based approach shows better discriminative capabilities during the visualization of the results than the linear methods PCA and LDA, with it facilitates the task of classification.

5. Conclusion and future challenges

In this chapter, a review of some of the current techniques based on deep learning and some of the functionalities that they may have within the environment of the diagnostic schemes of electromechanical systems is carried out. Having as reference the high complexity that is increasingly being found in the manufacturing processes, and the new challenges to face in the Industry 4.0 paradigm, it is necessary to improve the diagnostic capabilities of traditional schemes, which is why methodologies based on artificial intelligence and deep learning methods have increasingly called the attention of researchers. However, it remains to be discovered and identified the patterns that these deep neural networks learn, and specifically, within the industry environment, and electromechanical systems, what is the scope and benefits of applying these novel techniques.

Author details

Francisco Arellano Espitia* and Lucia Ruiz Soto
Technical University of Catalonia, Barcelona, Spain

*Address all correspondence to: Francisco.arellano@upc.edu

References

[1] Rosenblatt F. The perceptron: A probabilistic model for information storage and organization in the brain, Cornell Aeronautical Laboratory. Psychological Review. 1958;**65**(6):386-408

[2] Stuart G, Spruston N, Sakmann B, Häusser M. Action potential initiation and backpropagation in neurons of the mammalian CNS. Trends in Neurosciences. 1997;**20**(3):125-131. DOI: 10.1016/s0166-2236(96)10075-8

[3] Krizhevsky A, Sutskever I, Hinton GE. ImageNet classification with deep convolutional neural networks. Neural Information Processing Systems. 2012;**25**(2):84-90. DOI: 10.1145/3065386

[4] Sun W, Shao S, Zhao R, Yan R, Zhang X, Chen X. A sparse auto-encoder-based deep neural network approach for induction motor faults classification. Measurement. 2016;**89**:171-178

[5] Sun J, Yan C, Wen J. Intelligent bearing fault diagnosis method combining compressed data acquisition and deep learning. IEEE Transactions on Instrumentation and Measurement. 2018;**67**(1):185-195

[6] Olshausen BA, Field DJ. Emergence of simple-cell receptive field properties by learning a sparse code for natural images. Nature. 1996;**381**:607-609

[7] Ma X, Wang X. Convergence analysis of contrastive divergence algorithm based on gradient method with errors. Mathematical Problems in Engineering. 2015: Article ID 350102, 9 p

[8] Liu R, Yang Y, Zhao Z, Zhou J. A novel scheme for fault detection using data-driven gap metric technique. In: IEEE 7th Data Driven Control and Learning Systems Conference (DDCLS); Enshi. 2018. pp. 1207-1212

[9] Zheng J, Cao X, Zhang B, Zhen X, Su X. Deep ensemble machine for video classification. IEEE Transactions on Neural Networks and Learning Systems. 2019;**30**(2):553-565

[10] Yuan Y, Mou L, Lu X. Scene recognition by manifold regularized deep learning architecture. IEEE Transactions on Neural Networks and Learning Systems. 2015;**26**(10):2222-2233

[11] Albarqouni S, Baur C, Achilles F, Belagiannis V, Demirci S, Navab N. AggNet: Deep learning from crowds for mitosis detection in breast cancer histology images. IEEE Transactions on Medical Imaging. 2016;**35**(5):1313-1321

[12] Thirukovalluru R, Dixit S, Sevakula RK, Verma NK, Salour A. Generating feature sets for fault diagnosis using denoising stacked auto-encoder. In: 2016 IEEE Inter. Conf. on Progn. & Hlth. Manag. Ottawa, ON: ICPHM; 2016. pp. 1-7

[13] Li C, Zhang W, Peng G, Liu S. Bearing fault diagnosis using fully-connected winner-take-all autoencoder. IEEE Access. 2018;**6**:6103-6115

[14] Ding X, He Q. Energy-fluctuated multiscale feature learning with deep ConvNet for intelligent spindle bearing fault diagnosis. IEEE Transactions on Instrumentation and Measurement. 2017;**66**(8):1926-1935

[15] Abolhasanzadeh B. Nonlinear dimensionality reduction for intrusion detection using auto-encoder bottleneck features. In: 2015 7th Conference on Information and Knowledge Technology. Urmia: IKT; 2015. pp. 1-5

[16] Zhang J, Chen Z, Du X, Xu X, Yu M. Application of stack marginalised sparse denoising auto-encoder in fault diagnosis of rolling bearing.

The Journal of Engineering. 2018;**2018**(16):1772-1777

[17] Pimentel MA, Clifton DA, Clifton L, Tarassenko L. A review of novelty detection. Signal Processing. 2014;**99**:215-249

[18] Carino JA, Delgado-Prieto M, Zurita D, Millan M, Ortega Redondo JA, Romero-Troncoso R. Enhanced industrial machinery condition monitoring methodology based on novelty detection and multi-modal analysis. IEEE Access. 2016;**4**:7594-7604

[19] Amini A, Schwarting W, Rosman G, Araki B, Karaman S, Rus D. Variational autoencoder for end-to-end control of autonomous driving with novelty detection and training De-biasing. IEEE/RSJ International Conference on Intelligent Robots and Systems (IROS), Madrid. 2018;**2018**:568-575

[20] Lu W, Liang B, Cheng Y, Meng D, Yang J, Zhang T. Deep model based domain adaptation for fault diagnosis. IEEE Transactions on Industrial Electronics. 2017;**64**(3):2296-2305

[21] Wen L, Gao L, Li X. A new deep transfer learning based on sparse auto-encoder for fault diagnosis. IEEE Transactions on Systems, Man, and Cybernetics: Systems. 2019;**49**(1):136-144

Chapter 4

Smart Monitoring Based on Novelty Detection and Artificial Intelligence Applied to the Condition Assessment of Rotating Machinery in the Industry 4.0

Saucedo-Dorantes Juan Jose, Jaen-Cuellar Arturo Yosimar and Elvira-Ortiz David Alejandro

Abstract

The application of condition monitoring strategies for detecting and assessing unexpected events during the operation of rotating machines is still nowadays the most important equipment used in industrial processes; thus, their appropriate working condition must be ensured, aiming to avoid unexpected breakdowns that could represent important economical loses. In this regard, smart monitoring approaches are currently playing an important role for the condition assessment of industrial machinery. Hence, in this work an application is presented based on a novelty detection approach and artificial intelligence techniques for monitoring and assessing the working condition of gearbox-based machinery used in processes of the Industry 4.0. The main contribution of this work lies in modeling the normal working condition of such gearbox-based industrial process and then identifying the occurrence of faulty conditions under a novelty detection framework.

Keywords: smart monitoring, condition assessment, novelty detection, artificial intelligence, Industry 4.0, rotating machinery

1. Introduction

Nowadays industrial applications are straightly involved with intelligent manufacturing processes, and the importance of this issue is reflected in many different activities of the human being, for example, in health, economy, and even comfort. Thus, it is possible to say that most of the daily activities carried out by humans have a direct relationship with those elements produced in the industry that facilitate its making. On the other hand, during the last years, industrial sites have been continuously subjected to several transformations, aiming to improve the effectiveness of its processes and to increase the production quality. Consequently, the integration of multiple technologies in the industry has been performed by the composition of actuators and sensors with cyber-physical systems and Internet of Things devices. Such integration leads to the Industry 4.0 that is the fourth phase of manufacturing and industrial sectors where the automated manufacturing and process monitoring have been enhanced [1]. Consequently, under the integration of such complex systems, it should be highlighted that it is important to ensure its safety and reliability by the implementation of condition-based monitoring approaches. Thereby, in order to guarantee the proper operation in manufacturing processes and aiming to avoid undesirable downtimes, the working condition of the machine components must be continuously assessed. Commonly, most of the industrial applications and processes are involved with the use of mechanical and electrical rotating machines, where electric motors and gearboxes represent the most used elements to perform specific manufacturing processes [2].

In fact, this statement is validated and justified because electric motors, gearboxes, couplings, and shafts represent approximately more than 90% of the elements that compose any industrial process [3]. Indeed, these elements that integrate the main operating system of industrial machinery are also considered, and also known, as the electromechanical machine system. In this sense, electric motors are considered as the most important element in electromechanical systems since its performed functions cannot be carried out and replaced by any other element; additionally, these elements play also an important role in most of the industrial applications because two-thirds of the total electricity is consumed by them. Therefore, these issues make suitable the application of condition monitoring approaches to avoid the occurrence of unexpected breakdowns; even more, it must be noted that under the appearance of a faulty condition, such damaged element can also have influence over the proper operation of the whole elements that are linked to the electromechanical system and crucial damages may be produced [4].

As it has been mentioned, industrial sites have been subjected to several transformations, and through the integration of multiple technologies, a significant improvement in the production efficiency has been obtained. Accordingly, complex electromechanical systems compose most of the industrial machinery that is used in different applications of modern industry. In this regard, several condition monitoring-based approaches have been developed aiming to guarantee the appropriate working condition of industrial machinery. Thus, data-driven condition monitoring strategies represent the most common and suitable approach for carrying out the condition assessment in electromechanical systems; this approach has been preferred since it only takes into account the use of information of available data; therefore, based on known and available information, an accurate diagnosis of the machine under inspection is obtained [2, 4, 5].

In this sense, most of the data-driven approaches mainly include the continuous monitoring of different physical magnitudes that contain significant information related to the machine working condition. Indeed, stator current signals, vibrations, temperatures, and operational rotating speeds, among others, are some of the most accepted and reliable magnitudes used in condition monitoring strategies. On the other hand, aiming to provide the condition assessment, such monitored signals are then analyzed by different signal processing techniques, where time-domain analysis, frequency-domain analysis, and time-frequency domain analysis have been commonly implemented in several condition monitoring strategies [5]. However, although there exist different signal processing, it has been demonstrated that statistical time-based domain features contain significant information that describes the behavior related to the rotating machine working condition. Thereby, the calculation of a high-performance set of features is achieved because statistical time domain-based features have advantages for describing changes and trends of time-domain signals [6].

On the other side, although other sophisticated techniques such as fast Fourier transform (FFT) and discrete wavelet transforms (DWT), among others, also lead to the calculation of features related to the machine condition, the implementation of such techniques considers additional knowledge and experience about the proper usage of the techniques and also complete information of the parameters of the machine operation. Accordingly, it should be highlighted that it is not totally true that sophisticated and complex signal processing may always lead to the estimation of the most representative set of features to describe the machine condition. In this regard, from a practical application viewpoint and based on practical experience, the simplest way to evaluate and identify the early occurrence of faults is by means of analyzing trends of physical magnitudes acquired during the continuous working operation of the machine. Thus, as aforementioned, the appropriate early detection of faults may help in the reduction of monetary losses caused by unscheduled maintenance task.

Certainly, the detection and identification of faulty operating modes involve a critical procedure in which the signal processing or feature calculation must be carefully performed. Another important issue to perform and improve the condition assessment is the consideration of artificial intelligence (AI) for carrying out the automatic fault diagnosis. Indeed, the use of AI in condition monitoring strategies has been rapidly increased, and its application to identify the occurrence of faults in rotating machinery is an adequate and coherent option to obtain high-performance results. Additionally, it has been shown that an appropriated application of AI in condition monitoring approaches provides a powerful capacity for detecting and classifying the appearance of single or multiple faults in electromechanical systems. This potential provided by AI is reached because the limitations of classical space-transform techniques, when nonlinearities characterize the analyzed system, are overcome [6].

Hence, several AI techniques have been addressed with the main purpose of being applied in monitoring tasks of industrial machinery, for instance, artificial neural networks, genetic algorithms, fuzzy logic, support vector machines, Bayesian networks, self-organizing maps (SOM), and case-based reasoning, among others, represent some of the most techniques used in condition monitoring approaches [7]. However, there are still great challenges for developing new condition monitoring strategies; indeed, the use of AI techniques has increased because the main challenge of the condition assessment in industrial sites is that nonlinearities are inherent to the working operation [8].

Thereby, the contribution of this chapter lies in the proposal of a condition monitoring strategy for detecting and assessing unexpected working conditions in rotating machines. Such proposal performs the condition assessment under a novelty detection approach based on self-organizing maps. Thus, the proposed condition monitoring method includes the estimation of a statistical time-based set of features from acquired vibration signals; then, the data modeling is carried out through SOM and then the evaluation of novelty detection events. Finally, if novelties are detected, a retraining and incremental learning procedure is considered by including a dimensionality reduction stage by means of the linear discriminant analysis. This proposal is validated and applied to a real laboratory gearbox-based electromechanical system.

2. Fault detection and identification

The condition monitoring assessment is involved with the behavior analysis of the machine working operation; thus, the consideration of stator currents or vibrations as informative physical magnitudes for condition monitoring represents the most preferred and accepted approaches in the related literature. Also, although different information fusion levels are considered, such as signal-level or decision-level, dealing with electromechanical condition monitoring, the feature-level represents the most appropriate, since many numerical fault indicators from aforementioned physical magnitudes have been proposed as suitable fault indexes in multiple studies [9, 10]. In this regard, time-domain, frequency domain, and time-frequency domain are the three feature estimation approaches widely applied during the physical magnitude characterization process. Although techniques based on frequency and time-frequency domain, such as classical Fourier transform or wavelet analysis have been widely applied, most of these techniques require a deep knowledge of the fault effects over the resulting frequency distributions of the physical magnitudes. Indeed, as stated by Zhang et al. in [11], dealing with complex electromechanical systems, where the resulting interaction among multiple parts is reflected in the acquired physical magnitudes, the consideration of statistical time-domain features represents a performing trade-off between computational simplicity and characterization capabilities of general patterns. Such feature-level fusion scheme needs to consider the processing of a high-dimensional set of numerical features estimated during the characterization of the available physical magnitudes that, although increases the fault detection and identification capabilities, inevitably contain redundant and nonsignificant information.

Dimensionality reduction procedures are applied in order to avoid low fault diagnosis performances and overfitting responses of the condition monitoring schemes. In this regard, classical dimensionality reduction techniques have been widely applied, as the principal component analysis (PCA). However, PCA aims to identify orthogonal components that maximize the preservation of the data variance. That is, PCA seeks for global data representation; thus, considering the unsupervised operation, a set of non-connected data clusters have a negative impact over the resulting representation. Other classical approaches, as linear discriminant analysis, overcome such data topology limitation by means of a supervised approach, as the LDA, where the resulting set of features is a mathematical combination of the original ones maximizing distances among classes [12, 13].

Finally, the classification algorithms, play an important role in data-driven condition monitoring schemes to perform the automatic and final diagnosis outcome. In this regard, neural networks and fuzzy inferred systems classically represent the most used classifiers, but also classifiers like decision trees and support vector machines have been widely applied [14–16]. The use of these techniques, however, is related with the maximization of the classification ratio by means of the feature set decomposition following supervised training schemes. According to Shannon's rate-distortion theory, mutual dependencies among various sources and between the input and output spaces contain the actual intrinsic dimension of the data and allow avoiding over-fitted responses. Thus, unsupervised learning approaches applied over the available feature space represent the most coherent processing procedure in order to maintain the underlying physical phenomenon of the system under monitoring. Concerning this problem, manifold learning methods have been applied in the last years to preserve the information in a lower dimensional space. Among them, the self-organizing map, SOM, is the most used, which is based on developing a neural network grid to preserve most of the original distances between feature vector representations in the original feature space [17]. Indeed, the SOM allows a high-dimensional input data mapping over a two-dimensional output layer while preserving as much as possible the structure of the input data. Although SOM leads to model the original data distribution following an unsupervised approach, each of the neuron units used during the original space characterization can be later associated with a class label; thus, through distance criteria, the diagnosis can be estimated during the assessment of a new measurement. Thus, both fault detection and identification tasks can be faced at the same time and, what is more important, considering the same criteria for both outcomes, that is, topological aspects of the data distribution.

3. Novelty detection and diagnosis methodology

The proposed condition monitoring strategy that is applied to the condition assessment of an electromechanical system under a novelty detection framework is composed of five important stages as depicted in **Figure 1**.

The first stage is based on the fact that initially the machine condition is known; in this sense, it is considered as an initial condition that only the available information belongs specifically to the behavior of the healthy condition of the electromechanical system under evaluation. This assumption is asserted and taken into account since all the machinery used in most of the industrial applications starts its life cycle from an initial healthy condition, which means that all elements work properly. Therefore, under this assumption, such available information is obtained from the continuous monitoring of one vibration signal that is monitored during the working operation of the electromechanical system.

In the second stage, the characterization of the machinery behavior is performed; thus, the available vibration signal is processed and analyzed, aiming to carry out a characterization of the machine working condition and also with the aim of highlighting those representative features that can represent the occurrence of abnormal operations. Precisely, the calculation of a representative set of eight statistical time-based domain features is estimated from the acquired vibration signal; this proposed set of features consists of some well-known statistical features such as mean, rms, standard deviation, variance, shape factor, crest factor, skewness, and kurtosis. Indeed, and as it has been mentioned, statistical time-based domain features provide meaningful information leading to the estimation of high-performance feature characterization due to its capability of describing trends and changes in signals; additionally, this proposed set of statistical features has been included in several condition monitoring approaches to perform the assessment of the operating working condition of electromechanical systems used in industrial application [3, 11, 16]. The corresponding mathematical equations of such numerical features are shown in **Table 1**.

Subsequently, in the third stage, the set of statistical features estimated from vibrations is modeled through SOM; the data modeling is performed by SOMs since

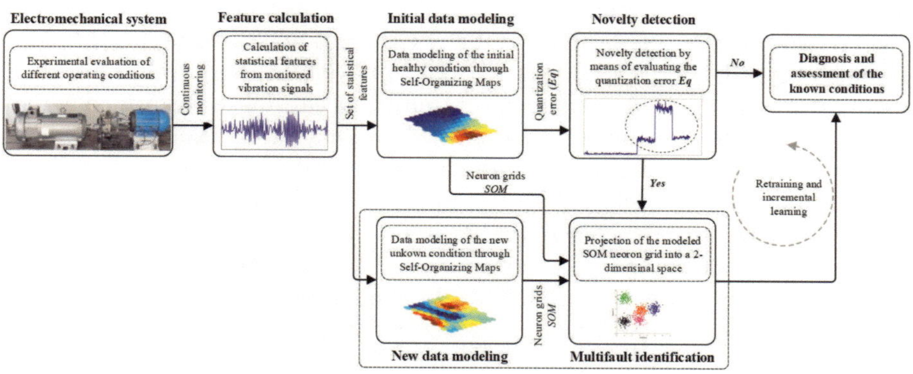

Figure 1.
Rotating machinery-based electromechanical system used to demonstrate the practical implementation of the proposed method.

Mean	$\overline{x} = \frac{1}{n} \cdot \sum_{k=1}^{n} \lvert x_k \rvert$	(1)
Root mean square	$RMS = \sqrt{\frac{1}{n} \cdot \sum_{k=1}^{n} (x_k)^2}$	(2)
Standard deviation	$\sigma = \sqrt{\frac{1}{n} \cdot \sum_{k=1}^{n} (x_k - \overline{x})^2}$	(3)
Variance	$\sigma^2 = \frac{1}{n} \cdot \sum_{k=1}^{n} (x_k - \overline{x})^2$	(4)
Shape factor	$SF_{RMS} = \frac{RMS}{\frac{1}{n} \sum_{k=1}^{n} \lvert x_k \rvert}$	(5)
Crest factor	$CF = \frac{\hat{x}}{RMS}$	(6)
Skewness	$S_k = \frac{E\left[(x_k - \overline{x})^3\right]}{\sigma^3}$	(7)
Kurtosis	$k = \frac{E\left[(x_k - \overline{x})^4\right]}{\sigma^4}$	(8)

Table 1.
Set of statistical time-domain features.

this approach allows to preserve the data topology. Due to the proposed condition, monitoring strategy is based under a novelty detection framework, and the initial and available information is modeled, aiming to represent the initial known condition which is the healthy condition. As a result, a pre-defined neuron SOM grid model is first obtained to characterize the healthy condition of the electromechanical system. Then, in case additional conditions appear, the data modeling is also performed by a specific neuron SOM grid model for each one of the additional operating condition.

Afterward, the novelty detection is performed in the fourth stage; in this sense, there exist different approaches for carrying out the detection of novel events. Classic novelty detection approaches are based on the evaluation of numerical threshold values, and the definition of such values depends on different criteria. Thereby, for this proposal, the novelty detection is performed by evaluating the average quantization error, Eq, obtained during the data modeling through SOMs; indeed, the novelty detection based on the Eq is a coherent option according to the data modeling to detect whether the electromechanical system condition is known or unknown. Certainly, because the healthy condition is initially the unique known and available condition, the evaluation of any other new measurement that does not belong to the known condition will exhibit a different Eq value. Thus, any change presented in the Eq value should be analyzed because this value is an important measurement related to the occurrence of unexpected and unknown events which results in the novelty detection. Otherwise, the diagnosis and condition assessment of the known conditions is carried out if any change is presented in the Eq value.

Finally, the last stage is carried out in case of novelty detection; thus, this stage considers a retraining process where an incremental learning is performed with the aim of updating the available information with new data that belongs to new operating conditions. In this sense, during the detection of a novelty event, the available information that describes such novel condition is also processed, and from the acquired vibration signal, the statistical time-domain features are also estimated. Then, such new available information represented by the estimated statistical features is modeled through SOMs, and a new neuron SOM grid represents the new condition. Accordingly, as aforementioned, each new operating condition detected under this novelty detection approach has to be modeled by a specific neuron SOM model. Finally, when novelty detection occurs, such neuron SOM grids are subjected to a dimensionality reduction procedure by means of the linear discriminant analysis in order to obtain a maximum linear separation between the considered conditions and also with the aim of obtaining a visual representation the assessed conditions.

4. Case study

In order to demonstrate the practical implementation of the proposed smart monitoring based on novelty detection in an industrial application, a case of study is proposed next.

A rotating machinery-based electromechanical system has been considered; such electromechanical system includes a three-phase IM of 1492-W (model WEG00236ET3E145T-W), a gearbox with 4:1 ratio (model BALDOR GCF4X01AA), and a DC used as a mechanical load (model BALDOR CDP3604). The IM is coupled shaft to shaft to the gearbox, and the gearbox is also coupled shaft to shaft to the DC generator, and a VFD (model WEGCFW08) is also used to feed and control the different operating frequencies of the IM. Besides, the DC generator is used as a non-controlled mechanical load representing around 20% of the nominal load. A picture of the second electromechanical system based on a gearbox is shown in **Figure 2**.

Aiming to detect and assess the appearance of unexpected conditions, a database of different experiments is generated. The data acquisition is carried out by means of a data acquisition system (DAS) that is a proprietary low-cost design based on a field programmable gate array; such DAS uses two 12-bit 4-channel serial-output sampling analog-to-digital converters, model ADS7841 from Texas Instruments. Different physical magnitudes have been acquired during the experiments; that is,

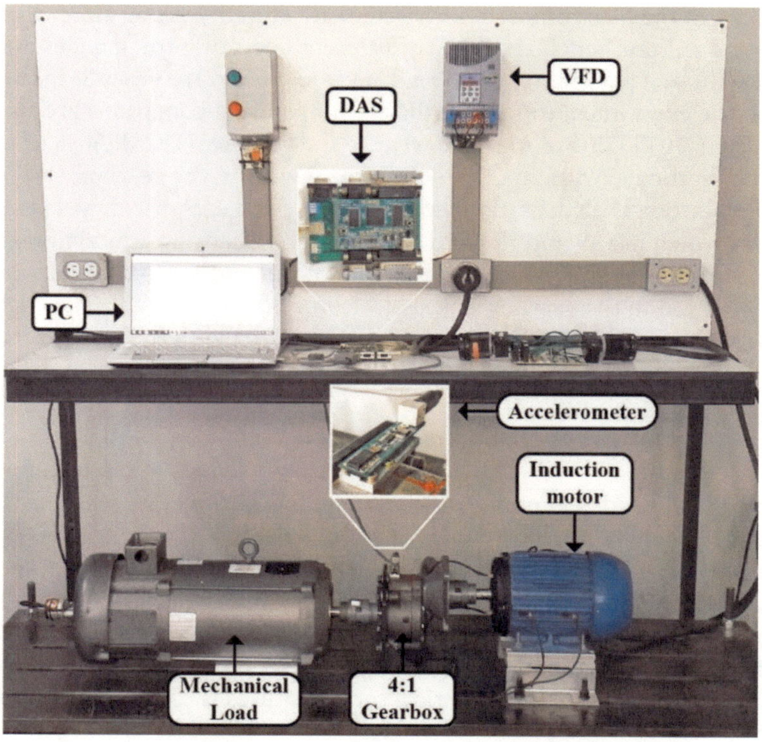

Figure 2.
Rotating machinery-based electromechanical system used to demonstrate the practical implementation of the proposed method.

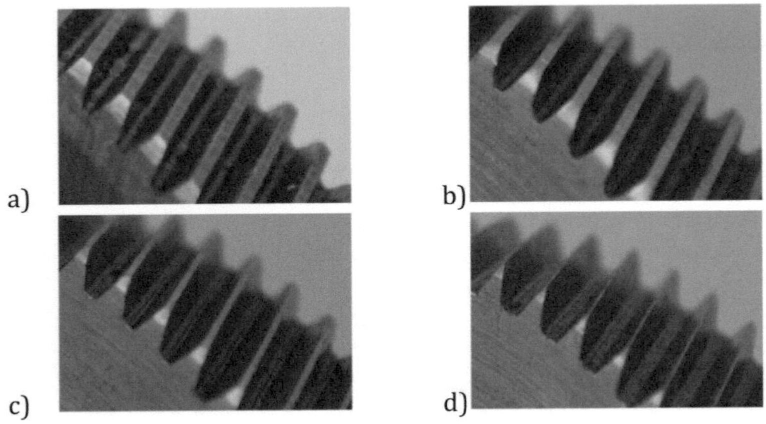

Figure 3.
Set of the faulty conditions evaluated in the gearbox-based electromechanical system: (a) healthy gear, (b) 25% of uniform wear, (c) 50% of uniform wear, and (d) 75% of uniform wear.

the appearance of mechanical vibrations is acquired by means of a triaxial accelerometer (LIS3L02AS4). In this regard, the accelerometer sensor is fixed on the top of the gearbox. For this proposed work, the occurrence of vibrations is analyzed because they are inherent to the rotating condition of the rotating elements that compose the electromechanical system, i.e., electric motors, gearboxes, and bearings, among others [2].

The accelerometer sensor is individually mounted on a board with its corresponding signal conditioning and anti-alias filtering. During the acquisition of vibration signals, the sampling frequency is set to 3 kHz; as a result, 270 kS are stored during 90 s of continuous sampling of the working condition, in the steady-state regime, of the electromechanical system are stored. Furthermore, the IM of the experimental test bench is driven at different operating frequencies during the experimentations; specifically, the operating frequencies are set at 5, 15, and 50 Hz.

During the experimentation, four different operating conditions are also evaluated: healthy (HLT), 25% of uniform wear in the gearbox (W25), 50% of uniform wear in the gearbox (W50), and 75% of uniform wear in the gearbox (W75). In this regard, the gearbox with 4:1 ratio is composed of two gears, the driver gear and the driven gear which has 18 and 72 teeth, respectively. The wear was artificially induced uniformly in all teeth of three similar driven gears: from **Figure 3a–d**, the set of gears tested in the gearbox-based electromechanical system. The experiments are performed by replacing iteratively the healthy gear with the damaged ones.

5. Competency of the method/results

The proposed condition monitoring strategy is based on a novelty detection approach; the implementation of such proposal has been done in Matlab that is a sophisticated software used in several engineering applications. Indeed, the use of Matlab facilitates the signal processing for carrying out the condition assessment of the electromechanical system. Thus, the available vibration signal is first continuously monitored and acquired during the operating condition of the electromechanical systems, and then the statistical set of features is estimated from the vibration signal.

As aforementioned, the initial condition belongs to the healthy condition; in this sense, the data modeling is carried out aiming to obtain a neuron SOM grid model that represents such initial condition. As a result of the data modeling, the first

SOM_1 model obtained and this SOM model only characterize the healthy condition of the electromechanical system. During the data modeling, an average *Eq* error of 0.4932 has been obtained during the training procedure, and during the evaluation the *Eq* error reaches a value of 19.4419. It should be noted that during the evaluation different data information has been used; indeed, the evaluated data belong to a faulty condition tested in the gearbox. In **Figure 4**, a visual representation of the novelty detection achieved by the first modeled neuron SOM_1 grid is shown.

After the first novelty detection, the process and incremental learning is carried out; in this regard, the available data that belong to the first faulty condition (25% of uniform wear) is modeled by a second neuron SOM_2 grid. Thus, the data information related to the working condition of the machine consist of two known conditions which are healthy and 25% of uniform wear. Indeed, during the training of the second SOM model, a *Eq* of 0.8997 is achieved during the training and during the evaluation with available data, which belongs to another unknown condition; the *Eq* error was 7.0773; thus, such significant increase in the *Eq* error depicts that an anormal condition is detected by the novelty detection approach. The visual representation of the *Eq* error is shown in **Figure 5** where it is possible to appreciate the abrupt change due to the occurrence of the unexpected faulty condition.

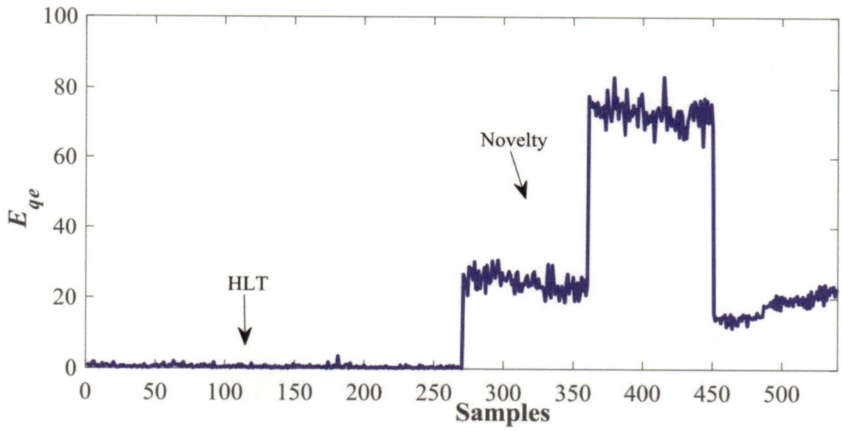

Figure 4.
Novelty detection performed by SOM_1 during the evaluation of the first faulty condition tested in the electromechanical system, 25% of uniform wear in the gearbox.

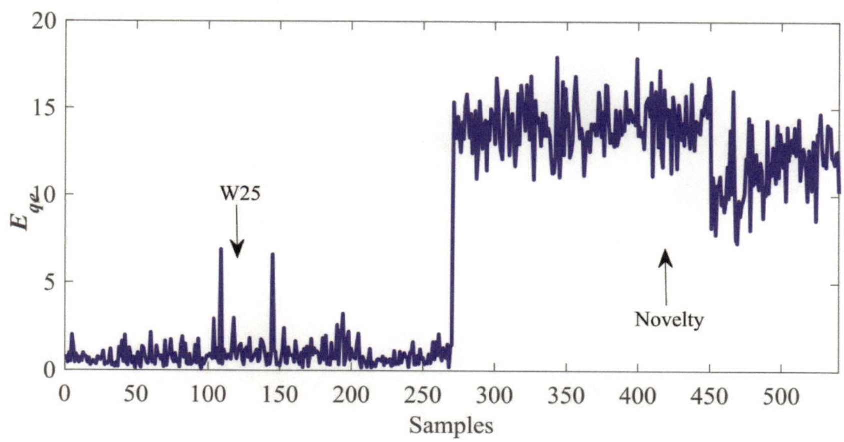

Figure 5.
Novelty detection performed by SOM_2 during the assessment of the second faulty condition, 50% of uniform wear in the gearbox.

The data information to the electromechanical system condition is currently composed of three different conditions, healthy, 25%, and 50% of uniform wear in the gearbox. Later, available information related to another faulty unknown condition is evaluated after performing the retraining process and incremental learning. In this regard, during the training procedure of the third neuron SOM_3 grid, the obtained Eq value was around 0.7077, and during the evaluation of the last faulty condition the achieved Eq was around 6.4367. Thus, the SOM_3 model represents the available information to the third faulty condition that is 50% of uniform wear. In **Figure 6**, the visual representation of the novelty detection performed is shown during the evaluation of the SOM_3 model.

Subsequently, after the last retraining and incremental learning, the available information related to the faulty condition of 75% of uniform wear is also modeled

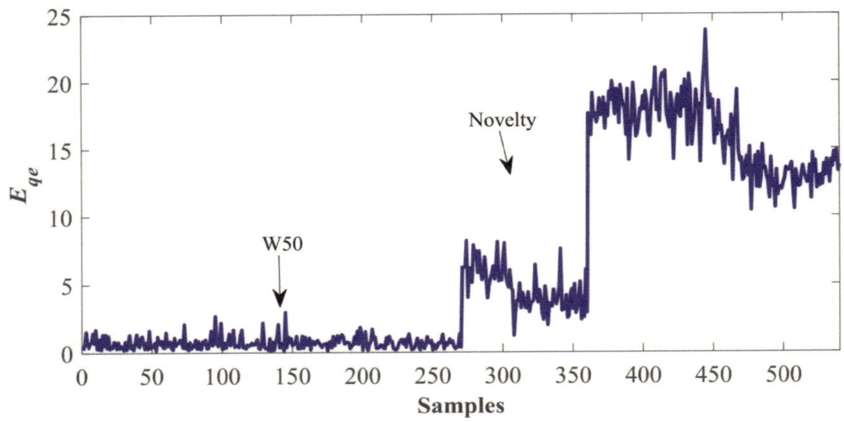

Figure 6.
Novelty detection carried out by SOM_3 obtained for the evaluation of the third faulty condition, 75% of uniform wear in the gearbox.

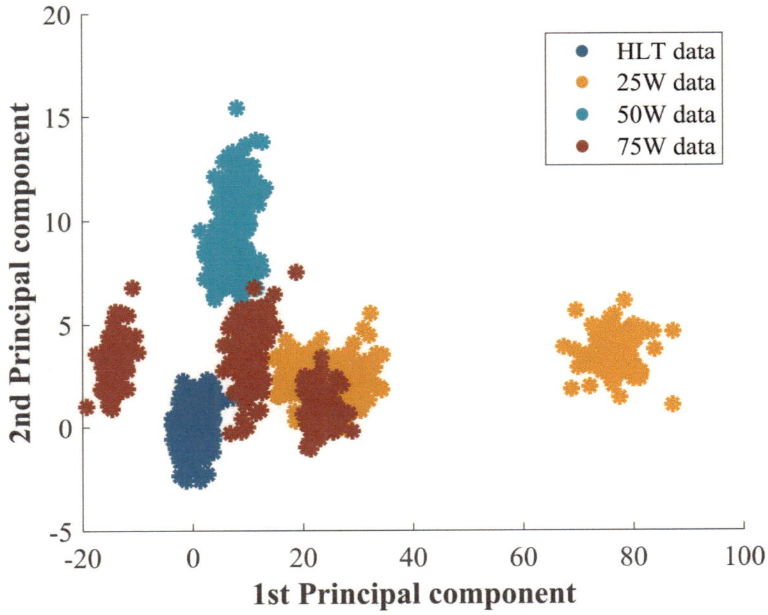

Figure 7.
Resulting two-dimensional projection obtained by considering the four neuron SOM grids modeled for each one of the detected conditions.

by a fourth SOM model, such model is the neuron SOM_4 model, and the E_q error achieved during the training was 0.7700. Because four different operating conditions are detected during the operating condition of the electromechanical system, the final available information stored by the proposed novelty detection approach consist of information capable of detecting four different operating conditions. In case of more novelty detections, the retraining process and incremental learning are again performed, and the information related to the different operating conditions is updated.

Finally, a visual representation of the operating conditions detected during the application of the proposed diagnosis methodology is obtained by means of applying a dimensionality reduction technique, PCA. In this sense, in **Figure 7**, a visual representation of the data distribution of all detected conditions is shown; in this visual representation, it is appreciated that different operating conditions appears. Indeed, different clusters appear for each detected condition because different operating frequencies were considered during the experimental evaluation of the considered conditions.

6. Conclusions

Modern industrial production is characterized by the consideration of machine learning data-based models to support the main aspects of the manufacturing process. In this regard, two main data science challenges related with condition monitoring of electromechanical assets in the Industry 4.0 framework are (i) the premise that only information of the healthy condition is initially available and (ii) the adaptation of the fault detection and identification scheme in order to incorporate new operating conditions. Thus, this paper proposes a new methodology for multifault detection and identification based on incremental learning applied to novel fault detection on electromechanical systems by analyzing vibrations and stator current signatures of the electric motor drive.

Moreover, the proposed condition monitoring strategy based on a novelty detection approach is capable of being applied to other electromechanical systems, and also the consideration of other different physical magnitudes can be also included in such proposal.

Acknowledgements

This research work has been partially supported by the FOFIUAQ2018 under the registered project FIN201811.

Conflict of interest

The authors declare no conflict of interest.

Author details

Saucedo-Dorantes Juan Jose*, Jaen-Cuellar Arturo Yosimar
and Elvira-Ortiz David Alejandro
HSPdigital CA-Mecatronica, Engineering Faculty, Autonomous University of Queretaro, Mexico

*Address all correspondence to: jsaucedo@hspdigital.org

References

[1] Frank AG, Dalenogare LS, Ayala NF. Industry 4.0 technologies: Implementation patterns in manufacturing companies. International Journal of Production Economics. 2019; **210**:15-26

[2] Contreras-Hernandez JL, Almanza-Ojeda DL, Ledesma S, Ibarra-Manzano MA. Motor fault detection using quaternion signal analysis on FPGA. Measurement. 2019;**138**:416-424

[3] Saucedo-Dorantes JJ, Osornio-Rios RA, Delgado-Prieto M, Romero-Troncoso RJ. Diagnosis methodology based on statistical-time features and linear discriminant analysis applied to induction motors. IEEE 11th International Symposium on Diagnostics for Electrical Machines, Power Electronics and Drives (SDEMPED). 2017;**2017**:517-523. DOI: 10.1109/DEMPED.2017.8062404

[4] Ribeiro DA, Ferreira DD, Pereira DA, Braga Junior RA, Nunes RD. Mechanical fault detection in electric motors measured by a digital signal processing device in an optical mouse. Measurement. 2019;**138**:350-355

[5] Frini M, Soualhi A, El Badaoui M. Gear faults diagnosis based on the geometric indicators of electrical signals in three-phase induction motors. Mechanism and Machine Theory. 2019; **138**:1-15

[6] Zhao Y, Li T, Zhang X, Zhang C. Artificial intelligence-based fault detection and diagnosis methods for building energy systems: Advantages, challenges and the future. Renewable and Sustainable Energy Reviews. 2019; **109**:85-101. DOI: 10.1016/j.rser. 2019.04.021

[7] Nasiri S, Khosravani MR, Weinberg K. Fracture mechanics and mechanical fault detection by artificial intelligence methods: A review. Engineering Failure Analysis. 2017;**81**: 270-293. DOI: 10.1016/j.engfailanal. 2017.07.011

[8] Liu R, Yang B, Zio E, Chen X. Artificial intelligence for fault diagnosis of rotating machinery: A review. Mechanical Systems and Signal Processing. 2018;**108**:33-47. DOI: 10.1016/j.ymssp.2018.02.016

[9] Kang Md. M, Islam R, Kim J, Kim JM, Pecht M. Hybrid feature selection scheme for reducing diagnostic performance deterioration caused by outliers in data-driven diagnostics. IEEE Transactions on Industrial Electronics. 2016;**63**(5):3299-3310

[10] Wang S, Yub J, Lapirac E, Lee J. A modified support vector data description based novelty detection approach for machinery components. Applied Soft Computing. 2013;**13**: 1193-1205. DOI: 10.1016/j.asoc. 2012.11.005

[11] Zhang X, Chei W, Wang B, Chen X. Intelligent fault diagnosis of rotating machinery using support vector machine with ant colony algorithm for synchronous feature selection and parameter optimization. Neurocomputing. 2015;**167**:260-279

[12] He Q, Ding X, Pan Y. Machine fault classification based on local discriminant bases and locality preserving projections. Mathematical Problems in Engineering. 2014;**2014**: 1-12. Article ID: 923424

[13] Prieto-Moreno A, Llantes-Santiago o, Garcia-Moreno E. Principal components selection for dimensionality reduction using discriminant information applied to fault diagnosis. Journal of Process Control. 2015;**33**:12-24

[14] Cunha-Palacios RH, Goedtel A, Godoy WF, Fabri JA. Fault identification in the stator winding of induction motors using PCA with artificial neural networks. Journal of Control, Automation and Electrical Systems. 2016;**27**(4):406-418

[15] Manimala K, Getzy David DI, Selvi K. A novel data selection technique using fuzzy c-means clustering to enhance SVM-based power quality classification. Soft Computing. 2015; **19**(5):3123-3144

[16] Sadooghi MS, Khadem SE. Improving one class support vector machine novelty detection scheme using nonlinear features. Pattern Recognition. 2018;**83**:14-33

[17] Li W, Zhang S, He G. Semisupervised distance-preserving self-organizing map for machine-defect detection and classification. IEEE Transactions on Instrumentation and Measurement. 2013;**62**(5):869-879

Section 2

AI Technologies and Tools

Chapter 5

AI for Improving the Overall Equipment Efficiency in Manufacturing Industry

Francesc Bonada, Lluís Echeverria, Xavier Domingo and Gabriel Anzaldi

Abstract

Industry 4.0 has emerged as the perfect scenario for boosting the application of novel artificial intelligence (AI) and machine learning (ML) solutions to industrial process monitoring and optimization. One of the key elements on this new industrial revolution is the hatching of massive process monitoring data, enabled by the cyber-physical systems (CPS) distributed along the manufacturing processes, the proliferation of hybrid Internet of Things (IoT) architectures supported by polyglot data repositories, and big (small) data analytics capabilities. Industry 4.0 paradigm is data-driven, where the smart exploitation of data is providing a large set of competitive advantages impacting productivity, quality, and efficiency key performance indicators (KPIs). Overall equipment efficiency (OEE) has emerged as the target KPI for most manufacturing industries due to the fact that considers three key indicators: availability, quality, and performance. This chapter describes how different AI and ML solutions can enable a big step forward in industrial process control, focusing on OEE impact illustrated by means of real use cases and research project results.

Keywords: machine learning, supervised learning, unsupervised learning, classification, regression, ensembles, artificial intelligence, data mining, data-driven, industry 4.0, smart manufacturing, cyber-physical systems, predictive analytics

1. Introduction

Industry 4.0 has emerged as the perfect scenario for boosting the application of novel artificial intelligence (AI) and machine learning (ML) approaches to industrial process monitoring and optimization. Artificial intelligence is a set of techniques and methodologies aimed at allowing machines, especially computer systems, to simulate human intelligence processes. Machine learning is a subset of artificial intelligence, which provides a set of methodologies and strategies to allow systems for improvement. ML relies in automatic learning procedures, which generate knowledge from previous experiences (data).

One of the key elements on this new industrial revolution, aligned with the disruptive capabilities that AI and ML provide, is the hatching of massive process monitoring data, enabled by the cyber-physical systems (CPS) distributed along the manufacturing processes, the proliferation of hybrid IoT architectures supported by polyglot data repositories, and big (small) data analytics capabilities. Industry 4.0 paradigm is data-driven, and the smart exploitation of this data can provide a large set of competitive advantages impacting productivity, quality, and efficiency key performance indicators (KPIs), which are of utmost importance in the current competitive scenario. Moreover, the manufacturing companies are evolving to low volume with high personalization manufacturing environments [1, 2], where their competitiveness depends on the industries' facilities, considering asset and resource availability, but also in the optimal execution of production processes [3].

Therefore, there is an opportunity on improving the performance of manufacturing processes taking as input those new streams of information; going through analytical processes; creating new supporting models, tools, and services; and benchmarking their recommendations and outcomes against classical approaches. To that end, the overall equipment effectiveness (OEE) is aimed at measuring types of production losses and indicating areas of process improvement [4, 5], ideal to be used as a benchmarking KPI, and one of the main indicators used in manufacturing execution systems (MES) [6, 7].

In the recent years, research projects are aiming to develop novel stand-alone solutions covering the entire monitoring and control value chain: from the CPS for retrieving the data, to wireless communication protocols, big data storage for traceability and advanced artificial intelligence techniques for production control, optimization, and maintenance.

The use of artificial intelligence algorithms is enabling a big step forward in industrial process control and monitoring: from statistical process control (SPC) and statistical quality control (SQC) methodologies, which require a high prior knowledge of the process, to AI optimized process boundaries that provide valuable insights of the monitored process. Industrial applications of AI have its particular requirements. Not only prediction and forecasting capabilities are desired but also increasing the process knowledge with the right selection of AI algorithms, providing a competitive edge over traditional approaches.

AI provides the right set of tools for automatic quality prediction and full part traceability, process optimization, and preventive maintenance. These sets of benefits are directly impacting into productivity KPIs such as OEE and breakdowns, among others.

This chapter will describe the application of different AI and ML algorithms, including classifiers, regressors, or ensembles such as random forest trees, gradient boosting, or support vector machines, to some real-case industrial scenarios, such as quality prediction or process characterization for plastic injection molding or iron foundry, predictive maintenance for industrial water treatment processes, and means of leveraging production data (quality control, time series, batch data, etc.) at different granularity levels and its impact to OEE: from soft real-time to batch analysis and how this can be translated to valuable production insights.

2. Overall equipment effectiveness as KPI

As introduced before, the current scenario for manufacturing industries can be summarized as high demanding, very competitive, with dynamic market demand, and last but not least, hyperconnected and digital. Low-volume and more personalized parts or product work orders are replacing old high-volume ones without personalization, and this implies that effectiveness may not only focus on specific process optimization but also, for example, on improving changeover setup times, reducing scrap, or improving quality. Therefore, there is a clear need on improving and optimizing all manufacturing processes to overcome this demanding situation with effective response, also considering the efficient adaptation and usage of production lines. Traditional approaches tended to focus on throughput and utilization rate, but nowadays this is insufficient. The main reason relies on the importance of unconsidered context information, or even small details, which are making a difference.

The overall equipment effectiveness indicates how good the equipment is being used. OEE has emerged as the target KPI for most manufacturing industries due to the fact that considers three key indicators:

- Availability: Percentage of time that an equipment can operate
- Quality: Percentage of good produced parts
- Performance: Percentage of maximum operation speed used

But before going deep into OEE calculation, we must first understand in which phases of the manufacturing process AI can impact, so that we can relate all together. To that end, please refer to **Figure 1**, where OEE components are summarized, and **Figure 2**, where a standard manufacturing process is compared with an AI-powered one.

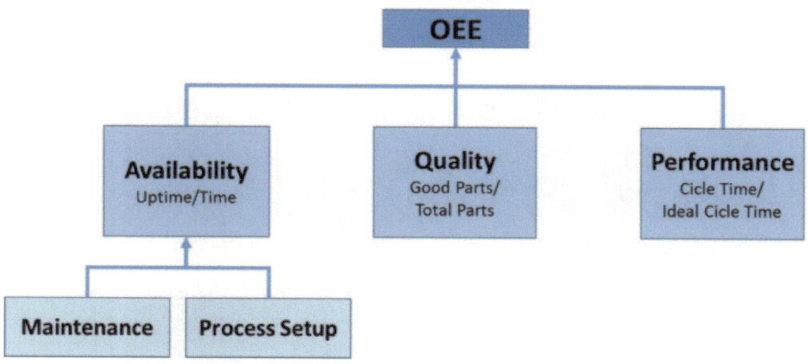

Figure 1.
OEE components and focus.

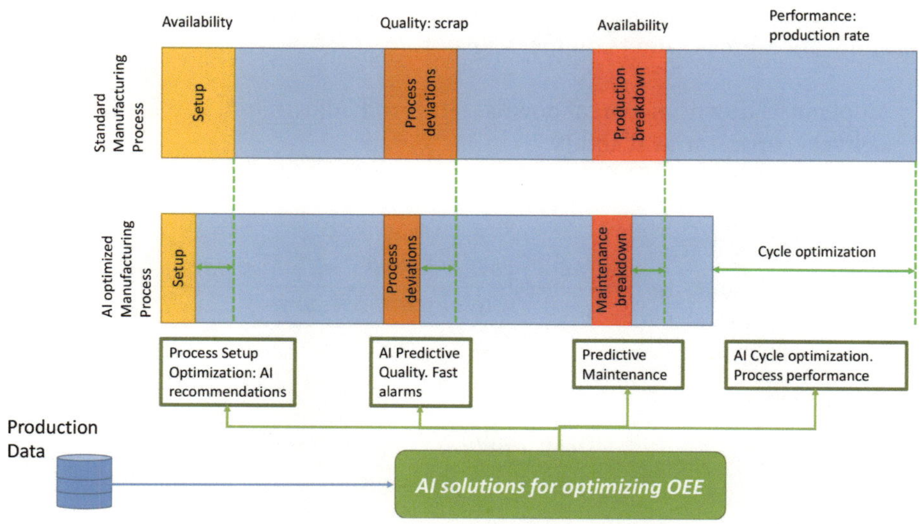

Figure 2.
OEE optimization using AI.

Focusing on **Figure 2**, let us introduce some simple examples of how AI impacts in the manufacturing process:

- Setup: We can improve the time needed to set up or adapt the environment, lines, and tools when a new incoming work order arrives, considering results from previous similar experiences. As we are able to do it in less time, and in a more effective way, we are impacting to the availability of the assets, and consequently, improving the OEE.

- Process deviations: In a similar way, AI allows for quality prediction relying on process parameters, which combined with real-time tuning of execution parameters, results in better quality outcomes, and scrap reduction, again, improving OEE.

- Maintenance: Predictive maintenance allows us to plan and provision with the needed spare parts so that impact in production is minimized. With this management we improve availability, and therefore, OEE is also improved.

In the text below, we define how the literature calculates the OEE, while in the following sections, we'll provide some real examples in which the OEE performance indicator has improved thanks to AI.

According to [8], the overall equipment effectiveness can be calculated as follows:

$$OEE = Availability * Performance\ rate * Quality\ rate. \tag{1}$$

where

- Availability

$$Availability = \frac{(available\ time - unplanned\ downtime)}{available\ time} \tag{2}$$

$$Availability\ time = \text{total available time–planned downtime} \tag{3}$$

Planned downtime: excess capacity, planned breaks, planned maintenance, communication break, and team meetings

- Unplanned downtime: breakdowns, setup and adjustment, late material delivery, operator availability

- Quality rate

$$Quality\ rate = \frac{(total\ produced\ parts - defective\ parts)}{total\ produced\ parts} \tag{4}$$

- Performance

$$Performance = \frac{(total\ production\ parts / operating\ time)}{idle\ run\ rate} \tag{5}$$

$$Operating\ time = Available\ time - unplanned\ downtime. \tag{6}$$

$$Idle\ run\ rate = number\ of\ parts\ per\ minute. \tag{7}$$

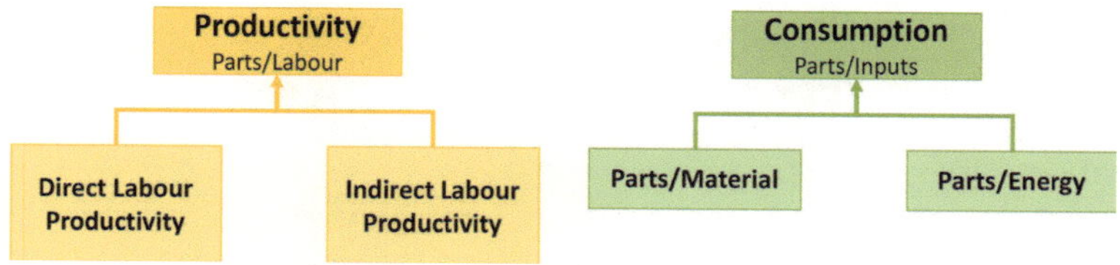

Figure 3.
Productivity indicators.

Other productivity indicators can also be very helpful when evaluating a manufacturing process and benchmarking how AI and ML solutions can provide tangible benefits (**Figure 3**).

Productivity indicators:

- Good produced parts/operator
- Good produced parts/total produced parts (scrap, setup, testing, etc.)

Consumption indicators:

- Material consumption (MC): weight of material consumed per time unit

$$MC\left(\frac{kg}{h}\right) = \frac{part\ weight\ g}{cycle\ time\ sec} * \frac{3600\ sec}{1\ hr} * \frac{1\ kg}{1000\ g} \tag{8}$$

- Specific energy consumption

The specific energy consumption (SEC) can be defined in terms of the amount of power (P) input into the system, divided by the process rate ($\dot{m}$):

$$SEC = \frac{P}{\dot{m}} \tag{9}$$

3. Artificial intelligence for availability

While guarantying high OEE, availability is key. OEE considers availability loss, which considers any event that stops the production plan for a significant amount of time, including unplanned and planned stops. An availability of 100% means the process is always running during planned production time.

There are other considerations which should be included in the availability computation, such as the changeover times. Changeovers are a source of setup and adjustment time, which is one of the main time loss reasons, and thus represent a valuable opportunity for improvement. Changeover times are most commonly improved (reduced) through the application of single-minute exchange of dies (SMED), which relies on performing as many changeover steps as possible while the equipment is running. In fact, these days equipment manufacturers tend to provide an availability rate in the specifications of their equipment, considering, among others, these changeovers.

But what can AI do for us? If we think in data processing and analytical capacities that can be run over information coming from equipment, we rapidly think in predictive maintenance to anticipate problems or virtual sensors to simulate, when feasible, some defective or malfunctioning sensors. Let us see some examples of this in the following subsections.

3.1 Virtual sensors

Virtual sensors (VS) are implemented with software to emulate real-world or even newly artificially defined sensors and are commonly used to (i) compute extra parameters derived from real sensors that are impossible to be measured, contributing to a better understanding of the whole environment, and (ii) simulate real sensor outputs. In the scope of this chapter, the second functionality becomes useful to mitigate system stops due to equipment failure or even planned maintenance, increase the availability of complex systems, and therefore improve the OEE.

For example, in a water treatment facility, where a lot of processes are continuously and simultaneously working to improve the quality of water, the decisions taken to manage the global system depends directly on the observations obtained by the sensors that are deployed along the premises. When any of those sensors is not working, the system cannot operate correctly because sometimes those input values are of utmost importance to determine which decision is correct.

In this case, a VS can be used to simulate and replace that lost sensor during the downtime. For this purpose, the VS is implemented through machine learning algorithms and is based on different inputs or sensors that are operating in the different parts of the water treatment cycle in the system.

Following this procedure, we showcase a VS simulating a measurement of one of the water quality parameters in a water treatment facility. In this case, this measurement is of utmost importance in the system because, depending on its observations, the processes adapt their execution parameters to fit the required quality requirements.

Therefore, we must overcome three main challenges, the combination of which increases considerably the complexity of the problem to be solved using AI/ML algorithms:

- The complexity of the processes: In water treatment facilities, physical and biological processes are combined to clean the water and achieve the expected levels of quality.

- The delayed responses: The water flow may be slow, so a change in the input state will not be immediately reflected in the rest of the system.

- The bad quality of the signals: In this kind of environments, where the sensors are in direct contact with dirty water, the observations usually contain anomalous values.

We start implementing the needed filters and preprocessing steps to clean and improve the data, but usually this is not enough, and ML algorithms cannot achieve the desired performance. Consequently, extra efforts are needed to obtain better models.

This example is a regression problem, where the target is a continuous value, and the predictors are composed of current and past values from other sensors which are part of the same process.

During the first iterations of the analysis, one of the main tasks was to select the optimal past values of each observation/sensor to be used as predictors. This process was done through the analysis of the importance of the variables once a model has been trained, selecting the N last values with the most importance. Also different frequencies of lags were tested using the same approach.

It is important to note that the target variable was not used to make next predictions, avoiding accumulated errors and allowing an infinite horizon of predictions, since the only requirement was the observations of the other sensors.

Different ML algorithms were tested and compared, and **Figure 4** showcases the three ML models that have better performance:

- XGBoost: Extreme gradient boosting. Optimized distributed gradient boosting library. Gradient boosting is a ML technique which produces a prediction model in the form of an ensemble of weak prediction models. It builds the model in a stage-wise fashion, training the weak models sequentially, each trying to correct its predecessor, and it generalizes them by allowing optimization of an arbitrary differentiable loss function [9].

- KNN: K-nearest neighbors. Nonparametric algorithm. Predictions are computed based on the mean of the labels of its nearest neighbors [10].

- RF: Random forests. Ensemble of decision trees, where each tree is usually built from a sample drawn with replacement (bagging method) from the training set. If the sample is obtained without resampling, the method is called pasting. When splitting each node during the construction of a tree, the best split is found either from all input features or a random subset of size *max_features* (RF algorithm hyperparameter) [11].

In order to compare the performance between model results, we are using the following metrics:

- Mean squared error (MSE) measures average squared error of our predictions, calculating the square difference between the predictions and the target and then the average of those values:

$$MSE = \frac{1}{N}\sum_{i=1}^{N}(y_i - \hat{y}_i)^2 \tag{10}$$

- Mean absolute error (MAE) is calculated as an average of absolute differences between the target values and the predictions:

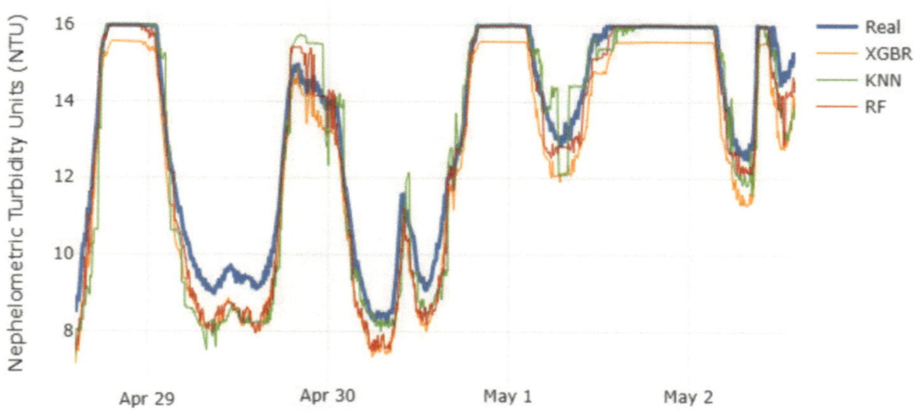

Figure 4.
Initial predictions.

$$MAE = \frac{1}{N}\sum_{i=1}^{N}|y_i - \hat{y}_i| \tag{11}$$

- Explained variance score (EVS) measures the proportion to which a mathematical model accounts for the variation (represented as σ^2, s^2, or Var (X)) of a given data set:

$$EVS = 1 - \frac{Var\{y_i - \hat{y}_i\}}{Var\{y_i\}} \tag{12}$$

The best performance is achieved by random forests followed by KNN (MSE, 0.69; MAE, 0.43; EVS, 0.86) and XGBoost (MSE, 0.81; MAE, 0.85; EVS, 0.98). In all the cases, grid search [12] has been used to tune the hyperparameters.

The scorings seem to be acceptable, but analyzing one by one the predicted values (**Figure 5**), unusual behaviors appear in the predictions. So, in order to try to improve the outputs, an ensemble model is implemented combining the previous algorithms and following the stacking methodology (**Figure 6**, [13]), where a new ML algorithm (called blender or meta learner), in this case a ridge regressor [14], takes the previous predictions as inputs and makes the final prediction, usually better. The blender has been trained following the hold-out set approach.

Basically, the main idea is to, instead of taking the best model and use it to make predictions, try to combine the predictions of completely different ML algorithms, which are based on really different approaches and are good to operate in specific conditions, into a new ensemble which combines the best of each one, is able to operate in all the cases, and reduces the global error.

This process improves significantly the predictions (**Figures 7** and **8**), achieving the following scores, MSE, 0.27; MAE, 0.40; EVS, 0.98, and resulting in a ML model that is able to simulate the real sensor during downtimes, allowing the system to continue working normally.

3.2 Maintenance

We define predictive maintenance as the set of techniques used to determine the condition of equipment, allowing for a better and more personalized maintenance

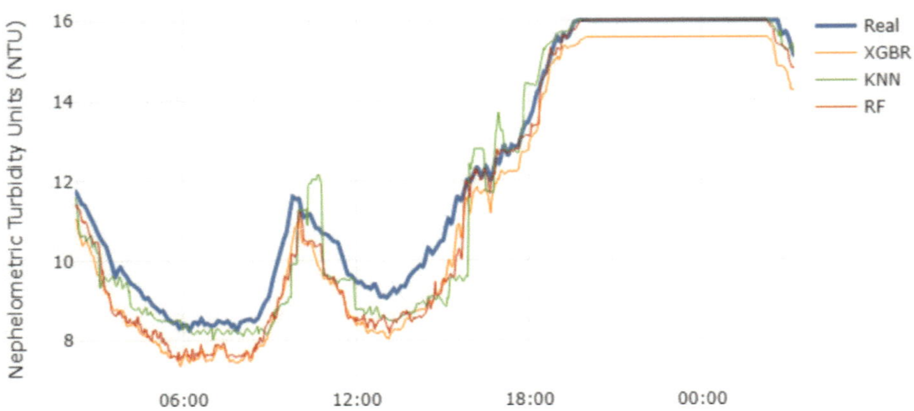

Figure 5.
Initial predictions detail.

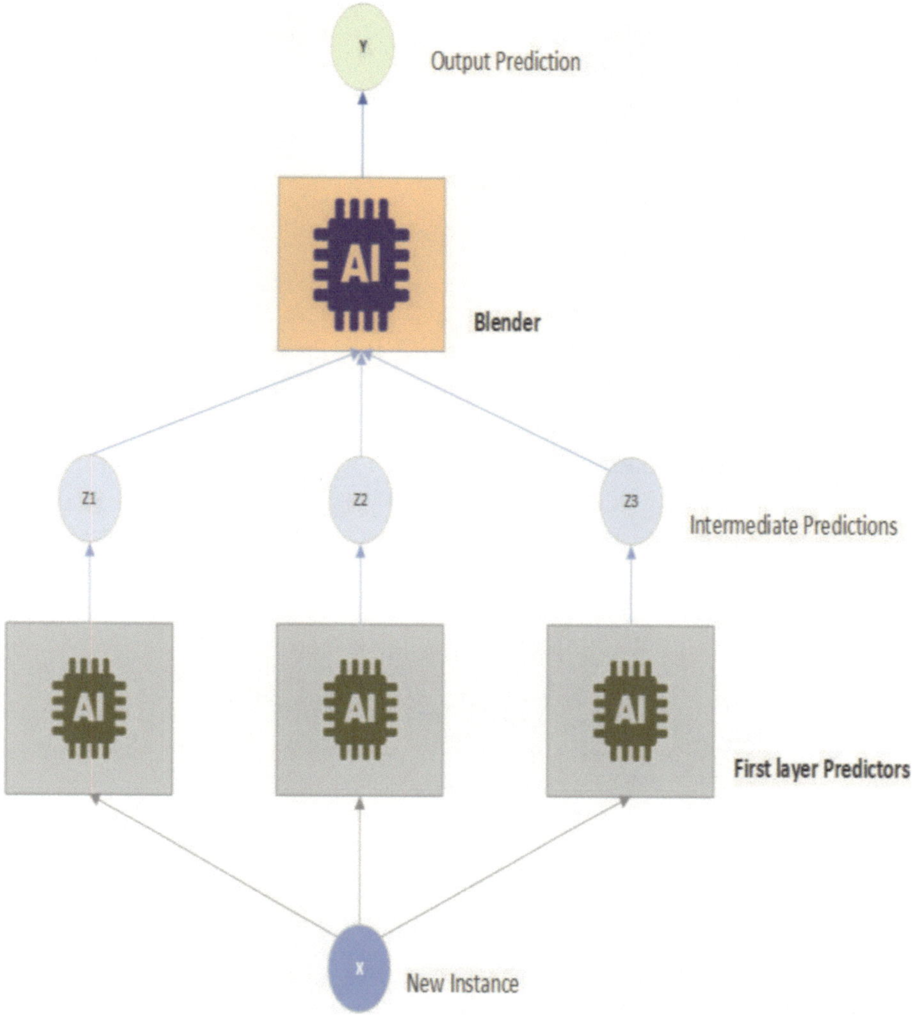

Figure 6.
Blending predictor schema.

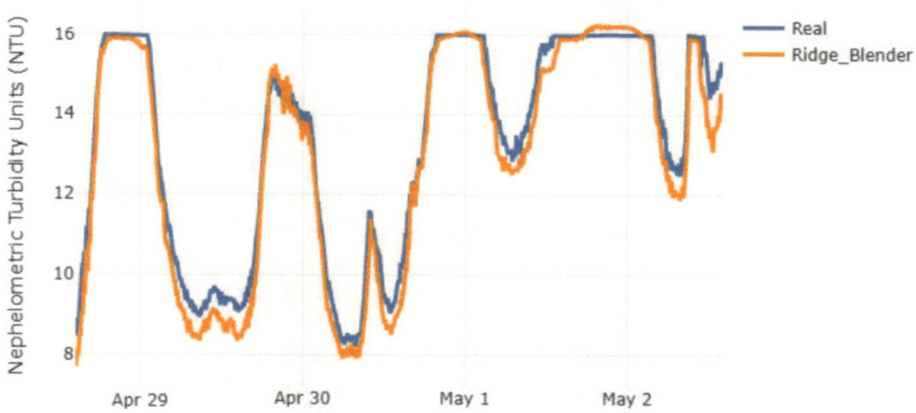

Figure 7.
Final virtual sensor predictions.

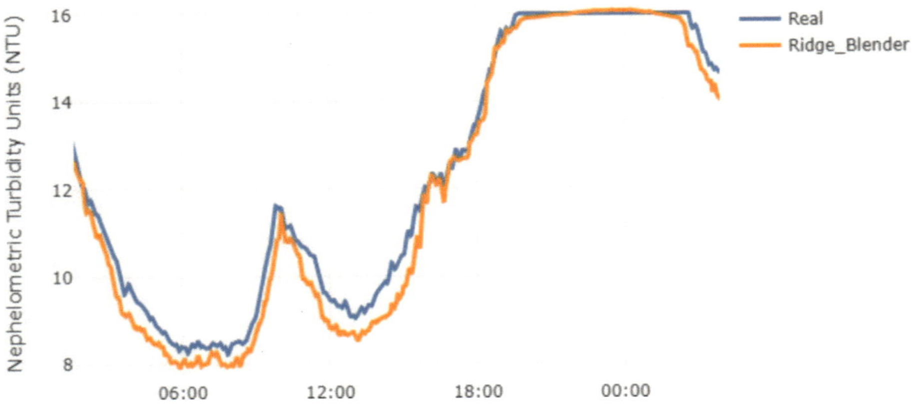

Figure 8.
Final virtual sensor predictions' detail.

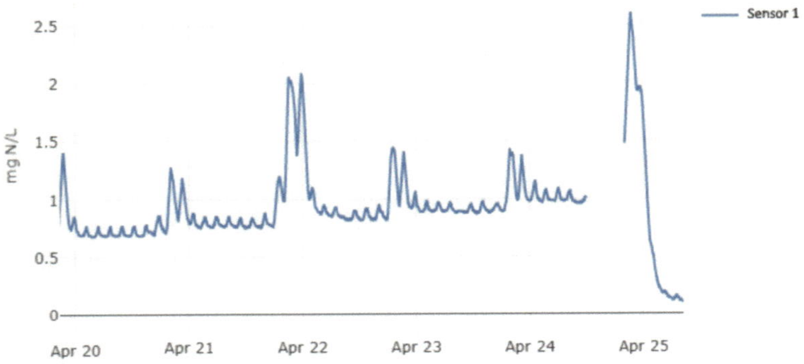

Figure 9.
Drift over the time.

plan. This plan depends on the performance, among other indicators, of the specific equipment (actual condition), instead of only relying on periodic maintenance routines, and this enables spare parts optimization, better maintenance actuations planning, and of course, OEE improvement due to its impact in availability, performance, or even quality.

Continuing on the water treatment facilities case introduced previously, one of the main problems faced in this environment is related to those sensors that are in direct contact with dirty water.

Over the time, a continuous and incremental drift appears in the observations of the sensors, thereby generating incorrect measurements. Since these measurements are the base of the system which takes operational decisions, the sequent of the taken actions will be incorrect, resulting in an unnecessary waste of resources or, even worse, an immediate stop of the system to repair and calibrate the sensors.

This pattern can be easily identified in **Figure 9**, having an incremental drift over the time until day 25, when the sensor was stopped during some hours for maintenance. Once the sensor is turned on again, the real value of the observations is shown, approximately 0.

Before the proposed approach, trying to prevent these problems, a set of preventive maintenances was defined, which consisted of manually taking measurements to compare them in the laboratory with the values of the sensors. Despite this, these actions were not enough, and the drift usually appeared before the scheduled maintenance, making necessary a better approach: a predictive maintenance-based approach.

There are different ways to implement a ML predictive maintenance solution. For example, it is possible to predict the remaining useful life of an equipment, which is a regression problem. But in this case, it has been defined as a binary classification problem, where the goal is to, given an observation (and the previous values), predict if there will be an anomaly in the following 24 hours (estimated minimum range of time to define a maintenance).

In the presented problem, the term anomaly refers to a sensor deviation or a drift in the observations measured by it, due to the contact with dirty water, making necessary a maintenance action in this specific sensor to clean or even replace it if it is necessary.

As in other classification problems, the basic requirement is labeled data, in this case, labeled anomalies. This was the main problem, there was a lot of historical data, but the anomalies were not labeled so the first step consisted of an anomaly detection problem.

Through unsupervised anomaly detection algorithms, such as:

- Isolation forest: Isolation forest algorithm isolates observations by randomly selecting a feature and then randomly selecting a split value between the maximum and minimum values of the selected feature. Since recursive partitioning can be represented by a tree structure, the number of splittings required to isolate a sample is equivalent to the path length from the root node to the terminating node. This path length, averaged over a forest of such random trees, is a measure of normality [15].

- Local outlier factor: Local outlier factor algorithm computes a score reflecting the degree of abnormality of the observations. It measures the local density deviation of a given data point with respect to its neighbors. The idea is to detect the samples that have a substantially lower density than their neighbors [16].

And thanks to an intensive data preprocessing steps such as data segmentation or feature engineering (which made the task easier to detect this specific anomaly), the historical dataset was labeled. Finally, a simple clustering algorithm was run to discard different anomalies.

The result of the anomaly detection analysis is shown in **Figure 10**, where sensor 1 is measuring a value different than 0 (anomaly), and therefore the system tries to force a response increasing excessively the resource measured by sensor 2.

Finally, we face the predictive maintenance classification problem, where the key was the definition of the target variable: a binary column indicating whether in

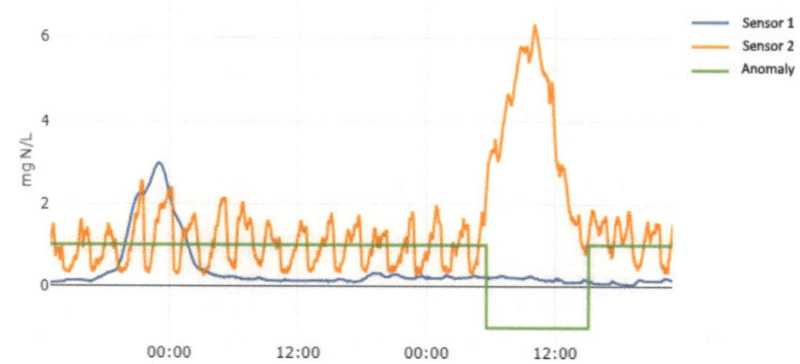

Figure 10.
Anomaly detection results.

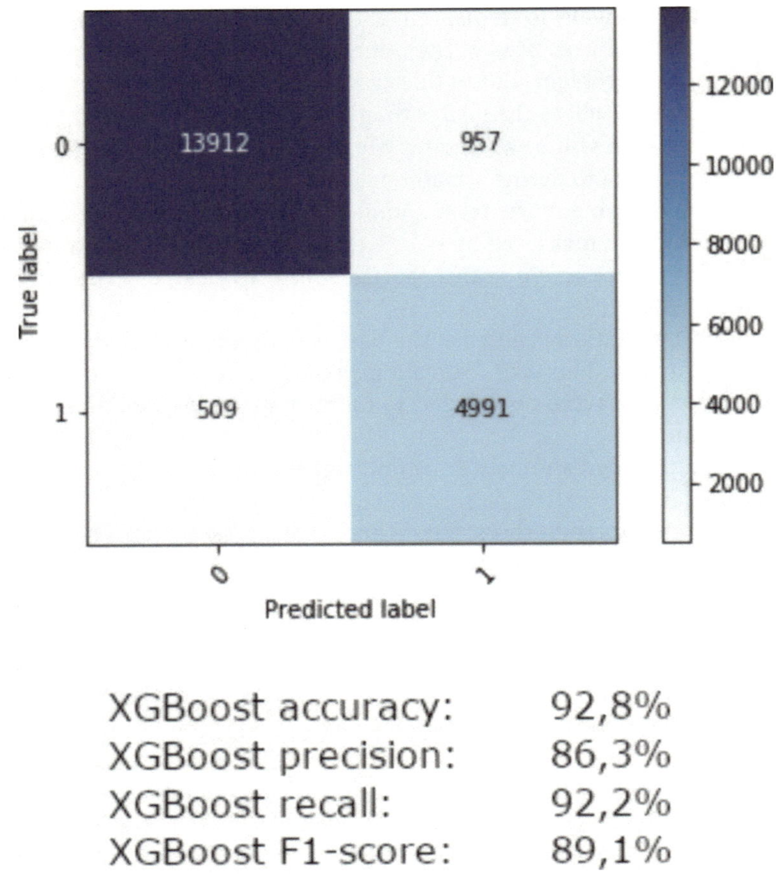

Figure 11.
Confusion matrix.

the next 24 hours an anomaly is detected or not. At this point, different ML classification algorithms were tested, and the best performance was achieved by XGBoost, obtaining the following classification results (**Figure 11**) in a test set.

In order to measure the algorithm performance in the classification task, we are using confusion matrix and the following metrics:

- Confusion matrix: In a ML classification problem, a confusion matrix is a specific table that simplifies the analysis of the performance of an algorithm. Each column of the matrix represents the instances in a predicted class, while each row represents the instance's real class (or vice versa) [17].

- Accuracy: Classification metric that computes the fraction of correct predictions:

$$\text{accuracy}(y, y') = \frac{1}{n_{\text{samples}}} \sum_{i=0}^{n_{\text{samples}}-1} 1(y'_i = y_i) \tag{13}$$

- Precision: Classification metric that computes the fraction of relevant instances among the retrieved instances. It is also called positive predictive value:

$$\text{precision} = \frac{\text{True Positive}}{\text{True Positive} + \text{False Positive}} \tag{14}$$

- Recall: Classification metric that computes the fraction of relevant instances that have been retrieved over the total amount of relevant instances. It is also called positive predictive value:

$$\text{recall} = \frac{\text{True Positive}}{\text{True Positive} + \text{False Negative}} \tag{15}$$

- F1-score: Classification metric that computes a weighted harmonic mean of the precision and recall. F1 score reaches its best value at 1 and worst score at 0.

$$\text{F1 score} = 2 * \frac{(\text{precision} * \text{recall})}{(\text{precision} + \text{recall})} \tag{16}$$

As depicted in **Figure 11**, the final version of the model provides good results while predicting anomalies with time enough to articulate the needed preventive actions. Not only the accuracy is important, but we would also like to remark that the false negative rate is low, that is, the algorithm performs very well in detecting anomalies, and only a few of them are undetected.

3.3 Process setup

Process setup, especially during changeover operations, can affect the availability indicator and thus represents an opportunity for manufacturing AI and ML based solutions. New production trends based on a high degree of flexibility, customization, and small batches require for an extra effort in terms of process setup and scheduling. For instance, in plastic injection molding quite often due to production flexibility and scheduling, a mold needs to be re-installed and set up for production again in order to deliver a new production batch to the final customer. This situation requires for a new tuning process involving an important waste of time, material, and energy. This situation opens the opportunity for developing supervised ML models to compare past production data with real-time data for recommending tuning parameters and reach in a shorter time frame the optimal process operation.

To this end, the real-time evolution of a key process parameter can be used as training of the manufacturing process setup or configuration. By comparing the actual real-time evolution within the manufacturing cycle versus the known optimal (acquired from previous production runs), a set of recommendations can be provided. This strategy can boost the process setup, providing recommendations to reach the optimal targeted key parameter cycle evolution, following an iterative method as depicted in **Figure 12**.

Following the plastic injection molding example, within the PREVIEW project [18], a set of experimental trials were performed in order to create the historical database that supports the AI system in charge of providing process tuning recommendations. Within the AI solution, different algorithms were tested for comparing new sensor data versus historical data to provide tuning recommendations. **Figure 13** shows a PREVIEW project result using random forest trees [19] to provide tuning recommendations when the injection speed parameter was changed to different operational points. As can be seen, for lower than optimal injection speeds, the AI system based on RF recommends increasing the injection speed, while for higher injection speeds recommends a reduction, driving always the parameter toward the optimal operational window that leads to optimal cavity pressure evolution within the manufacturing cycle.

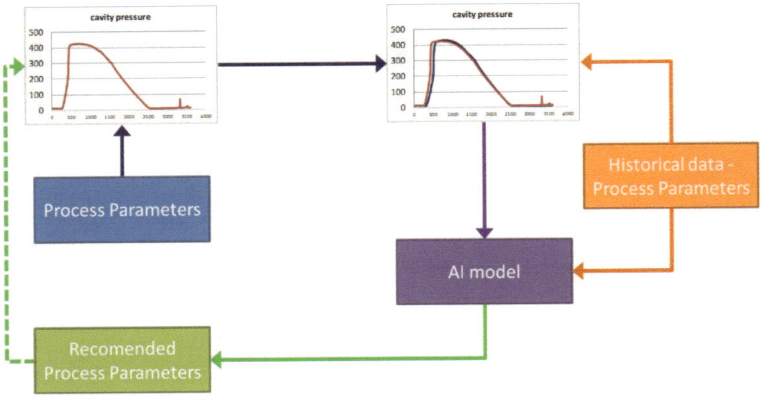

Figure 12.
Iterative comparison to optimized production setup comparing known optimal process parameters versus new acquired ones.

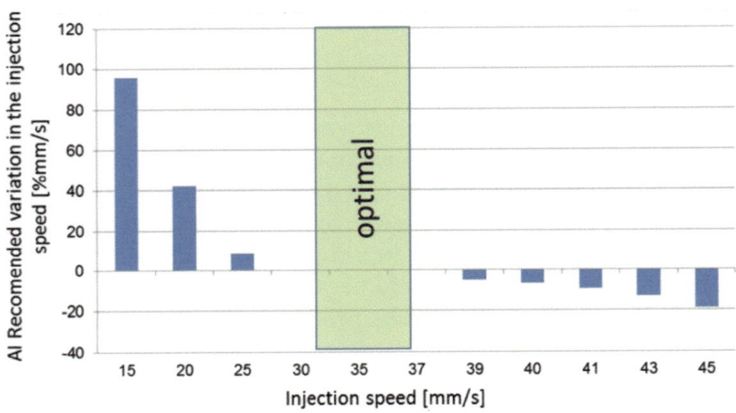

Figure 13.
Process optimization recommendation. The PREVIEW project result.

4. Artificial intelligence for quality

It is a well-known problem that high added-value industrial and manufacturing processes combining several operations (welding, milling, etc.) and thus heterogeneous data sources do not always reach their maximum performance potential due to the lack of powerful and tailored solutions for data analysis toward the zero defects manufacturing paradigm. Today's artificial intelligence and machine learning based solutions are mature enough to boost production processes by means of exploiting the process data generated thanks to the in-line sensors, workers' feedback, reports, quality control, etc. Thus, developing a tailored predictive quality solution based on artificial intelligence and machine learning has become a crucial key element for impacting OEE to prevent the manufacturing of non-quality parts and its exportation to the final client. Several research works have been carried out for different manufacturing processes, including plastic injection molding, foundry, milling, welding, etc. (e.g., see [20–24]) showing the potential benefits of applying AI and ML to exploit process data.

Continuous quality estimation at each step of the manufacturing process by means of machine learning and artificial intelligence, applied on the in-line acquired data, enables predictive warnings and alarms even before the target quality is affected and thus quality indicator of OEE is degraded. Two different approaches can be implemented when developing AI predictive quality tools: supervised versus unsupervised solutions. Supervised solutions can provide a better accuracy when predicting undesired quality deviations, but a properly tagged dataset is required. Unsupervised methods have the benefit of not requiring the tagged dataset and are typically used for anomaly detection, meaning strong quality deviations. Moreover, supervised system results can be tracked down and analyzed to provide process insights which can lead to knowledge discovery [25] solutions that help to address the root cause of the undesired quality deviation and thus improve quality and, therefore, OEE.

Focusing on supervised solutions, a proper dataset labeling is a key element. It is highly recommended to perform a Design of Experiments (DOE) where quality deviations are forced in order to obtain a more balanced dataset compared to the typical production dataset where non-quality parts are rare. In the case of qualitative quality labels (e.g., good, bad, type of defect, etc.), a classifier will be preferred, while for quantitative quality indicators (e.g., weigh, tensile strength, etc.), a regressor will be implemented.

Let us consider as illustrating example a plastic injection molding quality prediction problem. The four-cavity mold used for the experimental trials can be seen in **Figure 14**. Only one cavity was sensorized to obtain the pressure and temperature evolution of the melt during the production cycle. The machine pressure and screw position were also acquired for each one of the 199 injected parts of the trial. The injection cycle was 7.2 seconds and was sampled at 500 Hz. Thus, the dataset is the time series evolution of the key parameters of the process.

The DOE was designed in order to obtain seven different part qualities: good, short shot, shrinkage, flash, jetting, over-compaction, and flow lines. The different qualities were obtained by means of varying the injection machine configuration. A total of 199 parts were produced (**Figure 15**).

Depending on the data granularity (continuous, cycle, or batch), different preprocessing techniques can be implemented to boost the performance of the later machine learning classifier. For instance, entropy analysis and complexity reduction algorithms such as principal component analysis (PCA) [27] can provide a substantial advantage as seen in **Figure 16**, where the PCA projection of the screw position sensor is plotted.

In order to compare the performance of different machine learning classifiers, a benchmark based on cross-validation techniques was implemented, using a stratified shuffle split [28] strategy to preserve the percentage of samples of each class

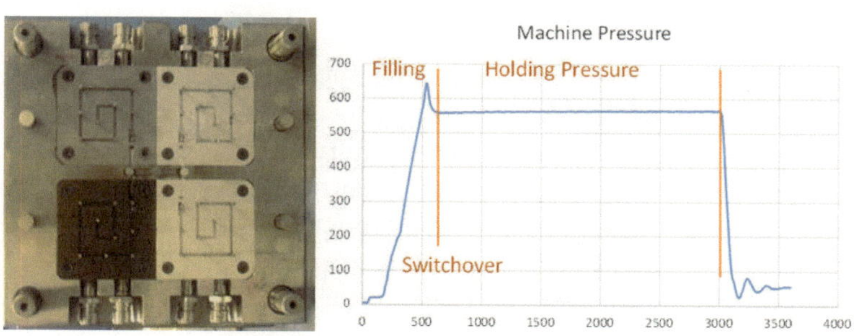

Figure 14.
Mold cavity picture and example of acquired machine pressure. Experimental data provided by EURECAT [26].

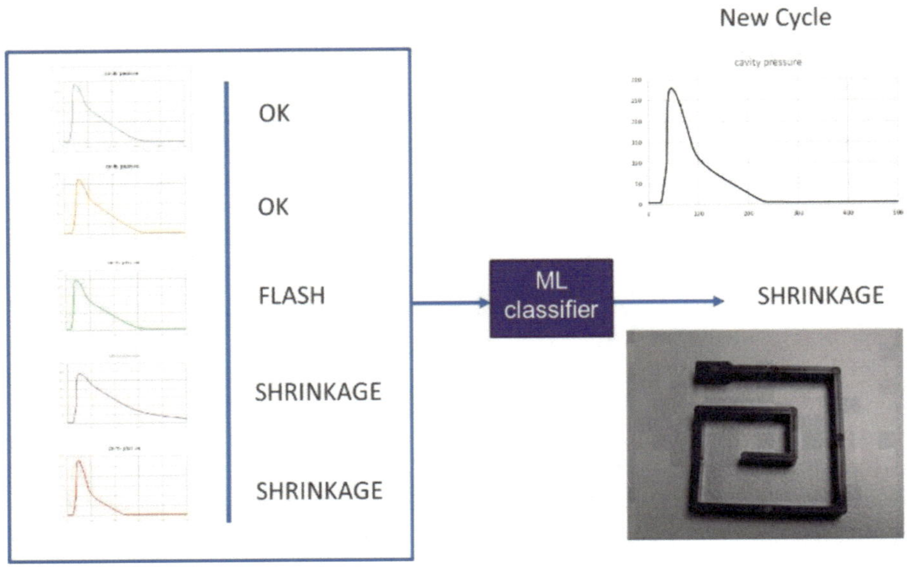

Figure 15.
Supervised approach for quality prediction.

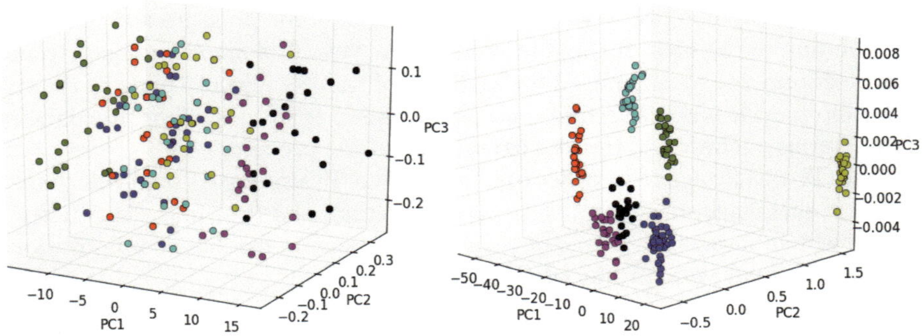

Figure 16.
3D PCA data projection using the raw data or a preprocessed data where the 10 time stamps with higher entropy are selected. Each color represents a different part quality or defect.

(quality). This test can be run for each sensor or by applying data fusion and combining all sensors in a single dataset (**Figures 17** and **18**).

As can be seen in **Figure 19**, support vector machines [29] with a linear kernel show a low performance, while ensemble algorithms like random forest trees and gradient boosting [30] present higher accuracy rates, especially when 50 estimators or more are used.

When combining all sensor information by means of applying data fusion, the quality prediction accuracy increases near to 100%, as can be seen in **Figure 18**. This result and system allow for an in-cycle quality preventive alarm that can lead to an important reduction of scrap rate and exported non-quality, which automatically translate to a higher quality rate and a reduction of costs due to wasted raw material and energy consumption while improving OEE.

Other manufacturing processes can have different sampling rates or even create batch datasets where for each part a set of relevant values are recorded. Typically, large batch datasets present a high degree of data heterogeneity, compiling sensor values, reports, environmental data, etc. Moreover, part traceability may not be

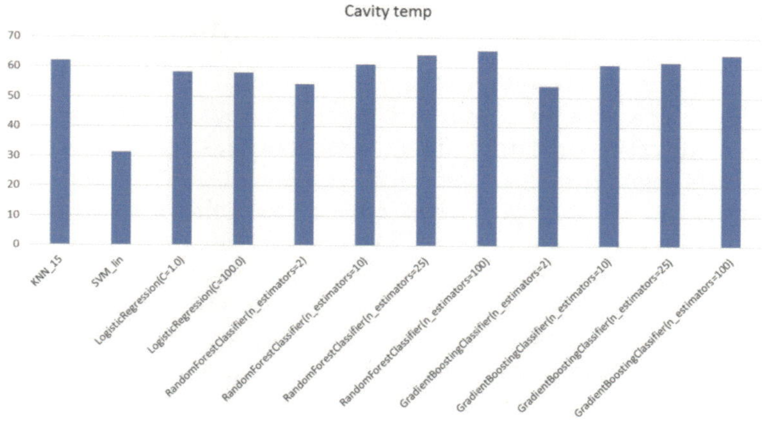

Figure 17.
Quality prediction mean accuracy for a 20-round cross-validation test using 70% for training and 30% of samples for test, using only the cavity temperature sensor data.

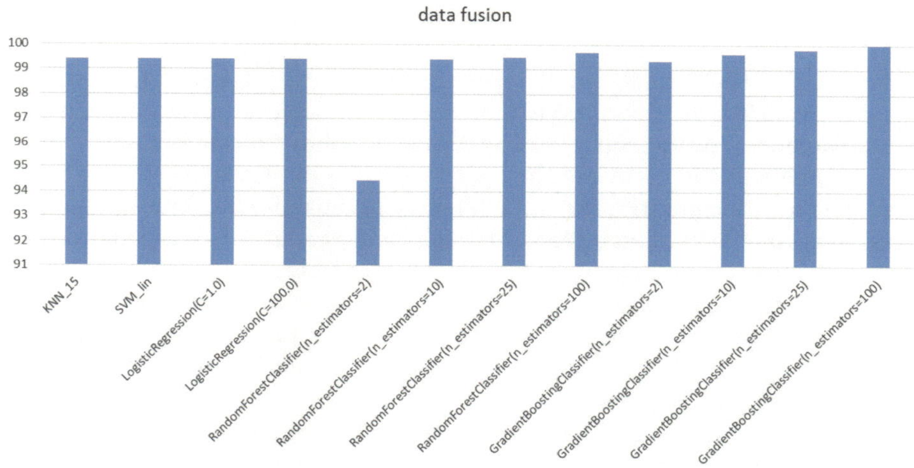

Figure 18.
Quality prediction mean accuracy for a 20-round cross-validation test using 70% for training and 30% of samples for test, combining the available cavity and machine sensor data.

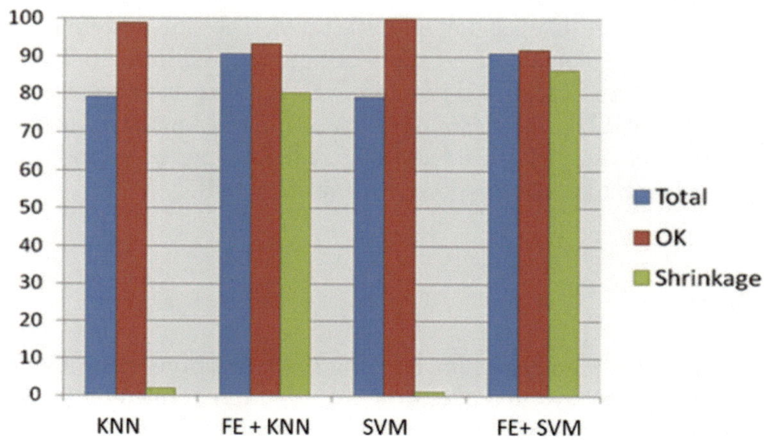

Figure 19.
Batch quality prediction with and without feature engineering (FE) for a heterogeneous and class-unbalanced dataset. Iron foundry case.

guaranteed, and thus quality rates may refer to the entire batch. In these scenarios, feature engineering [31] can provide a clear advantage for boosting the performance of the ML and AI algorithms. **Figure 19** shows the performance of KNN and SVM classifiers for a foundry dataset with more than 250 different parameters (chemical composition of the iron, climate, process data, sensor data, etc.) with and without feature engineering.

The dataset had two main difficulties: the extreme unbalance between classes (qualities) and the data heterogeneity. By applying feature engineering, the number of parameters can be reduced, focusing on the relevant ones. Bagging [32] and cost functions were used to face the class unbalance. Batch quality prediction based on process data can help in reducing the exported non-quality while providing knowledge discovery insights to find and correct the root causes of the undesired quality deviation.

5. Artificial intelligence for performance

Performance indicators consider any factor that causes the manufacturing process to run at lower speed than its maximum possible speed. For instance, slow cycle time affects performance indicators. For this reason, it is key to know the ideal cycle time, which is the fastest cycle time that can be achieved in optimal circumstances. Moreover, performance is also affected by idling time and minor stops.

Cycle time reduction is one of the main factors for improving productivity. A cycle time reduction contributes to reaching the optimal production throughputs, reduction of time to market, better scheduling, and a reduction of associated costs in terms of labor, energy, and raw material when combined with quality prediction and assessment. The reduction of cycle time has become a relevant topic both in research and in practical applications. Neural networks and machine learning algorithms can help to predict and optimize manufacturing cycle time in different sectors (e.g., see [33, 34]).

Preventive alarms generated by predictive quality systems based on AI and ML can prevent manufacturing at nonoptimal operation setups and thus prevent minor stops. Minor stops can also be reduced thanks to preventive maintenance systems. Case-based reasoning [35] systems can leverage past experiences to help manufacturing processes run faster. For instance, a CBR system can provide helpful recommendations for optimizing the cooling time based on the type of material and the thickness of the part that is being manufactured. The CBR system provides the most similar cases based on a defined similarity metric, and thus a previous cooling times of well-known and optimized processes can be taken as reference. Illustrating this case, the Des-MOLD project [36] developed an AI system based on CBR and argumentation [37] to help plastic injectors share their experiences and benefit from mold design and manufacturing process optimization [38].

6. Conclusions

Artificial intelligence and machine learning based solutions can provide a competitive advantage in today's manufacturing paradigm, redefined by the Industry 4.0 revolution and the massive data available thanks to CPS, virtual sensors, and IIoT devices. Leveraging this data has become a very relevant topic both in research and for practical applications due to its massive potential. Data-driven solutions are becoming more and more popular due to its potential both in terms of prediction and to its capacity to provide process insights for enhancing process owner's expertise.

This chapter has focused on how the leverage of the available process data by means of AI and ML solutions can impact into one of the most relevant manufacturing indicators: overall equipment efficiency. OEE has three main components: availability, quality, and performance. Each OEE component tackles a different challenge and thus may require a different approach. Through different experimental examples, each OEE component and how AI solutions can impact it have been described. It has been shown how predictive maintenance and virtual sensor solutions can help in reducing the undesired production breakdowns and thus increase equipment availability. Predictive quality solutions based on supervised algorithms, for either real-time cycle data or batch data, have been described, showing the importance of feature engineering for boosting prediction accuracy. And finally, equipment performance focusing on cycle time has been addressed by CBR for leveraging past experiences and providing process tuning types to run at the highest throughputs.

OEE will be further improved thanks to the new AI trends and technologies that are being researched right now, providing even more powerful and tailored solutions. Availability and performance indicators could be greatly improved when mature reinforced learning approaches are available at the production level, reducing setup times and optimizing cycle times thanks to the collaboration between human expertise and AI systems. Image processing through deep learning and convolutional neural networks can impact quality, especially for visual defects. Collaborative human-AI systems are envisaged as key for the next Industry 5.0.

Author details

Francesc Bonada[1*], Lluís Echeverria[2], Xavier Domingo[2] and Gabriel Anzaldi[2]

1 Eurecat Technology Centre, Av. Universitat Autònoma, Cerdanyola del Vallès, Barcelona, Spain

2 Eurecat Technology Centre, Parc Científic i Tecnològic de Lleida, Lleida, Spain

*Address all correspondence to: francesc.bonada@eurecat.org

References

[1] Huang SH, Dismukes JP, Shi J, Su Q, Razzak MA, Bodhale R, et al. Manufacturing productivity improvement using effectiveness metrics and simulation analysis. International Journal of Production Research. 2003;**41**(3):513-527. Available from: https://doi.org/10.1080/00207540210000042391

[2] Jauregui Becker JM, Borst J, Van Der Veen A. Improving the overall equipment effectiveness in high-mix-low-volume manufacturing environments. CIRP Annals—Manufacturing Technology. 2015;**64**: 419-422. DOI: 10.1016/j.cirp.2015.04.126

[3] Fleischer J, Weismann U, Niggeschmidt S. Calculation and optimisation model for costs and effects of availability relevant service elements. Proceedings of LCE. 2006:675-680

[4] Muchiri P, Pintelon L. Performance measurement using overall equipment effectiveness (OEE): Literature review and practical application discussion. International Journal of Production Research. 2008;**46**(13):3517-3535. DOI: 10.1080/00207540601142645

[5] Singh R, Shah DB, Gohil AM, Shah MH. Overall equipment effectiveness (OEE) calculation—Automation through hardware & software development. Procedia Engineering. 2013;**51**:579-584. DOI: 10.1016/j.proeng.2013.01.082

[6] Hedman R, Subramaniyan M, Almström P. Analysis of critical factors for automatic measurement of OEE. Procedia CIRP. 2016;**57**:128-133. DOI: 10.1016/j.procir.2016.11.023

[7] Mâinea M, Dută L, Patic PC, Căciulă I. A method to optimize the overall equipment effectiveness. IFAC Proceedings Volumes (IFAC-PapersOnline). 2010;**43**(17):237-241. DOI: 10.3182/20100908-3-PT-3007.00045

[8] Gabahne L, Gupta M, Zanwar D. Overall equipment effectiveness improvement: A case of injection molding machine. The International Journal of Engineering and Science (IJES). 2014;**3**(8):1-10

[9] Chen T, Guestrin C. XGBoost: A scalable tree boosting system. In: Proceedings of the ACM SIGKDD International Conference on Knowledge Discovery and Data Mining. San Francisco, USA: ACM; 2016. pp. 785-794. DOI: 10.1145/2939672.2939785

[10] Song Y, Liang J, Lu J, Zhao X. An efficient instance selection algorithm for k nearest neighbor regression. Neurocomputing. 2017;**251**:26-34. DOI: 10.1016/j.neucom.2017.04.018

[11] Prasad AM, Iverson LR, Liaw A. Newer classification and regression tree techniques: Bagging and random forests for ecological prediction. Ecosystems. 2006;**9**:181-199. DOI: 10.1007/s10021-005-0054-1

[12] Bergstra J, Bengio Y. Random search for hyper-parameter optimization. Journal of Machine Learning Research. 2012;**13**:281-305

[13] Breiman L. Stacked regressions. Machine Learning. 1996

[14] Björkström A, Sundberg R. A generalized view on continuum regression. Scandinavian Journal of Statistics. 1999;**26**(1):17-30. DOI: 10.1111/1467-9469.00134

[15] Liu FT, Ting KM, Zhou ZH. Isolation forest. In: Proceedings of the IEEE International Conference on Data Mining, ICDM. Pisa, Italy: IEEE; 2008. pp. 413-422. DOI: 10.1109/ICDM.2008.17

[16] Breuniq MM, Kriegel HP, Ng RT, Sander J. LOF: Identifying density-based local outliers. In: SIGMOD Record (ACM Special Interest Group on Management of Data). New York, USA: ACM; 2000. pp. 93-104. DOI: 10.1145/342009.335388

[17] Ting KM. Confusion matrix. In: Encyclopedia of Machine Learning and Data Mining. Boston, USA: Springer; 2017. DOI: 10.1007/978-1-4899-7687-1_50

[18] PREVIEW (H2020-FoF-2014). 2014. Available from: http://www.preview-project.eu/

[19] Ho TK. Random decision forests. In: Proceedings of 3rd International Conference on Document Analysis and Recognition. Vol. 1. Montreal, Canada: IEEE; 1995. pp. 278-282. DOI: 10.1109/ICDAR.1995.598994

[20] Huggett DJ, Liao TW, Wahab MA, et al. Prediction of friction stir weld quality without and with signal features. The International Journal of Advanced Manufacturing Technology. 2018;**95**(5–8):1989-2003. DOI: 10.1007/s00170-017-1403-x

[21] Perzyk M, Kochanski A. Detection of causes of casting defects assisted by artificial neural networks. Proceedings of the Institution of Mechanical Engineers, Part B: Journal of Engineering Manufacture. 2003;**217**(9):1279-1284. DOI: 10.1243/095440503322420205

[22] Ribeiro B. Support vector machines for quality monitoring in a plastic injection molding process. IEEE Transactions on Systems, Man, and Cybernetics, Part C (Applications and Reviews). 2005;**35**(3):401-410. DOI: 10.1109/TSMCC.2004.843228

[23] Denkena B, Dittrich MA, Uhlich F. Augmenting milling process data for shape error prediction. Procedia CIRP. 2016;**57**:487-491. DOI: 10.1016/j.procir.2016.11.084

[24] Purr S et al. Stamping plant 4.0—Basics for the application of data mining methods in manufacturing car body parts. Key Engineering Materials. 2015;**639**:21-30. DOI: 10.4028/www.scientific.net/kem.639.21

[25] Maimon O, Rokach L. Data Mining and Knowledge Discovery Handbook. Berlin, Heidelberg: Springer-Verlag; 2005. DOI: 10.1007/978-0-387-09823-4

[26] Available from: www.eurecat.org

[27] Pearson K. On lines and planes of closest fit to systems of points in space. Philosophical Magazine. 1901;**2**(11):559-557. DOI: 10.1080/14786440109462720

[28] Available from: https://scikit-learn.org/stable/modules/generated/sklearn.model_selection.StratifiedShuffleSplit.html

[29] Vapnik V. The Nature of Statistical Learning Theory. New York: Springer-Verlag; 2000. DOI: 10.1007/978-1-4757-3264-1

[30] Friedman JH. Greedy function approximation: A gradient boosting machine. The Annals of Statistics. 2001;**29**(5):1189-1232. DOI: 10.1214/aos/1013203451

[31] Zheng A, Casari A. Feature Engineering for Machine Learning: Principles and Techniques for Data Scientists. Sebastopol, USA: O'Reilly Media Inc; 2018. ISBN: 1491953195, 9781491953198

[32] Breiman L. Bagging predictors. Machine Learning. 1996;**24**(2):123-140. DOI: 10.1023/A:101805431

[33] Gelmereanu C, Morar L, Bogdan S. Productivity and cycle time prediction using artificial neural network. Procedia

Economics and Finance. 2014;**15**: 1563-1569. DOI: 10.1016/S2212-5671(14) 00626-1

[34] Kuo C, Chien C, Chen J. Manufacturing intelligence to exploit the value of production and tool data to reduce cycle time. IEEE Transactions on Automation Science and Engineering. 2011;**8**(1):103-111. DOI: 10.1109/ TASE.2010.2040999

[35] Riesbeck CK, Schank RC. Inside Case-Based Reasoning. Hillsdale, USA: Lawrence Erlbaum Associates Publishers; 1989. ISBN: 9780898597677

[36] Des-MOLD (FP7-NMP2-SL-314581). Available from: www.desmold.eu

[37] Toni F. A tutorial on assumption-based argumentation. Journal of Argument and Computation. 2014;**5**(1): 89-117. DOI: 10.1080/19462166.2013. 869878

[38] Cabanillas D, Bonada F, Ventura R, Toni F, Evripidou V, Cartens L, et al. A combination of knowledge and argumentation based system for supporting injection mould design. In: Proceedings of 16th Catalan Congress of Artificial Intelligence (CCIA). Vic, Spain: IOS Press; 2013. pp. 293-296

Chapter 6

Decision Support Models for the Selection of Production Strategies in the Paradigm of Digital Manufacturing, Based on Technologies, Costs and Productivity Levels

Joaquim Minguella-Canela and Irene Buj Corral

Abstract

Digital manufacturing has opened a new window in the way to approach the manufacture of parts. The possible switch from manufacturing and holding physical stock to manoeuvring with a fully-digital one is promising but still has not been undertaken-or only in a small proportion-by the majority of the manufacturing companies. What are the cost and productivity frontiers that halt the transformation taking place so far? When does it make sense, in terms of production volume and costs, to undertake this transformation? What level of savings could be achieved and what investments would be favourable? The base line of the present chapter is to depict quantitative tools to address the potential impact of endeavouring digital transformation in manufacturing environments, considering costing and production variables, as well as technological decision-making parameters. Keeping the modelling of the demand very basic, some exploration on the degree of postponement of the production is discussed. Also, decision support systems (DSSs) for manufacturing selection are reviewed. Finally, a case study serves to apply the mathematical framework presented and to quantify the results in a realistic industrial case. Using this case, the chapter outlines and describes how to apply artificial intelligence (AI) techniques to implement the DSSs.

Keywords: productivity, digital transformation, digital manufacturing, costs, decision support systems, decision support models, 3D printing, machining, injection moulding

1. Introduction

The industrial reality nowadays is as open that, in order to manufacture a certain part, there are usually many different alternative processes. However, the different viable alternatives may imply different cost schemes, and so, the decision on which process should be selected may not be such straightforward but linked to the values of several parameters of both the processes and the demanded part(s).

Building on this basis, in most cases, there is not a single solution of manufacturing that is optimal in all cases, and the objective of the present chapter is to provide the necessary guidelines to facilitate the decision-taking when selecting from different manufacturing processes.

Starting with the depiction of a general cost scheme, the chapter provides a useful modelling artefact to be able to tackle questions such as the following:

- What process should be used to manufacture a certain batch of a specific part?
- What process should be used to manufacture a certain series of a specific part?
- What manufacturing costs will be incurred if a certain manufacturing process is selected?
- When will it be economically favourable to undertake a certain investment to optimise an existing manufacturing process to obtain a specific product?
- When will it be economically favourable to undertake a certain investment in a new manufacturing process in order to start the manufacturing to obtain a specific product?

Having defined what is optimal concerning the costs' modelling, the present chapter also wants to bring some attention to the effect of manufacturing strategies imposed from the demand side. More and more frequently, the variability and uncertainty in the demand tend to force the production paces, for example, switching from manufacturing-to-stock (MTS) to engineering-to-order (ETO) paradigms. This is approached in the literature as the *level of postponement* of the manufacturing operation and has an effect in the manufacturing and stocking costs, which is also addressed in the present chapter.

Postponement in manufacturing has an important double-edged consequence. On one end, in order to be able to defer some (or all of the) production stages, it is important to embrace the digital stocking of the parts. On the other end, tooling should be avoided, bearing in mind that flexibility is key to achieve a fast response capability.

Following these considerations, the present chapter also reviews and comments on some *artificial intelligence* approaches in the form of decision support systems (DSS) in order to fulfil the decision-taking when aiming at selecting the most favourable manufacturing processes for a certain part. Indeed, the final decision on the manufacturing strategy to be embarked will have to be taken based on (i) technology capabilities, (ii) production organisation constraints and (iii) market-demand orientation. For this reason, to achieve the best decision-taking, the entire mathematical framework presented will have to be combined with in-depth technological knowledge and the most appropriate market approach.

Finally, the chapter illustrates the decision-taking and results in a case study that serves to illustrate the opportunity to shift to digital manufacturing technologies. The case study starts analysing the cost levels and equilibrium point for shifting from a very rigid (traditional) manufacturing technology to a more flexible one (3D printing). Finally, the case study deals with the limits on the possible benefits yielded by the product optimisation in a digital perspective, looking at what results could enhance for further improved production results.

2. Modelling framework: costing levels per technology

Modelling the cost framework of a specific process is crucial in order to take proper decisions on which process to select among the several available choices. However, by the same token, it is important to utilise the most well-fitting models in order to be able to take accurate decisions. It is also important to handle models as simplest as possible in order to avoid being stuck in a process parameter-evaluation stage.

One of the most applicable cost structures that can be found in literature is the model formulated by Hopkinson and Dickens [1]. This model was elaborated to be applied to 3D printing manufacturing technologies but, in particular, can be applied to any manufacturing technology in which the energy consumption costs of the machines are negligible in comparison to the rest of the costs in the model (i.e., if the energy-associated costs account for less than 1% of the final total cost).

In this chapter, the cost framework presented as a general cost model will be a very broad (traditional) one. The idea is to elaborate a simple and incremental costing model that can be further complicated by the reader, but that, at the same time, can be kept simple to facilitate its use with little parameterisation information.

In addition, the assumptions and simplifications will be made inside the model-and so they could be reverted by the reader if necessary.

2.1 General model

One general cost model, simple and broad enough to model the total costs in monetary units per year (m.u./year) incurred by the operations associated to manufacturing and keeping the manufactured parts in stock, is the one presented in Eq. (1):

$$Ct\left[\frac{m.u.}{year}\right] = Cp + Cs + Ci + Cr \tag{1}$$

where *Ct* is the total annual cost of manufacturing and keeping in stock the number of annual desired units (m.u./year); *Cp* is the total annual cost of the preparation of the production of batches in order to manufacture the desired number of units (m.u./year); *Cs* is the total annual cost to keep in stock the necessary parts to properly serve the desired number of units (m.u./year); *Ci* is the total annual cost of investments needed in the specific manufacturing system (m.u./year); *Cr* is the total annual cost caused by the rest of the factors independent from the lot or series size in order to manufacture the number of desired parts (m.u./year).

At this point, it is important to mention that this general model does not address additional costs generated in the entire product value chain than those strictly concerning the manufacturing and stocking in the production premises. For example, the costs of shipping the products across the globe as well as some costs associated to the inventory in the long term (obsolescence, spoilage, etc.) are not to be included within the factors declared in Eq. (1). Concerning this, some specific comments will be added when introducing the issues of production postponement in upcoming sections.

Then, starting from this very general model, it is possible to make some assumptions that are ordinary and that, at the same time, facilitate the evaluation of the associated costs. Specifically, the following is assumed:

- The demand stays constant throughout the year.
- The stock of parts is emptied linearly.
- The production is synchronised with the demand, so that the warehouse is filled again just when the corresponding stock is finished.

These assumptions regarding stocks can be summarised graphically as shown in **Figure 1**. As it can be seen, the average level of stocks throughout the year corresponds to B/2 (*B* being the size of the batches to be manufactured) and the number of annual preparations is equal to *D/B* (*D* being the annual demand of parts to be manufactured).

Accepting these assumptions, the *cost of the preparations* for the production process *Cp* can be calculated as indicated in Eq. (2):

$$Cp\left[\frac{m.u.}{year}\right] = \frac{D}{B}\cdot Tp \cdot Chp \tag{2}$$

where *Cp* is the total annual cost of the preparations of the production batches in order to manufacture the desired number of parts (m.u./year); *D* is the annual demand of parts to be manufactured (number of parts); *B* is the batch size to make (number of parts); *Tp* is the preparation time of the corresponding process (h); *Chp* is the cost of the time of preparing the corresponding process (m.u./h).

And the *cost of the stocks Cs* can be calculated as indicated in Eq. (3):

$$Cs\left[\frac{m.u.}{year}\right] = \frac{B}{2}\cdot Csp \tag{3}$$

where *Cs* is the total annual cost incurred to keep the necessary pieces in stock in order to properly serve the desired number of pieces (m.u./year); *B* is the batch size to manufacture (number of parts); and *Csp* is the cost of keeping a part in stock for a year (m.u./part_year).

On the other hand, assuming that investments are amortised in a number of years *y*, the *costs of annual investment Ci* can be calculated as indicated in Eq. (4):

$$Ci\left[\frac{m.u.}{year}\right] = \frac{Cet}{y} \tag{4}$$

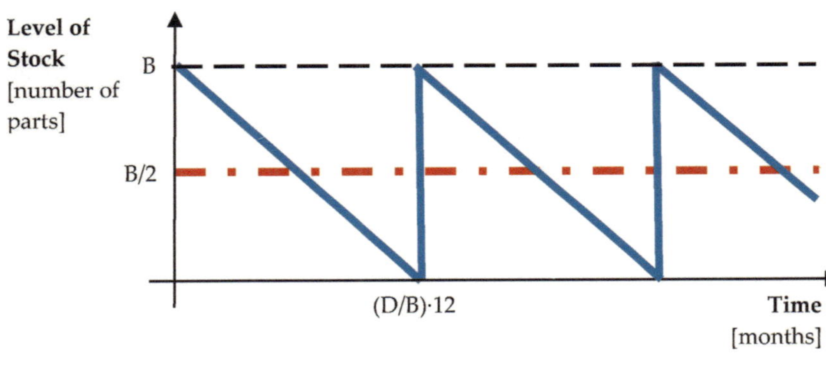

Figure 1.
Evolution of stock levels taking into account the considerations set on the inventory policy. B is the size of the batches to be manufactured and D is the total annual demand, both expressed in number of parts.

where *Ci* is the total annual cost incurred in investments for the manufacturing system (m.u./year); *Cet* is the total cost incurred in equipment and tooling for the manufacturing system (m.u.); and *y* is the timespan in which it is decided to amortise the tooling and equipment required (years).

Finally, there are other manufacturing costs, which are associated, among others, with the costs of raw materials and the costs derived strictly from manufacturing cycle times. Assuming that those costs are all proportional to the number of parts manufactured, the *rest of the costs Cr* can be calculated as indicated in Eq. (5):

$$Cr\left[\frac{m.u.}{year}\right] = D \cdot Cd \tag{5}$$

Where *Cr* is the total annual cost caused by the rest of the factors independent of the size of lot or series to make the number of desired pieces (m.u./year); *D* is the annual demand for parts to be manufactured (number of parts); and *Cd* is the direct cost per part caused by the rest of the factors independent of the size of lot or series (m.u./year).

In this way, the general model of production costs presented in Eq. (1) can be further detailed as the one described in Eq. (6):

$$Ct\left[\frac{m.u.}{year}\right] = \frac{D}{B} \cdot Tp \cdot Chp + \frac{B}{2} \cdot Csp + \frac{Cet}{y} + D \cdot Cd \tag{6}$$

Concerning the scope of this model, again, it is worth mentioning that the general model deployed in Eq. (6) does not approach the entire product value chain, but only the manufacturing and holding in the production premises.

Concerning the level of detail of the fundamental factors, it is also interesting to visit some other models in the literature, which introduce more parameters in the calculation of such factors. For example, the addition of a parameter for accounting an additional amount of money to ensure a proper treatment of perishable goods can be found. Moreover, the costs of warehousing management or even the cost of capital is usually considered within the stock cost calculation, although some authors advocate maintaining it as a separate cost factor [2]. Indeed, the costs generated by the stocks and their management have a huge effect on the manufacturing decision-taking and are at the grounds of the *lean manufacturing* approaches.

Because of this, other authors incorporate a special treatment to the demand, modelling it as a probability distribution function [3], which leads to results that are more accurate and opens the door to multi-scenario analysis, yet implying a much more complicated decision models than the general model discussed in the present chapter.

2.2 Determination of the optimal batch and its associated manufacturing costs

*2.2.1 Size of the optimum manufacturing batch B**

Starting from a cost model such as the one presented in the previous section (Eq. (6)), which takes into account the costs of preparation, manufacturing, amortisation of investments and also holding parts in the factory stock, it can be determined which batch size will minimise the total cost (i.e., the optimal batch B^*) as follows (Eqs. (7), (8) and (9)).

$$\frac{dCt}{dB} = \frac{0 \cdot B - 1 \cdot D \cdot Tp \cdot Chp}{B^2} + \frac{1}{2} \cdot Cs + 0 + 0 = 0 \tag{7}$$

$$\frac{D \cdot Tp \cdot Chp}{B^2} = \frac{Cs}{2} \Leftrightarrow \tag{8}$$

$$B^* = \sqrt{\frac{2 \cdot Tp \cdot Chp \cdot D}{Cs}} \tag{9}$$

Eq. (9) is coherent with the experience in manufacturing. The number of parts in an optimal batch B^* holds direct relation with the preparation time Tp, the preparation cost Cp and the total number of units to make D. The higher the values of these parameters, the bigger the value of the optimal batch size associated with its manufacture. On the other hand, the optimal batch size B^* has a reverse proportionality ratio with the cost Cs of keeping a part in the stock. Indeed, the more expensive it is to have a part in stock, the more favourable it will be to adopt manufacturing strategies based on small batches.

In fact, it is interesting to note that, based on the second derivative of the cost scheme presented in Eq. (6), it can be stated that this optimum point will always be a minimum for the total costs. This is because the values of D, Tp and B will always be positive numbers and, therefore, the value of the second derivative (Eq. (10)) will always be positive for any value of these variables.

$$\frac{d^2Ct}{dB^2} = \frac{0 \cdot B^2 - (2B \cdot (-D \cdot Tp \cdot Chp))}{B^4} + 0 = \frac{2 \cdot D \cdot Tp \cdot Chp}{B^3} > 0 \; \forall D, Tp, B \tag{10}$$

2.2.2 *Costs in the optimum manufacturing batch* C*

Starting from a cost model such as that obtained in Eq. (6), using the expression corresponding to the optimal batch B^* calculated in the previous section, the following is obtained:

$$Ct_{(if\ B=B^*)} \left[\frac{m.u.}{year}\right] = \frac{D}{\sqrt{\frac{2 \cdot Tp \cdot Chp \cdot D}{Cs}}} \cdot Tp \cdot Chp + \frac{\sqrt{\frac{2 \cdot Tp \cdot Chp \cdot D}{Cs}}}{2} \cdot Cs + \frac{Cet}{y} + D \cdot Cd \tag{11}$$

which, grouping terms, can be formulated as:

$$Ct_{(if\ B=B^*)} \left[\frac{m.u.}{year}\right] = \sqrt{2 \cdot D \cdot Tp \cdot Chp \cdot Cs} + \frac{Cet}{y} + D \cdot Cd \tag{12}$$

In some cases, it is not necessary to use specific tooling or take into account the amortisation costs of the equipment. For example, this can happen in case a manufacturing process without specific tooling (*a flexible process*) is used, and, at the same time, it has a very low cost of equipment in relation to its repayment period. If this is the case, the calculation of the total costs is further simplified, as it is presented in Eq. (13):

$$Ct_{(if\ B=B^*,\ \ Cet=0\ )} \left[\frac{m.u.}{year}\right] = \sqrt{2 \cdot D \cdot Tp \cdot Chp \cdot Cs} + D \cdot Cd \tag{13}$$

In any of these cost descriptions, it can be seen that, when working on the production of different parts requiring continuous production changes, reducing the preparation time will have a much greater effect on the total costs than it could seem at the very first glance.

2.3 Specific models for specific manufacturing technologies: 3D printing, machining and injection moulding

Disregarding the general costing model presented in the previous sections, which is powerful because of its generality, the manufacturing cost levels for specific manufacturing technologies can also be determined in an approximate manner by means of the most relevant cost factors in that certain technology.

For example, in 3D printing technologies, the cost factors that are the most important descriptors and that can be characterised relating to them are [4]: (i) part weight, (ii) part dimensions and (iii) construction time. In some works (e.g., see [5]), the cost modelling in the case of 3D printing technologies has been formulated as the function of the following factors: machinery costs, materials costs, energy consumption costs and labour costs. In any case, digging again in the method to obtain those terms, it is possible to find that the fundamental factors of mass z dimension and construction times correlate with the indicated (i) part weight, (ii) part dimensions and (iii) construction time.

Taking the simplification modelling to a further stage, there have been some recent attempts to construct and validate useful specific and simplified cost models, for example for 3D Printing, machining and injection moulding manufacturing technologies [6]. In this case, the results were found of relevance for 3D printing and machining, while the fit was not appropriate for the injection moulding technologies.

3. Manufacturing context: critical batches and critical series vs. ultrapostponement strategies

3.1 Critical batch

Given two processes A and B that allow to obtain the same part P, A being a process that requires the use of specific tooling and B a process that does not require them, the critical batch Bc is the one that implies the same productivity in time per manufactured part (that is, $T_A = T_B$).

Indeed, the manufacturing time per part in the case of a tooling process (T_A), assuming that it involves a process preparation time different than zero minutes ($Tp_A \neq 0$), can be determined as presented in Eq. (14):

$$T_A\left[\frac{min}{part}\right] = \frac{Tp_A}{B_A} + Tf_A = \frac{Tp_A + Tf_A \cdot B_A}{B_A} \tag{14}$$

where T_A is the manufacturing time per part in the case of an A process with tooling (min/part); Tp_A is the machine preparation time of the A process (min); Tf_A is the time of individual forming of a part using the process A (min/part); and B_A is the size of the batch to be manufactured using the A process (number of parts).

On the other hand, the manufacturing time per part in the case of a process without tooling (T_B), in which it is considered that the machine preparation time is null ($Tp_B = 0$), results as follows (Eq. (15)):

$$T_B\left[\frac{min}{part}\right] = \frac{Tp_B}{B_B} + Tf_B = Tf_B \tag{15}$$

where T_B is the manufacturing time per part in the case of a B process without tooling (min/part); TfB is the machine preparation time of the B process (min); TcB

is the time of individual forming of a part using the *B* process (min/part); and L_B is the size of the batch to be manufactured using the *B* process (min).

As can be seen, the fundamental reason for varying the cost schemes of two manufacturing processes such as the ones presented here is the effect of the preparation time *Tp* of the process (sometimes also called machine preparation time) on the manufacturing time T_B. In case this is not equal to zero, its impact will have to be taken into account in the determination of manufacturing time per unit produced. In this sense, the existence of non-zero machine preparation time will especially penalise the production of parts in small batches, accounting for a most diluted effect in the case of large batches.

In this way, regarding the determination of the critical batch *Bc*, it is important to emphasise that what will have effect is not the existence of some or other specific tooling, but the temporary impact of the preparation. Once the part is finished, such preparation is required to switch all the necessary and start making a different part.

Graphically, this behaviour is illustrated in **Figure 2**. The individual forming times of the *A* process (with tooling) are affected by the machine preparation time. As the batch size increases, manufacturing costs per part produced are reduced asymptotically with a horizontal limit Tf_A. Since the individual conformation times for the *B* process are constant and always equal to Tf_B, whenever Tf_A is less than Tf_B, there will be a cut-off point between T_A and T_B, which is called equilibrium point. The equilibrium point marks the critical batch (*Bc*) between processes *A* and *B*.

In the case referred here, for batches with number of units lower than the number of parts corresponding to *Bc*, it will be more productive to use the process without specific tooling *B*, since Tf_B will be equal to T_B. Instead, for cases where the number of units to be used as the working batch *B* is greater than *Bc*, the process with specific tooling *A* will be more productive.

As a practical detail, it should be noted that, given the way in which it is obtained, the equilibrium point can be any positive number, in particular, not necessarily a whole number. In the case of manufacturing in discrete processes, however, it should be noted that it is necessary to work with natural numbers of parts, as it would make no physical sense to manufacture decimal parts of products.

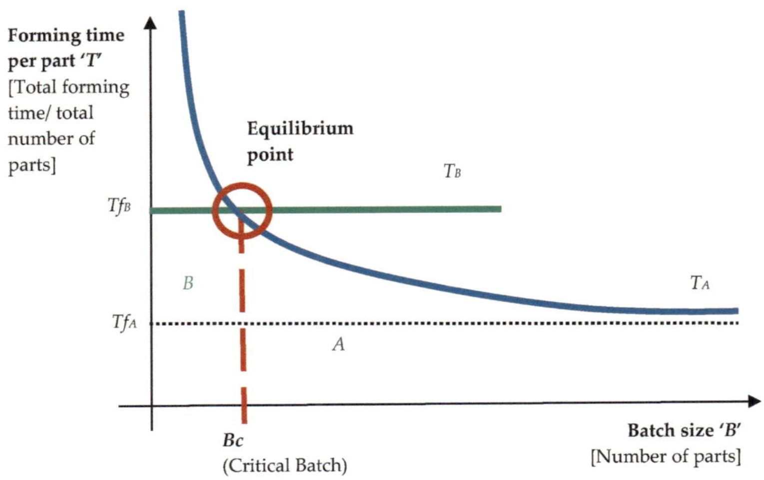

Figure 2.
Forming time per part as function of the batch size for different processes (A process with tooling-rigid process-and B process not requiring a specific tooling-more flexible process.)

For these cases, the immediately lower integer will be set as the upper limit of the number of units that make the *B* process more productive. Also, the immediately superior integer number will be set as the lower limit of the number of units which makes the process *A* more productive to obtain the product.

In case the size of the critical batch is a natural number, this number will be set as the upper limit of the number of units that make the *B* process more productive, since it will always be easier to work without the need for specific tooling.

3.2 Critical series

Suppose once again two processes *A* and *B* that allow obtaining the same part *P*. Given the two processes, it is called *critical series Sc*-the one that implies the same level of total costs for both processes (i.e., $C_A = C_B$).

In some cases, it will be possible to maintain the assumptions made in the previous section; namely supposing *A* a process that requires the use of specific tooling (a rigid process) and *B* a process that does not require it (a fully flexible process). However, many times these assumptions will not be straightforward when a process is assessed in the long run. This is due to the fact that all processes require some tooling and equipment, which can have a negligible impact on a very short batch manufacturing. Nevertheless, its amortisation cost has to be necessarily taken into account when setting its cost scheme and comparing it with other possible options.

On the other hand, many different discrete manufacturing processes, which are batch processes that obtain parts, work discontinuously with a maximum number of parts that can be manufactured in a single run and that cannot be exceeded. For example, this occurs in processes where parts are manufactured in green but require a subsequent thermal treatment in which the whole lot enters a non-continuous furnace at a time. It would also be a sample of this case: the manufacture of parts by means of 3D printing in a bed or in a building platform. These types of 3D printing manufacturing processes determine the maximum size of the batch to be manufactured from the available contact surface with the bed or the maximum mass volume available on the platform. Therefore, the selection of the manufacturing working batch cannot be done minimising the costs of a single function but will have separate cost functions depending on the number of production runs to be set in a demanded batch.

For this reason, in a general case, it is advised to determine the *critical series Sc* using the general cost model presented in Eq. (1) and replacing the demand *D* by the *critical series Sc*. In this way, as shown below, the expressions given are Eqs. (16)–(20):

$$Ct_A = Ct_B \Longleftrightarrow \tag{16}$$

$$Cp_A + Cs_A + Ci_A + Cr_A = Cp_B + Cs_B + Ci_B + Cr_B; \tag{17}$$

$$\begin{aligned} &\frac{Sc}{B_A} \cdot Tp_A \cdot Chp_A + \frac{B_A}{2} \cdot Cs_A + \frac{Cet_A}{y_A} + Sc \cdot Cd_A \\ &\quad = \frac{Sc}{B_B} \cdot Tp_B \cdot Chp_B + \frac{B_B}{2} \cdot Cs_B + \frac{Cet_B}{y_B} + Sc \cdot Cd_B; \end{aligned} \tag{18}$$

$$\begin{aligned} &Sc \cdot \left(\frac{Tp_A \cdot Chp_A}{B_A} + Cd_A \right) + \frac{B_A}{2} \cdot Cs_A + \frac{Cet_A}{y_A} \\ &\quad = Sc \cdot \left(\frac{Tp_B \cdot Chp_B}{B_B} + Cd_B \right) + \frac{B_B}{2} \cdot Cs_B + \frac{Cet_B}{y_B}; \end{aligned} \tag{19}$$

$$Sc = \frac{\left(\frac{B}{2} \cdot Cs_B + \frac{Cet_B}{y_B}\right) - \left(\frac{B_A}{2} \cdot Cs_A + \frac{Cet_A}{y_A}\right)}{\left(\frac{Tp_A \cdot Chp_A}{B_A} + Cd_A\right) - \left(\frac{Tp_B \cdot Chp_B}{B_B} + Cd_B\right)} \tag{20}$$

Depending on the values that the corresponding parameters included in Eq. (20) can take, there might be a cut-off point in the positive range of the number of parts to be produced. If this is the case, the crossing point between the two processes compared will be again referred as the *equilibrium point* and will determine the size of the critical series *Sc*.

This situation is described in **Figure 3**, which shows the total manufacturing costs as function of the size of the manufactured series for two different processes *A* and *B*. As assumed along this section, the use of tooling and equipment cannot be neglected in the cost calculation of neither process and has to be incorporated into the model. As it can be inferred from **Figure 3**, in the presented case, process *B* is contemplated to be more flexible than process *A-B* having lower equipment and tooling costs. Also, *A* presents lower costs per single forming, thus leading to the existence of an equilibrium point (*Sc*).

3.3 Ultrapostponement strategies

Nowadays, a large stake of the products that are sold to the general public is very complex combinations of parts that normally have numerous production stages. Regardless of what the specific technological aspects dictate to the optimal-economical or less time consuming-organisation of manufacturing, there is always a market effect that intervenes in the production strategies. Serving the demand *where* and *when* it is produced is even more complicated in the cases in which the demand is unstable and when the products sold are frequently customised to the specific customer demanding them.

Again, having a look at previous works, it is established as customer order decoupling point (CODP), the moment when the customer acquires the product [7]. The CODP marks just a moment in time, notwithstanding the product sold is finished, in an intermediate manufacturing stage or when its production process has not even started. However, the position of the CODP in the product value chain is important, as it is the milestone in which the product is effectively wanted by the

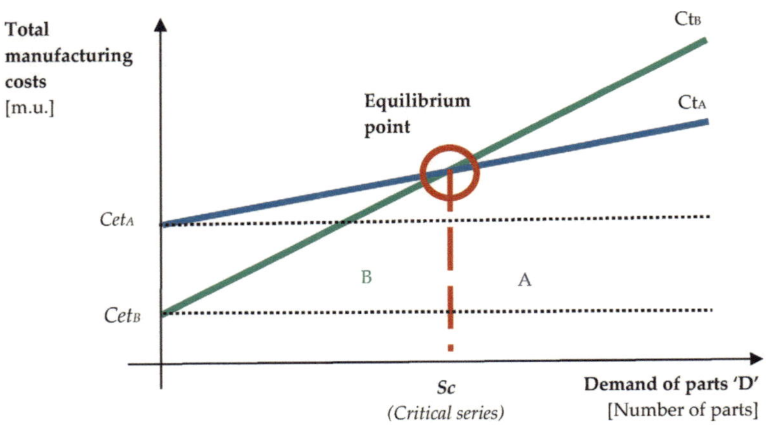

Figure 3.
Total manufacturing costs as function of the size of the series for two different processes A and B. In this case, the use of tooling and equipment is assessed in both processes, although process B is contemplated to be more flexible than process A.

customer, and it fixes the place in the product value chain where the so-called *postponement* effect occurs. The place where the postponement happens along the product value chain is referred as the *degree of postponement* of the production process.

Taking the postponement effect to one of its possible extreme positions, there is the possibility to operate in *pure-speculative* markets. These are, for example, the typical markets of regular alimentation products (i.e., yogurts, bread, bottles of water, etc.), which are goods that are produced and taken to the shops without any intervention of the customer in the production chain. In these production strategies, the selling side produces all the products in the quantities that match the selling expectations and just hopes that the demand will consume all the produced goods. Of course, these sorts of strategies are only adopted in markets with a very stable demand and with relatively low product costs. These strategies are also referred as make-to-stock (MTS) paradigms, as with them the production process works against the action of filling the product warehouse.

Moving then to the other possible extreme position, in some products, there exists the possibility of not even starting the design stage before the customer has effectively placed the order. These are considered the strategies of engineering-to-order (ETO) and are associated to products that must be completely customised to the customer, for example, a specific prosthesis for a health treatment or a bridge to be installed in a river. These sorts of strategies are common in markets with a very unstable demand (sometimes a demand that will only happen once in life) and with relatively high product costs.

Discussing a general case, as formulated by Yang et al. [8], moving upstream the CODP enhances the effectiveness and flexibility of the product supply chain. In effect, the ideal production process should only produce parts that it is sure that some customers will buy. However, in order to be capable of serving the demand in

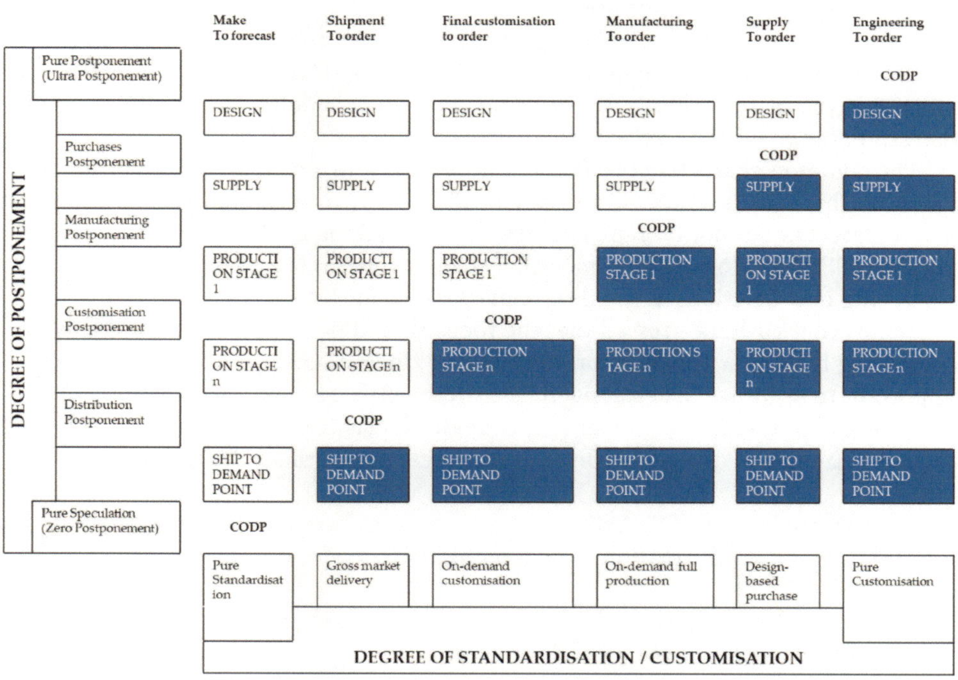

Figure 4.
Schematic representation of the CODP position in different situations along the value chain. Presented in [5] and elaborated from the findings of the study of Yang et al. [8].

the point and moment it is produced (*where* and *when*), some production processes may need to *start earlier* the manufacturing, as the product would not be ready if approached in a different manner.

The final strategy adopted, therefore, will have to be restricted due to many factors that could be grouped in: (i) technology capabilities, (ii) production organisation constraints and (iii) market-demand orientation. With all those constraints, it will be of interest to defer all the possible manufacturing stages. Some different levels of postponement that can be established as a product manufacturing policy are *make-to-forecast, ship-to-order, final customisation-to-order, manufacturing-to-order, supply-to-order* and *engineering-to-order* [5].

At this point, it will be key to be able to adopt digital manufacturing processes, more flexible than the traditional ones, which will imply lower manufacturing costs per part when addressing the forming of small batches of production. Having access to more and more flexible processes will make it viable to work economically and timely with nearly unitary batches of parts, thus allowing triggering the production only when the costumer has proceeded to pay for it.

Concerning to all this, **Figure 4** synthesises the many different possibilities on placing the CODP along the product value chain, and so the degree of postponement that could be associated to it: *pure-postponement (ultrapostponement), purchase postponement, manufacturing postponement, customisation postponement, distribution postponement and pure speculation (zero postponement).*

4. AI approaches for decision-taking: decision support systems (DSS)

The theoretical dissertation of computer systems to help in the decision-taking processes date as far as the late 1950s and early 1960s, probably being in the decade of the 1980s when it gained the most of its intensity. Regarding the interests in the present chapter, a decision support system (DSS) can be described in a general manner as a system capable of aiding the user to select the best option given the prospective results of the analysis of several scenarios. Curiously, it is interesting to know that the main authors have not agreed on a single definition of DSS and that, therefore, the their prescription may vary.

The common characteristics that described a DSS were enunciated by Alter [9]. Based on this description, DSS are specifically designed to facilitate the decision-making process but not on replacing the decision-taking role of the user. In addition, the DSS have to be fast in incorporating changes in the parameters and in producing new solutions in the new scenarios considered.

Some other authors stressed that the focus should be put on having systems containing both data and decision models [10]. In this sense, for a DSS, it is more important to optimise the effectiveness than the efficiency of the system.

Concerning taxonomy, Power [11] provided a classification of the DSS in 5 different categories depending on the assistance mode utilised by the system:

- Document-driven (DD-DSS): consisting of DSS based on the search and finding of the information in documentation

- Communication-driven (CD-DSS): consisting of DSS based on the communication between different users

- Data-driven or data-oriented (DO-DSS): consisting of DSS based on the utilisation of temporal data series

- Model-driven (MD-DSS): consisting of DSS based on statistical, financial models, being empirical, analytical or theoretical

- Knowledge-driven (KD-DSS): consisting of DSS based on the experience and knowledge in a particular area

Apart from the definition and categorisation, what is commonly agreed in the literature is what are the fundamental components of a DSS, namely: (i) the database or knowledge base, (ii) the model utilised-decision context and criteria rules- and (iii) the user-interface. Assuming that the decision-taking role is performed by the users, many authors agree that the users themselves are also a very important part in the system.

Concerning the level of interaction with the user, the DSS can be classified as passive, active or cooperative systems. Concerning the capability of interaction with the users, the DSS can be classified as single-user DSS and multi-user DSS.

4.1 Formal models and trends of DSS applied to manufacturing process selection

From the categorisation presented in the previous section, the majority of the DSS applied to manufacturing processes that can be found in the literature are KD-DSS. This may probably be since the decision taken in manufacturing technologies relies strongly on the experience and knowledge in the corresponding domain, and so the most ambitious experiences have been constructed over a nurtured manufacturing know-how database.

The selection of processes and process parameters encountered a research ignition with the emergence of the additive manufacturing technologies that took place during the late half of the 1980s. Following that, many research teams embarked on researching about consolidating the best possible advice for switching from one technology (normally a traditional manufacturing one) to a rapid (later considered additive) manufacturing technique.

In the 1990s, some authors completed a first model for yielding information about the election of additive manufacturing processes for applications of rapid prototyping (e.g., see [12, 13]). Since then, many AI-based advisory systems have focused on the manufacturing topics of *rapid prototyping*, *rapid tooling* and *rapid manufacturing* (e.g., see [14, 15]). Two outstanding achievements produced in the last 10 years at *Universitat Politècnica de Catalunya-BarcelonaTECH* are the *Rapid Manufacturing Advise System* (RMADS) proposed by Munguía in 2009 [16] and the *Design for Additive Manufacturing* (DFAM) for parts with high variability in the demand proposed by Morales in 2019 [17].

The RMADS software utilised a combination of several artificial intelligence (AI) techniques in order to deliver a concurrent and comprehensive concurrent engineering methodology to estimate the manufacturing costs and times comparing two different machines for selective laser sintering (SLS) technology. In Munguía's RMADS, expert systems were used, but also fuzzy logic, relational databases as well as neural networks. In comparison, the approach in Morales' DFAM system also utilised an expert system commanded by five layers of 'if-then' rules and a knowledge base. The system is prepared with information of the multi jet fusion (MJF) process and it also yields data on manufacturing costs that can be compared with injection moulding processes. However, the focus in this case is on assisting the 'non-expert' user on being able to redesign the parts-if needed-to better utilise the additive manufacturing (AM) capabilities.

Opening to the broad manufacturing advice, some solutions-the more specialised ones- focus only in providing technological advice on the process, material or even machine selection [18]. Some other solutions-much broader in content-take into consideration multiple manufacturing plants [19] or even the entire product value chain [20].

Concerning their architecture, most of the DSS incorporate expert systems based on rules for assessing the situations presented [21–23]. Some of the most recent ones also incorporate or assisted [17, 24, 25] machine learning procedures to enlarge its knowledge base during its operation. These later ones can be approached not only by a regular user but also by an expert that can feed the system with new knowledge on a continuous basis [26]. Some include fuzzy-logic learning features [15, 27].

As commented, some systems are intended to be proactive in the extension of its knowledge base. When not relying on the information directly provided by an external expert, the most utilised source of information reported by the academia is the link and download of on-line data that is finally incorporated in the knowledge base of the DSS [28–29].

Different to what is found in the literature for systems that manage and improve the performance of production lines, the self-learning capabilities that could be provided by the AI techniques have not been fully deployed in systems for decision-taking among different processes. In this sense, currently, the common use widely seen is the so-called hybrid intelligence learning use: the DSS is capable to produce a ranking or a statement on costs or other attributes [30]. However, the final decision-taking on the process and the follow-up and accumulation of new experiences still rely heavily on human operators.

The variables of study underlying the decision-taking are also diverse. Most of models use as parameters variables that evaluate economic and time aspects (i.e., costs and times), which are included at some point in almost every system developed. Many models incorporate technological rules and advise on manufacturing best practices [17, 23]. Finally, the newest models usually incorporate additional variables related to energy use [20], sustainability of the technology [31] and/or user-friendliness in order to build a balanced scorecard for decision-making.

Also, another trend that has been identified is the interest on providing advice on product design alternatives in the cases the system cannot derive a specific solution from the manufacturing processes database. Some recent contributions also give indications on complementary processes, such as those for post-processing and finishing the parts [32].

Being capable of yielding fully autonomous self-learning decision support systems is a paradigm that will only be able to be developed once advanced sensors would be fully deployed along the production means. Indeed, the deployment of self-learning sensor capabilities is currently in the strategic agendas and attracts the focus of research and development [33]. This achievement would lead to the materialisation of the so-called intelligent manufacturing systems (IMS) [34]. In this scenario, being in the Industry 4.0 era, the end users could gain access to collaborative services, having a more integrated human-machine interaction ecosystem, and the organisational, technical and decision-making levels could be synthesised at a unique level.

5. Case study application in an industrial product

Following what has been presented so far, most cases of application (products) will have the possibility to be manufactured by several (at least two) different production processes. Some of the processes will be more rigid and will usually lead

Order size	Machine preparation time of process *A*	Timely cost of preparing the corresponding process *A*	Cost of keeping a part in stock for a year	Cost caused by the rest of the factors independent of the series or batch size	Total cost incurred in new tooling for process *A*
D (parts/year)	Tp_A (h/batch)	Chp_A (m.u./h)	Cs_A (m.u./part_year)	Cd_A (m.u./part)	Ci_A (m.u.)
6000	2	30	2	0.15	6500

Table 1.
Size of the demand for the initial year, machine preparation time and different costs for the parts under initially planned process A.

to shorter forming times per unit (a priori) yet will imply higher costs in terms of tooling and batch preparation times that will have to be added to the forming times per unit.

Some other processes will be more flexible and will sometimes not require specific tooling, yielding smaller costs per produced part. However, the individual forming times per produced part will probably be higher than those in a more rigid production process, thus implying shorter production rates when the system achieves the stationary functioning.

With these two dissimilar choices (more rigid versus more flexible possible processes), the following application case tries to be useful to deploy the decision-taking framework that has been described along the chapter. The first part of the section concentrates on the characterisation of the available possibilities to manufacture the studied product and on determining the critical batches, total costs, costs per part and critical series for each of them. In this first part, the models presented are deployed as it must be done in a real application case, to compare cost levels and to quantify the outcomes of different levels of investment. Following that, the section recaps on how the DSS could be applied to this case and what structure could have to facilitate the user's decision.

5.1 Manufacturing of an accessory for an established product

A pharmaceutical company ordered to a workshop specialised on plastic the manufacture of a series of clip-type tweezers to add to one of its products: glucometers. With the incorporation of those tweezers, the product increases its added value a lot, yet the long run is not ensured with this first manufacturing order.

The initial planned manufacturing process is the injection of the plastic parts using steel moulds-an in-house technology already available in the production facility. The estimation of units, the preparation time and the different costs for the parts under initially planned process *A* is summarised in **Table 1**.

5.1.1 Size of the optimum manufacturing batch $B_A{}^*$ and total costs of process A (Ct_A)

The starting point about the manufacturing process to be adopted is to characterise the optimal manufacturing batch B^* and the total manufacturing costs Ct_A yielded by process A.

Assuming that in a year of production all the specific tooling has to be fully amortised and adopting the standard manufacturing cost model presented in the previous sections, $B_A{}^*$ and Ct_A can be calculated according to Eqs. (21) and (22):

$$B_A{}^* = \sqrt{\frac{2 \cdot Tp_A \cdot Chp \cdot D}{Cs}} = \sqrt{\frac{2 \cdot 2h \cdot 30\,\frac{m.u.}{h} \cdot 6000\,\frac{parts}{year}}{2\,\frac{m.u.}{year}}} = 600\,parts \tag{21}$$

$$\begin{aligned} Ct_A &= \frac{D}{B_A} \cdot Tp_A \cdot Chp + \frac{B_A}{2} \cdot Cs + Ci + D \cdot Cd_A \\ &= \frac{6000\,parts}{600\,parts} \cdot 2\,h \cdot 30\frac{m.u.}{h} + \frac{600\,parts}{2} \cdot 2\frac{€}{year} \\ &+ 6000\,parts \cdot 0,15\frac{m.u.}{part} + 6500\,m.u. = 8600\,m.u. \end{aligned} \tag{22}$$

Regarding the total cost of process A, it is important to stress that the injection moulding machine is considered an in-house technology with a very long period of amortisation. Therefore, the amortisation cost incurred for a very short run of production can be neglected in front of the other costs considered. In this regard, in case it should be taken into account, the costs of investment should be modified accordingly.

Within this context, the workshop has just introduced a new 3D printing technology, with which it is possible to manufacture the required parts without specific tooling. However, in this case, the parts must be manufactured in batches of 400 units. This technology is characterised by the time and costs summarised in **Table 2**, while the annual demand is considered to be the same.

5.1.2 Unit costs per part using each of the processes (A: injection, B: 3D printing)

In order to calculate the cost per part C_A for process A (injection moulding), it is possible to divide the result obtained in the previous section by the total number of parts to be manufactured:

$$C_A = \frac{CtA}{D} = \frac{8600\,m.u.}{6000\,parts} = 1.43\frac{m.u.}{part} \tag{23}$$

For process B (3D printing), using the general expression and taking into account that there is no specific tooling needed to be quantified, C_B can be obtained using the general costing model as follows (Eqs. (24) and (25)):

$$Ct_B = \frac{6000\,ud}{400\,ud} \cdot 1\,h \cdot 30\frac{€}{h} + \frac{400\,ud}{2} \cdot 2\frac{€}{\tilde{a}no} + 6000\,ud \cdot 2\frac{€}{ud} + 0 = 12850€ \tag{24}$$

Machine preparation time of process *B*	Timely cost of preparing corresponding process *B*	Batch size imposed by process *B*	Cost of keeping a part in stock for a year	Cost caused by the rest of the factors independent of the series or batch size
Tp_B (h/batch)	Chp_B (m.u./h)	B_B (parts)	Cs_B (m.u./ part_year)	Cd_B (m.u./part)
1	30	400	2	2

Table 2.
Machine preparation time and different costs for the parts under possible alternative process B.

And with this result, the cost per manufactured part equals to:

$$C_B = \frac{CtB}{D} = \frac{12850\ m.u.}{6000\ parts} = 2.14\frac{m.u.}{part} \tag{25}$$

Again, in the calculation of the total costs for process B, it is assumed that the amortisation cost of the overall equipment can be neglected in front of the other costs considered. In case it should be taken into account, the costs of investment should be modified accordingly.

5.1.3 *Critical series per part taking into account the two options (A: injection, B: 3D printing)*

To calculate the critical series of the two possible processes, it is important to take into account that the working batches set are different. In process A, it is possible to work in the situation of the optimal manufacturing batch $B_A{}^*$ calculated in Section 5.1.1. However, in process B, the manufacturing batch is fixed to 400 parts in every run.

In this situation, the size of the critical series can be determined by simply defining as equal the two general cost models (Eq. (26)):

$$Ct_A = Ct_B \tag{26}$$

And, since process B has no additional tooling to be considered, Eqs. (27)–(29) can be applied:

$$\frac{D}{B_A} \cdot Tp_A \cdot Chp_A + \frac{B_A}{2} \cdot Cs_A + D \cdot Cd_A + Ci_A = \frac{D}{B_B} \cdot Tp_B \cdot Chp_B + \frac{B_B}{2} \cdot Cs_B + D \cdot Cd_B; \tag{27}$$

$$\frac{D}{600} \cdot 2\,h \cdot 30\frac{m.u.}{h} + \frac{600\ parts}{2} \cdot 2\frac{m.u.}{year} + D \cdot 0,15\frac{m.u.}{part} + 6500€ = \frac{D}{400} \cdot 1\,h \cdot 30\frac{m.u.}{h} + \frac{400\ m.u.}{2} \cdot 2\frac{m.u.}{year} + D \cdot 2\frac{m.u.}{part}; \tag{28}$$

$$D = \frac{6700}{1.825} = 3671.23\ ud \tag{29}$$

Therefore, if the total demand were to be 3671 parts or less, it would be better to implement process B (3D printing). On the contrary, in a scenario with a demand starting from 3672 parts and more, it would be better to use the A (injection) process.

As the current situation is that the annual demand is of 6000 parts to be produced, the advice for process undertaking is to manufacture the parts using process A, which will require a specific tooling, but will also yield a smaller cost per produced part.

5.1.4 *Product optimisation with process B: 3D printing*

Given the opportunity offered by 3D printing technologies to make better designs, and in view that the demand for parts can grow, it is interesting to study a scenario of product optimization through weight reduction and modification of non-critical geometries. This is a very common procedure in the product design iteration for 3D printing and it is commonly retrieved in the literature as design for additive manufacturing (DFAM). In the present case study, it would be assumed that the envelope dimensions of the part to be manufactured do not change during this process; and so that the manufacturing batch size remain constant as in the previous case ($B_B = 400\ parts$).

By undertaking those steps, it would be easy to decrease the cost per part yielded by process *B*. However, how much should the cost per part manufactured by process *B* be reduced to achieve a situation in which the critical series is 10,000 parts per year?

To determine the maximum costs of process *B* in the case of a critical series equal to 10,000 units, the same expression as in the previous section can be utilised. Nevertheless, this time it is necessary to isolate the costs independently of the batch size for the "C_C" process (being *C* the process of 3D printing the optimised product), as it is done in Eqs. (30)–(32).

$$\frac{D}{B_A} \cdot Tp_A \cdot Chp_A + \frac{B_A}{2} \cdot Cs_A + D \cdot C_A + Ci_A = \frac{D}{B_B} \cdot Tp_B \cdot Chp_B + \frac{B_B}{2} \cdot Cs_B + D \cdot C_C; \tag{30}$$

$$\frac{10000}{600} \cdot 2\,h \cdot 30\frac{m.u.}{h} + \frac{600\,parts}{2} \cdot 2\frac{m.u.}{year} + 10\,000\,parts \cdot 0,15\frac{m.u.}{part} + 6\,500\,m.u. = \frac{10\,000}{400} \cdot 1\,h \cdot 30\frac{m.u.}{h} + \frac{400\,parts}{2} \cdot 2\frac{m.u.}{year} + 10\,000\,parts \cdot C_C\frac{m.u.}{part}; \tag{31}$$

$$C_C = \frac{8450}{10000} = 0,845\,\frac{m.u.}{part} \tag{32}$$

In order to interpret the results, it is interesting to represent graphically the unit cost per part versus the number of units manufactured using the three options proposed (*A*: injection moulding, *B*: 3D printing and *C*: 3D printing of optimised product).

To do so, Eqs. (33)–(35) can be used to obtain the figures presented in **Table 3**.

$$C_A = \frac{\left(\frac{X\,parts}{600\,parts} \cdot 2\,h \cdot 30\frac{m.u.}{h} + \frac{600\,parts}{2} \cdot 2\frac{m.u.}{year} + X\,parts \cdot 0,15\frac{m.u.}{part} + 6500\,m.u.\right)}{X\,parts} \tag{33}$$

$$C_B = \frac{\left(\frac{X\,parts}{400\,parts} \cdot 1\,h \cdot 30\frac{m.u.}{h} + \frac{400\,parts}{2} \cdot 2\frac{m.u.}{year} + X\,parts \cdot 2\frac{m.u.}{part} + 0\,m.u.\right)}{X\,parts} \tag{34}$$

X (parts)	C_A (m.u.)	C_B (m.u.)	C_C (m.u.)
1000	7.35	2.48	1.32
2000	3.80	2.28	1.12
3671.23	2.18	2.18	1.03
5000	1.67	2.16	1.00
10,000	0.96	2.12	0.96
15,000	0.72	2.10	0.95

The table contains the calculation of the costs for number of parts X = 3671.23 and X = 10,000 in order to see how the costs C_A and C_B as well as C_A and C_C are levelled in the equilibrium points.

Table 3.
Costs of manufacturing per part produced for different demands by processes A, B and C.

$$C_C = \frac{\left(\frac{X\ parts}{400\ parts} \cdot 1\,h \cdot 30\,\frac{m.u.}{h} + \frac{400\ parts}{2} \cdot 2\,\frac{m.u.}{year} + X\ parts \cdot 0,825\,\frac{m.u.}{part} + 0\ €\right)}{X\ parts} \quad (35)$$

As a summary of the entire case study, **Figure 5** shows graphically the three cost models that follow the three alternative processes.

In particular, process *A* is the more rigid one, requiring specific tooling that has a non-negligible impact in the manufacturing costs of small series of products.

Processes *B* and *C* are more flexible, yielding a more constant cost per manufactured unit along the entire study range (from 1000 to 15,000 parts). Process *C* derives from an optimisation of the product from the original case, and so the cost values remain all times below the ones in process *B*. Indeed, the evolution of the costs in processes *B* and *C* follow an evolution almost parallel throughout **Figure 5**.

The costs of process *A* experiment a strong decrease along the range represented in **Figure 5**. This causes the cost model of process *A* to cross the cost models for processes *B* and *C*, thus determining two equilibrium points marking the sizes of their associated critical series.

5.2 Application of the DSS to the process of decision-making

The application of DSS to compare and extract information from different processes in order to decide which one would be more favourable has usually a similar structure, based on three stages (e.g., see [35]): (i) identification of product requirements, (ii) proposition of feasible alternative processes and (iii) assessment of the outcomes obtained by each of the proposed processes, if possible, adding best practices information.

Within this scheme, the DSS configuration normally starts with the preparation of a knowledge base with the information of the processes that will be taken into consideration during the assessment. Manufacturing times, cost levels, limitations on the number of parts in a batch and in general all the information like the one contained in **Tables 1** and **2** are usually stored and managed in relational databases. In this way, the knowledge is easy to access, filter, select and represent graphically.

Stages (i) and (ii) are usually undertaken by expert systems (ESs), in which the inference engine launches queries to the knowledge base. The most typical use of

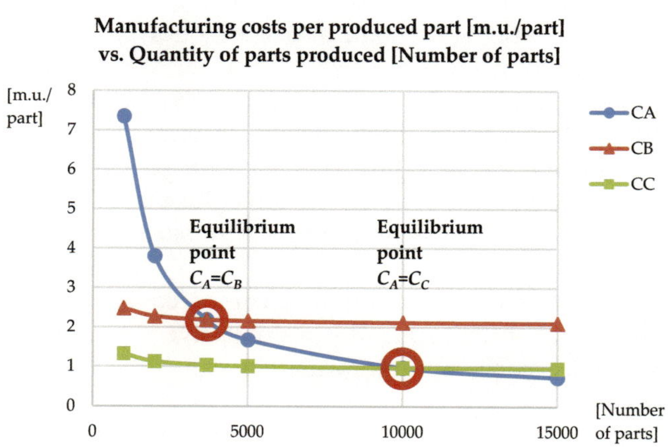

Figure 5.
Costs of manufacturing per part produced as function of the number of manufactured parts by processes A, B and C.

these techniques is by using the *'If-Then-Else'* queries supported on a rule-base knowledge (rule-based diagnosis). Sometimes, if the process complexity is high, it could be useful to implement the knowledge on cases (case-based diagnosis) or even models (model-based diagnosis). This screening technique is useful for the DSS during the first steps to understand the nature of the products that require to be manufactured and so to define the processes that should be shortlisted for in-detail analysis. In the case study discussed in the present chapter, the expert system could have prescribed either injection moulding (process *A*) or additive manufacturing (process *B*) as feasible alternatives.

Once the shortlist of two or three processes has been configured, it is time to provide qualitative and quantitative outputs (iii). In effect, the expert system can provide information on which features of the part can be manufactured straightforward and which cannot. In extreme impracticable cases, the ES would discard the processes that would not be feasible. However, for the processes shortlisted, some small tuning could be necessary or advisable to be performed before producing the part. At this stage, there is a general need to increase the system response in quantitative and qualitative aspects.

Concerning the quantitative aspects, further results can be achieved using artificial neural networks (ANNs). ANNs can be used, for example, to simulate the manufacturing process of the same part with the same technology in two different units of equipment-for example, two machines in different production sites-that yield different process variables-for example, because one is bigger than the other, or because they are placed in different regions with different cost schemes. Also, the ANNs could be used to assess the consequences of undertaking product modifications like the optimisation simulated in the case study to achieve the part as process *C* [16].

In addition, many times the qualitative analysis can be further deployed with fuzzy logic (FL) techniques. In this sense, the application of fuzzy ontologies can be helpful to translate linguistic terms and qualitative values into numerical properties and specific states. For example, it is common to receive the customer need of a product to have *'good mechanical behaviour'* and/or *'low permeability of liquid through its walls'*. In these cases, fuzzy can help in quantifying this information. The quantification could be good to help configure a balanced scorecard for decision-taking [17].

Finally, the user interface in the DSS should present the user the conclusions of the analysis. It is preferable to have it in a mix of quantitative and qualitative description. The numerical report is recommended to be as the one presented in **Table 3** and **Figure 5**, where the economical cost schemes and levels are clear. Also, other related information such as a scenario analysis for different batch sizes or the study of the different manufacturing delivery times would be highly acknowledged by the users. The qualitative report should include information on the best practices and some part improvement counselling. It would be highly recommendable to be presented in the form of a colour scale-for example, for which each assessed variable ranked from 0 to 5-and if possibly displayed in a visual mode (in a dot plot or a spider diagram form).

This *'vectors'* of information could finally be compared by the user, probably assisted by the numerical optimisation of some objective function in order to finish with a multi-criteria decision support information, capable of being run by non-expert users.

A further refinement of the DSS could deploy the use of AI techniques to increase autonomously the information contained in the knowledge base. The current systems installed frequently utilise on-line information as a procedure for data mining for the processes taken into consideration, while the most common practice is to incorporate it from human experts through specific expert user gates in the system. However, there is still a big opportunity to deploy systems that could incorporate information on the obtained results directly from the manufacturing facilities, or even better from the customer use point, once the part is performing the task for which it was originally acquired.

6. Conclusions

In the current paradigm of Industry 4.0, it is more than ever more necessary to be able to take the best decisions when it comes to manufacturing. Indeed, the industrial means available nowadays postulate that many different possibilities of processes and strategies can be viable in order to produce a specific part.

In this context, Section 2 of the present chapter has formalised a general model for evaluating costs in manufacturing process, which also considers the contribution to the costs of stocking the parts in the manufacturing premises.

Following that, Section 3 has formalised the necessary rules to determine the critical batch *Bc* between two different possible manufacturing processes for a part, serving as a decision-taking criterion for selecting the most productive scenario. In addition, Section 3 has also addressed the evaluation of the size of a critical series *Sc* for taking decisions based on the manufacturing long run. Complementary to the critical batch launch, Section 3 has also discussed the so-called *degree of postponement*, in order to give additional insight into how to raise the efficiency and effectiveness of the production processes.

Section 4 has drawn a concise review of the literature on decision support systems (DSS) used to tackle production strategies decision-taking. At this point, it is clear that the groups of factors affecting the decisions can be categorised into (i) technology capabilities, (ii) production organisation constraints and (iii) market-demand orientation.

Finally, Section 5 has illustrated the decision-taking processes and results with a simple yet realistic industrial case study in which it is possible to utilise two different existing in-house processes *A* or *B* for obtaining the same part *P*. In the case study, the cost models of both processes have been analysed and the determination of the critical batches, critical series as well as the total costs per process has been targeted. In addition, it has been numerically determined and the possibility to undertake some process optimisation to reduce the cost level of one of the technologies envisaged has been studied. Based on this case study, the possible application of a DSS to the decision-making framework has also been outlined and the different AI techniques that could be developed at each stage have been described.

Acknowledgements

The authors would like to acknowledge the programme '*Accenture Research Grants to Leading Universities to Promote Greater R&D Collaboration*', for supporting the project '*Studying the advantages of ultra-postponement with 3D printing by using analytical tools and mathematical optimization models and algorithms*' as well as the inputs of the companies participating in the study as the catalyst for the achievements yielded. The development of the project has been crucial for studying, understanding and modelling the impact of the postponement strategies on the decision-taking at a manufacturing level for highly customised products.

Additionally, the authors would like to acknowledge the Spanish Ministry of Economy and Competitiveness for the financial support of the research projects

Nhibrid32D: RTC-2015-3497-7 (MINECO/FEDER, UE) and Net3D+: DPI2016-80119-C3-1-R (MINECO/FEDER, UE). The possibility to develop new processes and hybrid (3D printing) manufacturing machinery in collaboration with leading manufacturing companies, as well as to be able to assess and compare the results obtained with other available technologies, has been eye-opening for raising awareness on what may be of interest from an industrial point of view.

Additionally, the authors would like to acknowledge the *Generalitat de Catalunya* and the *Agència per a la Gestió d'Ajuts Universitaris i de Recerca* (AGAUR) for the financial support of the research project 2015 DI 029. The possibility to have the framework for raising questions on decision-taking and discussing them with Prof. Dr. JR Gomà and Dr. S Morales at an academic/industrial level has been of much interest in shaping the contents of the present chapter.

Conflict of interest

The authors declare that they have no conflict of interest on this publication.

Author details

Joaquim Minguella-Canela[1,2]* and Irene Buj Corral[1]

1 Mechanical Engineering Department, Universitat Politècnica de Catalunya – BarcelonaTECH (UPC), Barcelona, Spain

2 Fundació Privada Centre CIM, (CIM UPC), Barcelona, Spain

*Address all correspondence to: joaquim.minguella@upc.edu

References

[1] Hopkinson N, Dickens P. Analysis of rapid manufacturing—Using layer manufacturing processes for production. Proceedings of the Institution of Mechanical Engineers, Part C: Journal of Mechanical Engineering Science. 2003;**217**:31-39. DOI: 10.1243/095440603762554596

[2] Berling P. The capital cost of holding inventory with stochastically mean-reverting purchase price. European Journal of Operational Research. 2008; **186**:620-636. DOI: 10.1016/j.ejor.2007.02.022

[3] Lesmono D. Limansyah T. a multi item probabilistic inventory model. IOP Conf. Ser. Journal of Physics Conference Series. 2017;**893**:012024. DOI: 10.1088/1742-6596/893/1/012024

[4] Minguella-Canela J, Morales S, Gomà JR, De los Santos MA. Assessment of the potential economic impact of the use of am technologies in the cost levels of manufacturing and stocking of spare part products. Materials. 2018;**11**:1429. DOI: 10.3390/ma11081429

[5] Minguella-Canela J, Muguruza A, Lumbierres DR, Heredia FJ, Gimeno R, Guo P, et al. Comparison of production strategies and degree of postponement when incorporating additive manufacturing to product supply chains. Procedia Manufacturing. 2017; **13**:754-761. DOI: 10.1016/j.promfg.2017.09.181

[6] Minguella-Canela J, Morales Planas S, Gomà Ayats JR, De los Santos López MA. Study and comparison of the different costs' schema associated to geometry, material and processing between 3D printing, injection molding and machining manufacturing technologies. In: Book of Abstracts of the 8th Manufacturing International Society International Conference (MESIC '19); 19–21 June 2019; Madrid. Spain: SIF; 2019. p. 48

[7] Wikner J, Rudberg M. Introducing a customer order decoupling zone in logistics decision-making. International Journal of Logistics Research and Applications. 2005;**8**:211-224. DOI: 10.1080/13675560500282595

[8] Yang B, Burns N. Implications of postponement for the supply chain. International Journal of Production Research. 2003;**41**:75-90. DOI: 10.1080/00207544031000077284

[9] Alter SL. Decision Support Systems: Current Practice and Continuing Challenges. Reading, Mass: Addison-Wesley Pub; 1980. 316 p. ISBN 0-201-00193-4. DOI: 10.1002/bs.3830270109

[10] Turban E, Aronson JE, Liang TP. Decision Support Systems and Intelligent Systems. 7th ed. Prentice Hall: Upper Saddle River, NJ; 2004. 960 p. ISBN: 978-0130461063

[11] Power DJ. Decision Support Systems: Concepts and Resources for Managers. Westport, CT: Greenwood/Quorum Books; 2002. 251 p. ISBN: 156720497X

[12] Hornberger LE. Rapid prototyping program [thesis]. Santa Clara: California Santa Clara University; 1993

[13] Campbell RI, Bernie MRN. Creating a database of rapid prototyping system capabilities. Journal of Materials Processing Technology. 1996;**61**(1–2): 163-167. DOI: 10.1016/0924-0136(96)02481-8

[14] Xu F, Wong YS, Loh HT. Toward generic models for comparative evaluation and process selection in rapid prototyping and manufacturing. Journal of Manufacturing Systems. 2001;**15**(5):

283-286. DOI: 10.1016/S0278-6125(01) 89001-4

[15] Byun HS, Lee KH. A decision support system for the selection of a rapid prototyping process using the modified TOPSIS method. International Journal of Advanced Manufacturing Technology. 2005;**26**:1338-1347. DOI: 10.1007/s00170-004-2099-2

[16] Munguía J. RMADS: Development of a concurrent rapid manufacturing advice system [thesis]. Barcelona, Spain: Universitat Politècnica de Catalunya-Barcelona TECH; 2009

[17] Morales S. Contribución al Desarrollo de una metodología de diseño para la fabricación con tecnologías aditivas de piezas con alta variabilidad de demanda [thesis]. Barcelona: Spain. Universitat Politècnica de Catalunya-Barcelona TECH; 2019

[18] Taha Z, Rostam S. A hybrid fuzzy AHP-PROMETHEE decision support system for machine tool selection in flexible manufacturing cell. Journal of Intelligent Manufacturing. 2012;**23**: 2137-2149. DOI: 10.1007/s10845-011-0560-2

[19] Yu VF, Hu K-J. An integrated fuzzy multi-criteria approach for the performance evaluation of multiple manufacturing plants. Computers and Industrial Engineering. 2010;**58**(2): 269-277. DOI: 10.1016/j.cie.2009.10.005

[20] Watson JK, Taminger KMB. A decision support model for selecting additive manufacturing versus subtractive manufacturing based on energy consumption. Journal of Cleaner Production. 2018;**176**:1316-1322. DOI: 10.1016/j.jclepro.2015.12.009

[21] Kaschka U, Auerbach P. Selection and evaluation of rapid tooling process chains with Protool. Rapid Prototyping Journal. 2000;**6**(1):60-66. DOI: 10.1108/ 13552540010309886

[22] Panda BN, Biswal BB, Deepak BBLV. Integrated AHP and fuzzy TOPSIS approach for the selection of a rapid prototyping process under multi-criteria perspective. In: Proceedings of the 5th International and 26th all India Manufacturing Technology, Design and Research Conference (AIMTDR '14), 12–14 December 2014. Guwahati, India: IIT; 2014. pp. 1-6

[23] Park H-S. Tran N-H. a decision support system for selecting additive manufacturing technologies. In: Proceedings of the International Conference on Information System and Data Mining (ICISDM '17); 2017. Charleston, SC, USA: ACM; 2017. pp. 151-155

[24] Zhang Y, Xu Y, Bernard A. A new decision support method for the selection of RP process: Knowledge value measuring. International Journal of Computer Integrated Manufacturing. 2014;**27**(8):747-758. DOI: 10.1080/ 0951192X.2013.834474

[25] Masood SH, Al-Alawi M. The IRIS rapid prototyping system selector for educational and manufacturing users. International Journal of Engineering Education. 2002;**18**(1):66-77

[26] Arjona-Montes J, Minguella-Canela J, Vivancos Calvet J. SelecTool: Software tool for the search and comparison of cutting tools depending on standard, geometric and cutting properties and user's criteria. In: Proceedings of 37th International MATADOR Conference (MATADOR '12); 2012. Manchester, UK: Springer; 2012. pp. 157-161

[27] Mahesh M, Fuh JYH, Wong YS, Loh HT. Benchmarking for decision making in rapid prototyping systems. In: Proceedings of the 2005 IEEE Conference on Automation Science and Engineering (IEEE-CASE '05); 2005. Edmonton, Alberta, Canada: IEEE; 2005. pp. 19-24

[28] Gibson I, Rosen DW, Stucker B. Guidelines for process selection. In: Gibson I, Rosen DW, Stucker B, editors. Additive Manufacturing Technologies. Rapid Prototyping to Direct Digital Manufacturing. Springer; 2015. pp. 333-356. ISBN 978-1-4939-2113-3

[29] Krais S, Al-Hawari T, Al-Araidah O. A fuzzy logic application for selecting layered manufacturing techniques. Expert Systems with Applications. 2011; **38**(8):10286-10291. DOI: 10.1016/j.eswa.2011.02.061

[30] Hagemann S, Sünnetcioglu A, Stark R. Hybrid artificial intelligence system for the design of highly automated production systems. Procedia Manufacturing. 2019;**28**: 160-166. DOI: 10.1016/j.promfg.2018.12.026

[31] Vimal KEK, Vinodh S, Brajesh P, Muralidharan R. Rapid prototyping process selection using multi criteria decision making considering environmental criteria and its decision support system. Rapid Prototyping Journal. 2016;**22**(2):225-250. DOI: 10.1108/RPJ-03-2014-0040

[32] Ghazy MMSA. Development of an additive manufacturing decision support system (AMDSS) [thesis]. Newcastle, UK: University of Newcastle; 2012

[33] European Factories of the Future Research Association (EFFRA). Factories 4.0 and Beyond. Recommendations for the work programme 18-19-20 of the FoF PPP under Horizon 2020 [Internet]. 2016. Available from: https://www.effra.eu/sites/default/files/factories40_beyond_v31_public.pdf [Accessed: 29 August 2019]

[34] Zhong RY, Xu X, Klotz E, Newman ST. Intelligent manufacturing in the context of industry 4.0: A review. Engineering. 2017;**3**(5):616-630. DOI: 10.1016/J.ENG.2017.05.015

[35] Shende V, Kulkarni P. Decision support system for rapid prototyping process selection. International Journal of Scientific and Research Publications. 2014;**4**(1):2250-3153

Chapter 7

Developing Cognitive Advisor Agents for Operators in Industry 4.0

Alejandro Chacón, Cecilio Angulo and Pere Ponsa

Abstract

Human cyber-physical systems (CPS) are an important component in the development of Industry 4.0. The paradigm shift of doing to thinking has allowed the emergence of cognition as a new perspective for intelligent systems. Currently, different platforms offer several cognitive solutions. Within this space, user assistance systems become increasingly necessary not as a tool but as a function that amplifies the capabilities of the operator in the work environment. There exist different perspectives of cognition. In this study cognition is introduced from the point of view of joint cognitive systems (JCSs); the synergistic combination of different technologies such as artificial intelligence (AI), the Internet of Things (IoT) and multi-agent systems (MAS) allows the operator and the process to provide the necessary conditions to do their work effectively and efficiently.

Keywords: cognition, multi-agent system, advisor, operator

1. Introduction

The continuous introduction of technology in the industrial environment is a main generator of changes in architectures, models and work styles in the industry. Currently, Industry 4.0 signifies a great opportunity for operators to become a part of the new manufacturing systems [1]. On the one hand, operators generate information and data to programme machines and robots and optimise process flows; on the other hand, they receive useful support for their work as well as effective cooperation with intelligent systems [2]. This bidirectional dialogue allows new types of powerful interactions between operators and machines. Hence, a new kind of workforce should be trained in order to obtain a significant impact on the development of the industry [3].

The use of artificial intelligence (AI) techniques to enhance the lifelong learning experience of humans has evolved in literature from the early works on *intelligent tutor systems*, where AI is used as a tool to monitor and facilitate the user learning process, to the creation of *human-computer collaborative learning* systems (HCCL) [4], where AI entities become members of a group of mixed human and artificial learners. Through HCCL systems, humans acquire problem-solving or decision-making capabilities in a particular domain in simulated or real situations.

In the Industry 4.0 scenario, AI entities can be endowed as cognitive advisor agents implemented in the form of either voice assistants or embodied agents, in

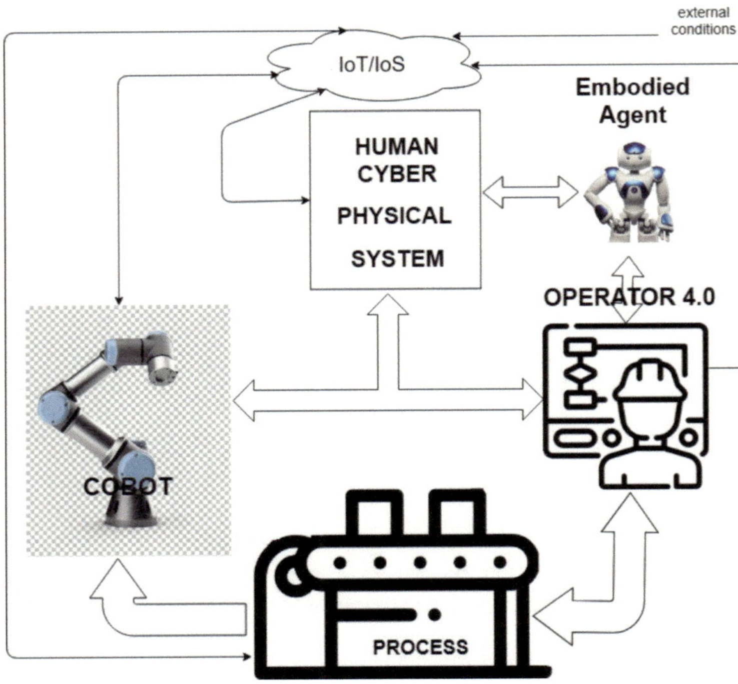

Figure 1.
Proof of concept. The operator 4.0 is assisted by the embodied agent to collaborate with the cobot in the process.

order to propose collaborative working behaviours between machines and humans. The implementation of these systems in manufacturing pushes towards factories characterised by the symbiosis of human automation [5], where machines cooperate with humans, both parts having the opportunity to lead the cooperative task at hands.

The challenge motivating this research is to define a human-centred architecture to design, implement and evaluate cognitive advisor agents in the framework of a human cyber-physical production system (H-CPPS) [2, 6] which supports the operator in Industry 4.0 to accomplish their job into an automation system [7] in a more efficient and effective form. The proposed overall H-CPPS architecture will be evaluated through a proof of concept based on a multi-agent system (MAS) implementing a cognitive robot (embodied agent) to assist the operator (operator 4.0) in a collaborative work with a cobot. A scheme of the operator—cobot—assistant robot symbiotic system is shown in **Figure 1**.

This chapter is structured as follows. Firstly, the current Industry 4.0 paradigm is introduced, and the role of human operator in this domain is shown. Next, the proposed human cyber-physical production system architecture is introduced. Moreover, the approach of this architecture to cognitive tasks is presented. The cognitive advisor vision to be endowed into the previous architecture is finally introduced. Conclusions and future research lines are closing the chapter.

2. The operator's workspace in Industry 4.0

The *operator 4.0* concept is defined in [2, 8] in a general form as an operator in an industrial setting assisted by technological tools. Although the increase in the degree of automation in factories reduces costs and improves productivity, in the Industry 4.0 vision, differently of computer-integrated manufacturing (CIM), human operators are yet key elements in the manufacturing systems. In fact, the increasing degree of automation 'per se' does not necessarily lead to enhanced operator performance.

The continuous innovations in the technological areas of cyber-physical systems (CPS), the Internet of Things (IoT), the Internet of Services (IoS), robotics, big data, cloud and cognitive computing and augmented reality (AR) result in a significant change in production systems [9, 10]. Empowered with these new skills, cyber-physical systems can take part, for instance, in tasks of planning and disposition, eventually to manage them. Machines take care of the adequate supply of material, change the production method to the optimal one for the real product or devise a new plan themselves [11]. This technological evolution generates, among others, the following impacts on the operator:

- The qualification of manual tasks decreases.
- The operator can access all the necessary information in real-time to take decisions.
- Intelligent assistance systems allow decisions to be taken more quickly and in a short space of time.
- Co-working in the workspace between machines and people requires less effort and attention.
- Human implementation and monitoring are more relevant than ever.

The emerging technologies in Industry 4.0 [12] as well as current development of AI technologies are allowing that cyber-physical systems oriented to human-machine interaction be moving from only a physical interaction vision paradigm to also a cognitive one (see **Table 1**). The operator should be able to take the control and supervise the automated production system. However, the increasing information and communication power of these systems leads to a complexity that is not understandable by the current standard user interfaces employed in the industry. Consequently, the operator would need support to keep the system under stable requirements. Moreover, the operator could get the system work plan (factory, not shift supervisor), and therefore the operator would need additional information during field operation, which requires access to location-independent information as well as a situation-oriented and task-oriented information offer [13].

As a result of this paradigm shift, new forms of interaction appear in the field of human-machine interface (HMI), in the form of intelligent user interfaces, such as operator support systems (OSS), assistance systems, decision support systems and intelligent personal assistants (IPAs) [7]. In the context of smart, people-centred service systems, cognitive systems can potentially progress from tools to assistants to collaborators to coaches and be perceived differently depending on the role they play in a service system.

	Physical	Cognitive
Routine	Traditional automation	Automated learning techniques
Nonroutine	Collaborative robots	Intelligent assistants (IA)

Table 1.
Vision of physical and cognitive automation.

Assistance systems support the operator as follows [14]:

- From a human-centred design approach, it expressly considers the identification of user context, the specification of user requirements, the creation of design solutions, and the evaluation of design solutions. Moreover, it provides an appropriate amount of information in a clear way.

- As a decision-maker in production control, with information acquisition, data aggregation/analysis of information and operation choice.

However, it should be clarified that the final decision always remains in the human operator side, thus maintaining the principle of human centrality.

Regarding the tasks and the role of the operator, an increase in the proportion of *complex cognitive tasks* is expected, hence increasing the needs for coordination or organisation of production resources, as well as the control and monitoring of complex production systems.

The literature shows that a significant change in this relationship from purely physical to cognitive refers to the human-machine interface, which encompasses the interaction between operators and a set of new forms of collaborative work. The interaction between humans and CPS is produced by either direct manipulation or with the help of a mediating user interface. Such a close interaction between humans and CPS also raises socio-technological issues regarding autonomy and decision-making power. Cybernetics provides an answer on how a system that controls another system can compensate for more errors in the control process by having more operational variety. As the most flexible entity in the cyber-physical structure, the human will assume the role of a higher-level control instance [10]. Through technological support, it is guaranteed that operators can develop their full potential and adopt the role of strategic decision-makers and flexible problem solvers, thus managing the increasing technical complexity.

3. Human cyber-physical production systems

Cyber-physical systems are one of the fundamental pillars of Industry 4.0 [10, 15, 16]. According to the National Institute of Standards and Technology (NIST), cyber-physical systems are intelligent systems, including interactive networks, designed of physical and computational components. These systems integrate computing, communication, detection and performance with physical systems to fulfil time-sensitive functions with varying degrees of interaction with the environment, including human interaction (see **Figure 2**). These systems are conceived as components in the production system able of executing physical processes in cooperation with other entities. Systems can adapt independently to changing circumstances, by learning from the additional information coming from the sensors [6].

Usually, each component of the CPS takes the necessary control decisions related to the physical aspects of the underlying production system and communicates control decisions, system states and behaviour patterns. Currently, the possibility to combine existing technologies such as multi-agent systems, service-oriented architectures (SOA), the Internet of things, cloud communication, augmented reality, big data or machine-to-machine communication (M2M) [9] has empowered the features and functions of these systems so that levels of cognition in the cooperation, beyond physical interaction, can be also considered.

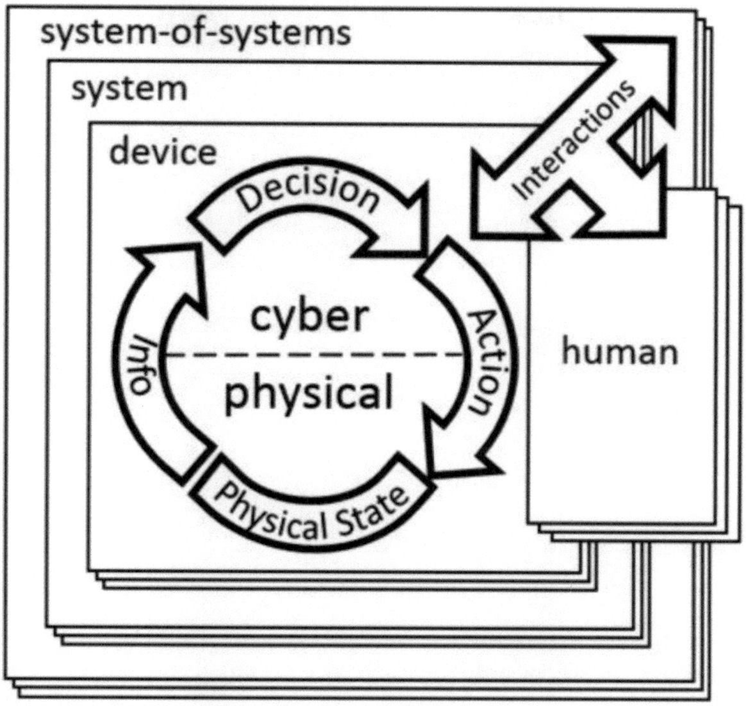

Figure 2.
CPS conceptual model [17].

In the approach with humans in the interaction, new models of CPS have emerged which focused on improving the capabilities of operators, such as cyber-physical human system (CPHS) [17] and human cyber-physical production system [2]. CPHS is defined as "a class of sociotechnical systems critical for security in which the interactions between the physical system and the cybernetic elements that control its operation are influenced by human agents." Our research, however, focuses on H-CPPS, defined as "a work system that improves the capabilities of operators thanks to a dynamic interaction between humans and machines in the cyber and physical worlds through intelligent human-machine interfaces." The objectives for H-CPPS are achieved through the interactions between the physical system (or process) to be controlled, cybernetic elements (i.e. communication links and software modules) and human agents that monitor and influence the functioning of the cyber-physical elements.

In both definitions we can highlight the role of the operator within the control loop. In human-oriented architectures, there is the ability to feedback the information (see **Figure 3**) at each level, because inherent intelligence of human operators can be used naturally for self-adaptation, corrective and preventive actions. For the H-CPPS approach, its levels' configuration acts as a supervisory control to ensure that decisions made at the cognitive level are implemented and that corrective or adaptive actions are carried out by the human worker [18].

H-CPPS are very dynamic and complex systems being subject to a certain degree of unpredictable behaviour of both the environment and the user. These conditions generate several challenges related to the administration of H-CPPS that require run-time capabilities allowing the system to detect, monitor, understand, plan and act on those not predicted changes while minimising (and potentially eliminating) system downtime. In order to develop our cognitive advisor agent for operators, we start by defining three dimensions of H-CPPS: *cybernetic*, *physical* and *human*. Each

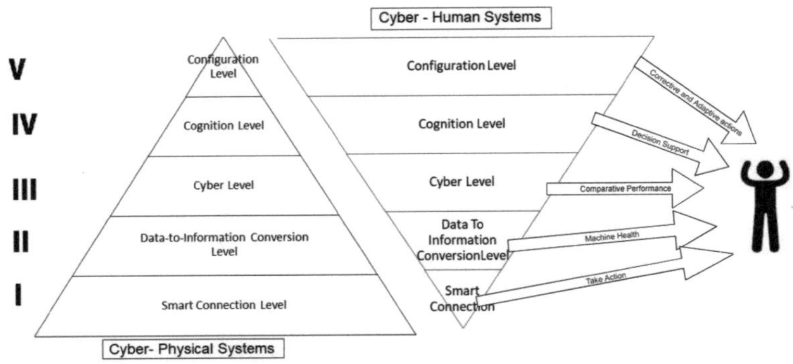

Figure 3.
CPS vs. H-CPPS model.

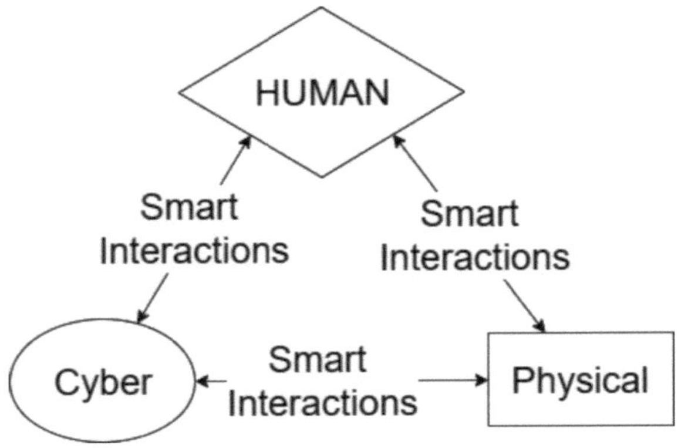

Figure 4.
Three dimensions of H-CPPS.

dimension is connected to the other ones through intelligent interactions (see **Figure 4**).

The physical dimension includes all the resources connected to the production system through sensors and actuators. The cybernetic dimension describes all computing, network and cloud infrastructures that communicate data, processes and software resources. Finally, the human dimension describes human elements, as well as their situations based on their objectives and context. The human dimension is especially relevant for this research, focused in aligning the objectives of H-CPPS with the achievement of the personal goals of the users.

3.1 Agent-based approach to H-CPPS

The applications of artificial intelligence techniques related to humans in the work environment are guided by four possible paths in human cyber-physical systems (see **Table 2**). As the 'human in the loop' is considered in H-CPPS, intelligent assistance systems are the approach to be developed in our research.

Nowadays, different architecture patterns and implementation technologies have been developed and applied to process and exchange information allowing H-CPPS components to make their decisions. They range from service-oriented architectures that exploit technologies such as web services to agent-based architectures that exploit solutions compatible with Foundation for Intelligent Physical Agents (FIPA) [19]. However, they also come with their own set of challenges.

	Human in the loop	No human in the loop
Hardwired specific systems	*Assisted intelligence*: AI system that assist human in making decisions or taking actions, hardwired systems that do not learn from their interactions	*Automation*: Automation of manual and cognitive tasks that are either routine or nonroutine. This does not involve new ways of doing things—automates existing task
Adaptative systems	*Assisted intelligence*: AI systems that augment human decision-making and continuously learn from their interactions with humans and the environment	*Autonomous intelligence*: AI systems that can adapt to different situations and can act autonomously without assistance

Table 2.
Path AI in human cyber-physical systems.

Multi-agent systems [20] are an example of architecture applicable to the implementation of H-CPPS. More specifically, industrial agents [21, 22] address industry requirements in productive systems. MAS expose system characteristics such as autonomy, cooperation, intelligence, reactivity and proactivity, which allows intelligence to be distributed among a network of control nodes and, consequently, adapts effectively to distributed control systems, that is, by implementing H-CPPS solutions [21]. While the use of MAS for control process can be considered as a mature architecture pattern, its application in the industry is still limited [23].

In order to define our agent-based approach to H-CPPS systems, two types of interactions should be identified (see **Figure 4**):

- Interaction between agents (only considering the cyber dimension)
- Interaction between agents (cyber dimension) and hardware automation control devices (physical dimension)

For the first type of interaction, FIPA has established guidelines to regulate the development of agent-based systems. It is a collection of standards that are grouped into different categories, that is, applications, summary architecture, agent communication, agent management and message transport agent. For the second type of interaction, related to the interconnection of the agent and the physical automation control device [24], standardised practices are not yet defined, allowing to simplify and make transparent the process of integration of physical and cybernetic counterparts.

Finally, it should be noticed that agents, as an enabling technology to manage smart approaches, endow inherent characteristics (including autonomy, negotiation, mobility) which could be more beneficial when combined with *distributed intelligence* approaches and lead to better services and applications at the edge [16].

3.2 Human roles in H-CPPS

For the moment, the cyber and the physical dimension have been considered in our agent-based approach. However, while in a human-centred architecture, the roles of humans in cyber-physical human systems (H-CPPS) must be also defined.

In the models of human-automation interaction, attention is paid to whether human assumes control of the system [25]. In H-CPPS systems, however, human intervention is focused in more aspects: the dialogue with other agents, decision-making and information supply. In this sense, one research line is about the definition of a human model as a part of the full H-CPPS model. However, human models defined as a transfer function leads to a poor approach. Some researchers expand this approach by developing analytic human models that reflect *cognitive abilities* in the interaction with cyber-physical systems [17]. On the other hand, a H-CPPS requires flexibility. An adaptive H-CPPS responds to unexpected or novel situations (replanning, setting new goals, learn from experience), and the definition of the role of human (passive or active performer) is required [17]. Human roles examples in H-CPPS are, for instance:

- Supervisor (human on the loop): Approve CPS decisions; reallocate tasks between human and CPS.

- Controller (human in the loop, operator 4.0): Interact with sensors and actuators; use of augmented reality technology; collaborative task with a cobot.

Merging human roles with CPS roles in order to define the functional architecture of a H-CPPS leads our research to the definition of a *joint cognitive system* (JCS), its basic aim being to achieve a high level of successful performance managing the human cognitive load in the process.

4. Joint cognitive system

The current development of technology allows us to reach the level of cognition in H-CPPS (see **Figure 3**) [18]. However, the understanding of cognition generates debates because it can be approached from several domains, mainly from psychology through mental models, and from cognitive systems engineering (CSE) to applications in practice.

A joint cognitive system acknowledges that cognition emerges as goal-oriented interactions of people and artefacts in order to produce work in a specific context and at the level of the work being conducted. It does not produce models of cognition but models of **coagency** that corresponds to the required variety of performance and thereby emphasises the functional aspects [26].

In this situation, complexity emerges because neither goals nor resources nor constraints remain constant, creating dynamic couplings between artefacts, operators and organisations. The CSE approach focuses on analysing how people manage complexity, understanding how artefacts are used and understanding how people and artefacts work together to create and organise joint cognitive systems which constitutes a basic unit of analysis in CSE. Human and machine need to be considered together, rather than separate entities linked by human-machine interactions [27].

In the domain of CSE, focus is on the mission that the joint cognitive system shall perform, avoiding vagaries into its human resemblances. It performs cognitive work via cognitive functions such as communicating, deciding, planning, and problem-solving (**Figure 5**). These sorts of cognitive functions are supported by cognitive processes such as perceiving, analysing, exchanging information and manipulating.

The importance of cognition, regardless of how it is defined, as a necessary part of the work has grown after the industrial revolution:

- Cognition is distributed rather than isolated in the human operator's mind.

- Operator does not passively accept technological artefacts or the original conditions of their work.

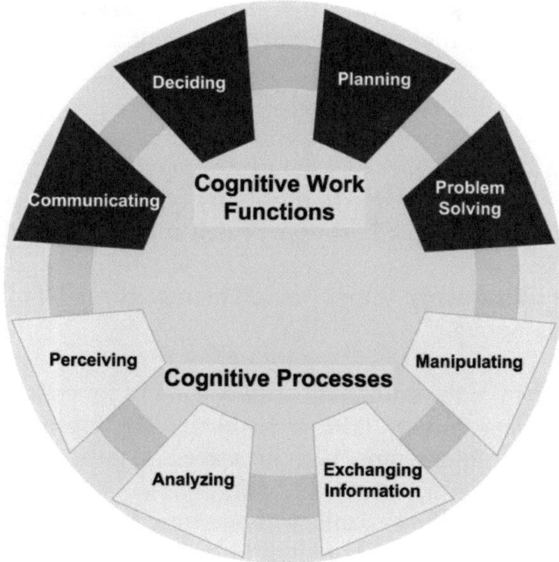

Figure 5.
Cognitive work functions and cognitive processes.

- Technological development is rampant; this entails the development of work with inevitably greater *operational complexity*.
- Technology is often used in ways that are not well adapted to the needs of the operator.

There is no turning back, the evolution of information technology, digital transformation and the Fourth Industrial Revolution requires that processes be more cognitive, automatic and efficient.

4.1 The cognitive design problem: the FRAM tool

As the automation of complex processes becomes more achievable, the need for engineering procedures that help decide what and how to automate becomes more important to the safety, flexibility and performance of automation use. The implementation must satisfy general criteria such as *minimising workload*, *maximising awareness of what is going on* and *reducing the number of errors*. The basic problem therefore is to reduce the cognitive demands of the tasks being performed by the operators involved in the system while maintaining fully their ability to function within their given roles [28].

JCSs are characterised by three principles [27]: (a) goal orientation, (b) control to minimise entropy (i.e. disorder in the system) and (c) coagency at the service of objectives.

In order to understand the sociotechnical system, the functional resonance analysis method (FRAM) [29] can be used, which allows to have a model generated by the application itself. The FRAM can be described as a method that is used to produce a model, instead of a method that is derived from a model. It proposes that everyday events and activities can be described in terms of *functions* involved without predefined specific relations, levels or structures. Instead, the FRAM assumes that the behaviour of functions, hence the outcomes of an activity or process, can be understood in terms of *four basic principles* described in the following statements. Moreover, the not predefined functions are described using *six aspects*.

The principles of FRAM are:

1. The equivalence of successes and failures: acceptable outcomes as well as unacceptable outcomes are due to the ability of organisations, groups and individuals successfully to adjust to expected and unexpected situations.

2. Approximate adjustments: things predominantly go well, but also they occasionally go wrong.

3. Emergent outcomes: the variability of two or more functions can be combined in unexpected ways that can lead to results that are unpredictable and disproportionate in magnitude, both negative and positive.

4. Functional resonance: the variability of one function may in this way come to affect the variability of other functions in analogy with the phenomenon of resonance.

In FRAM a function represents acts or activities—simple or composite—needed to produce a certain result. Examples of simple human functions are to triage a patient or to fill a glass with water. The organisational function of the emergency room in a hospital, for example, is to treat incoming patients, while the function of a restaurant is to serve food. Finally, composite functions include, for instance, a flight management system.

In the description of functions, an important distinction can be made between tasks and activities, corresponding to the distinction between work-as-imagined (WAI) and work-as-done (WAD). A task describes work as designed or as imagined by managers. An activity describes work as it is actually performed or done. FRAM primarily focuses on activities as they are done or WAD but can of course also be used to model WAI.

To basically illustrate the use of FRAM, a pick and place system with a robot is shown in **Figure 6**. The system is based on filling boxes with cylinders. The cylinder supplier is in position *Warehouse* and the destination box in position *Box*. The FRAM model should describe functions and their potential couplings for a typical

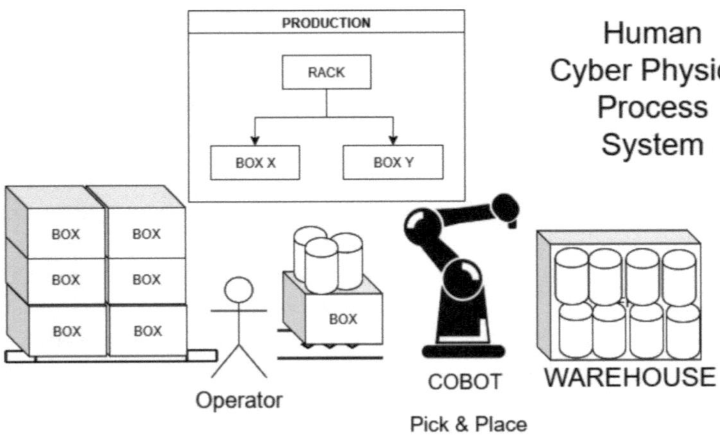

Figure 6.
Example of a H-CPPS.

situation but not for a specific one. Hence, it is not possible to certainly determine whether a function always will be performed before or after another function. It can only be determined when the model is instantiated. At the start, functions are identified in a first-independent version about execution (see **Figure 7**).

The development of the model can continue in several ways—none of them being preferable over the others. One way is to look at the other functions in the same way and try to define as many of their aspects as seems reasonable and possible. Another way is try to define aspects that are incompletely described in the current version of the model. The basis of the FRAM is the description of the functions that make up an activity or a process. The functions of different tasks have been assigned depending on who does it, (human, cobot, process) in the H-CPPS (see **Figure 8**). The relationships are not specified nor described directly, and the FRAM Model Visualiser (FMV) in fact does not allow lines or connectors to be drawn between functions. The relationships are instead specified indirectly via the descriptions of the aspects of functions. The common technical term for such relations is *couplings*.

Couplings described in a FRAM model through dependencies are called *potential couplings*. This is because a FRAM model describes the potential or possible relationships or dependencies between functions without referring to any particular situation. In an instantiating of a FRAM model, only a subset of the potential couplings can be realised; these represent the *actual couplings* or dependencies that have occurred or are expected to occur in a particular situation or a particular scenario [29].

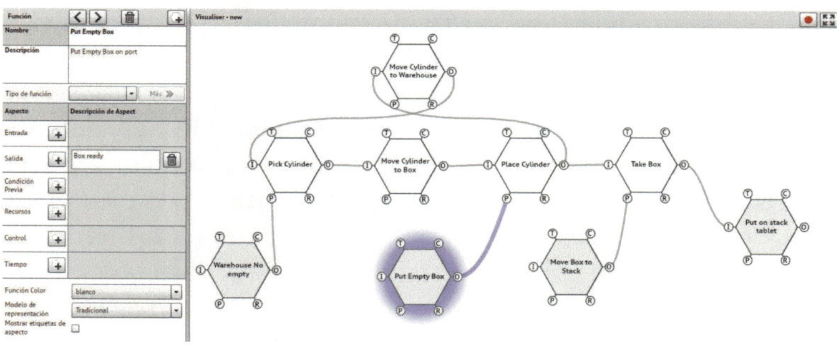

Figure 7.
The FRAM model for a pick and place function ver1.0.

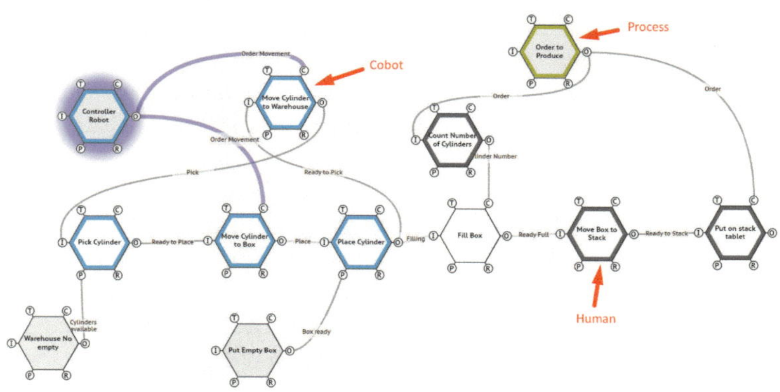

Figure 8.
The FRAM model for a pick and place function/assignation functions.

Hence, basically we can highlight the following useful features for our study:

- Purpose: A FRAM analysis aims to identify how the system works (or should work) for everything to succeed (i.e. everyday performance) and to understand how the variability of functions alone or in combination may affect overall performance.

- Model: A FRAM model describes a system's functions and the potential couplings among them. The model does not describe or depict an actual sequence of events, such as an accident or a future scenario.

- Instantiation: A concrete scenario is the result of an instantiation of the model. The instantiation is a 'map' about functions coupling or how they may become coupled, under given—favourable or unfavourable—conditions.

The use of FRAM as a tool for the analysis of cognitive tasks would allow us to understand about JCS works, identify its critical points and the propagation of the relationships between functions and understand the distributed cognition and coagency between the human and the machine.

5. Cognitive advisor agents

Cognitive systems are capable of humanlike actions such as perception, learning, planning, reasoning, self- and context-awareness, interaction and performing actions in unstructured environments. The functionality of the cognitive system includes enabling perception and awareness, understanding and interpreting situations, reasoning, decision-making and autonomous acting.

Due to their cognitive capabilities, humans are superior to fully automated mass production systems in adapting to flexible, customised manufacturing processes. Yet, the increasing specialisation is creating more and more complex production processes that require elaborate assistance in task execution. Furthermore, machines are much better at performing repetitive, heavy-load tasks with high precision and reliability.

The cognitive system provides the best possible assistance with the least necessary disruption. In this context, a cognitive system enables the realisation of an adaptive, sensitive assistance system that provides guidance only if needed and based on operator skill (e.g. a 1-day 1 trainee versus a worker who has been with the company for 30 years), cognitive load and perception capability—in other words, it provides the best possible assistance with the least necessary disruption. The adaptivity of the feedback design enables the education of novices in on-the-job training scenarios, integrating novices directly into the production process during their 1-month training period without the need for specialists [30].

At present, H-CPPS can be endowed with powerful intelligence by leveraging next-generation AI, which allows three main technological features: the first, most critical, characteristic is that the cyber systems have the ability to solve uncertain and complex problems; furthermore, problem-solving methods shift from the traditional model of emphasising causality to an innovative model of emphasising correlation and further towards an advanced model of deeply integrating correlation with causality. This shift will lead to fundamental improvements in the modelling and optimization of manufacturing systems.

The second most important feature is that cyber systems have capabilities such as learning, cognitive skills and the generation and better use of knowledge; this will

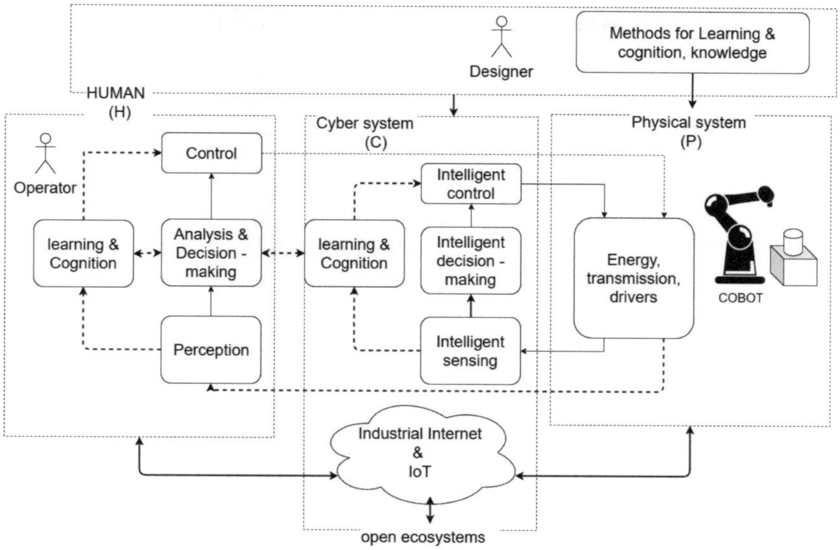

Figure 9.
H-CPPS for Industry 4.0.

lead to revolutionary changes in the efficiency of the generation, use, importation and accumulation of knowledge and to the significant promotion of the marginal productivity of knowledge as a central productive element.

The third feature is the formation of augmented human-machine hybrid intelligence, which provides full scope and synergistically integrates the advantages of human intelligence and artificial intelligence. This will result in the innovation potential of humans being completely released, and the innovation capabilities of the manufacturing industry greatly increase. With these technological advances and the advances in the Internet of Things and cloud computing, cognitive solutions are available that will allow the operator to develop their work in an efficient, effective and, above all, empowered position. **Figure 9** introduces an architecture with cognition for the Industry 4.0. Two characteristics are important to highlight, the first the Internet of Things and its solutions in the cloud which allow to reach levels of cognition for all operator functions and the second the cognitive capacity of H-CPPS systems.

6. Conclusions

The development of emerging technologies around Industry 4.0 is changing the paradigm of the intelligent industry to the cognitive industry, where it seeks to harness the cognitive capabilities of the systems to meet the new demands of the industry. Challenges presented by technological development that focused on industry require the integration of different areas of science, engineering and technology. Today, synergy combinations are required to support the development of intelligent and cognitive solutions. Understanding of sociotechnical systems from the perspective of joint cognitive systems shows in the first place the current ability to provide the operator with functions and tools that allow him to amplify his abilities, in particular the cognitive ones for which it can be seen that there are different cognitive tools, thanks to which cognitive solutions are capable of being applied.

Author details

Alejandro Chacón[1,2]†, Cecilio Angulo[2]*† and Pere Ponsa[2]

1 Universitad de las Fuerzas Armadas 'ESPE', Quito, Ecuador

2 Universitat Politècnica de Catalunya (UPC), BarcelonaTech, Barcelona, Spain

*Address all correspondence to: cecilio.angulo@upc.edu

† These authors contributed equally.

References

[1] Lu Y. Industry 4.0: A survey on technologies, applications and open research issues. Journal of Industrial Information Integration. 2017;**6**:1-10

[2] Romero D, Bernus P, Noran O, Stahre J, Åsa B. The operator 4.0: Human cyber-physical systems & adaptive automation towards human-automation symbiosis work systems. IFIP Advances in Information and Communication Technology. 2016;**488**: 677-686

[3] Ruppert T, Jaskó S, Holczinger T, Abonyi J. Enabling technologies for operator 4.0: A survey. Applied Sciences. 2018;**8**(9):1650

[4] Dillenbourg P, Baker M. Negotiation spaces in human-computer collaborative learning. In: Proceedings of COOP'96, Second International Conference on Design of Cooperative Systems. INRIA; 1996. pp. 187-206

[5] Romero D, Noran O, Stahre J, Bernus P, Fast-Berglund Å. Towards a human-centred reference architecture for next generation balanced automation systems: Human-automation symbiosis. IFIP Advances in Information and Communication Technology. 2015;**460**:556-566

[6] Bunte A, Fischbach A, Strohschein J, Bartz-Beielstein T, Faeskorn-Woyke H, Niggemann O. Evaluation of cognitive architectures for cyber-physical production systems. Computing Research Repository (CoRR). 2019

[7] Rauch E, Linder C, Dallasega P. Anthropocentric perspective of production before and within industry 4.0. Computers & Industrial Engineering. 2019;105644. DOI: 10.1016/j.cie.2019.01.018

[8] Longo F, Nicoletti L, Padovano A. Smart operators in industry 4.0: A human-centered approach to enhance operators' capabilities and competencies within the new smart factory context. Computers and Industrial Engineering. 2017;**113**:144-159

[9] Weyer S, Schmitt M, Ohmer M, Gorecky D. Towards industry 4.0—Standardization as the crucial challenge for highly modular, multi-vendor production systems. IFAC-PapersOnLine. 2015;**48**(3):579-584

[10] Gorecky D, Schmitt M, Loskyll M, Zühlke D. Human-machine-interaction in the industry 4.0 era. In: Proceedings—2014 12th IEEE International Conference on Industrial Informatics, INDIN 2014. 2014. pp. 289-294

[11] Wittenberg C. Human-CPS interaction—Requirements and human-machine interaction methods for the Industry 4.0. IFAC-PapersOnLine. 2016;**49**(19):420-425

[12] Pereira A, Romero F. A review of the meanings and the implications of the Industry 4.0 concept. Procedia Manufacturing. 2017;**13**:1206-1214

[13] Hollnagel E. Prolegomenon to cognitive task design. In: Handbook of Cognitive Task Design. Boca Raton, Florida: CRC Press; 2010. pp. 3-15

[14] Nelles J, Kuz S, Mertens A, Schlick CM. Human-centered design of assistance systems for production planning and control. In: Proceedings 2016 Ieee International Conference on Industrial Technology (Icit). 2016. pp. 2099-2104

[15] Fletcher S, Johnson T, Adlon T, Larreina J, Casla P, Parigot L, et al. Adaptive automation assembly: Identifying system requirements for technical efficiency and worker satisfaction. Computers & Industrial Engineering. 2019:105772

[16] Karnouskos S, Ribeiro L, Leitao P, Luder A, Vogel-Heuser B. Key directions for industrial agent based cyber-physical production systems. In: 2019 IEEE International Conference on Industrial Cyber Physical Systems (ICPS). 2019. pp. 17-22

[17] Madni AM, Sievers M. Model-based systems engineering: Motivation, current status, and research opportunities. Systems Engineering. 2018;**21**(3):172-190

[18] Krugh M, Mears L. A complementary cyber-human systems framework for Industry 4.0 cyber-physical systems. Manufacturing Letters. 2018;**15**:89-92

[19] Dale J, Lyell M. Foundation for intelligent physical agents. 2014. Online verfügbar unter: http://www.fipa.org/ [zuletzt aktualisiert am 4, 2014]

[20] Mas A, Belmonte MV, Garijo F. Agentes Software y Sistemas Multi-Agente. Upper Saddle River, New Jersey: Prentice Hall; 2004

[21] Leitão P, Karnouskos S. Industrial Agents: Emerging Applications of Software Agents in Industry. Burlington, Massachusetts: Morgan Kaufmann; 2015

[22] Leitão P, Karnouskos S, Ribeiro L, Lee J, Strasser T, Colombo AW. Smart agents in industrial cyber-physical systems. Proceedings of the IEEE. 2016; **104**(5):1086-1101

[23] Karnouskos S, Leitao P. Key contributing factors to the acceptance of agents in industrial environments. IEEE Transactions on Industrial Informatics. 2016;**13**(2):696-703

[24] Leitão P, Karnouskos S, Ribeiro L, Moutis P, Barbosa J, Strasser TI. Integration patterns for interfacing software agents with industrial automation systems. In: Proceedings: IECON 2018—44th Annual Conference of the IEEE Industrial Electronics Society. 2018. pp. 2908-2913

[25] Sheridan TB. Telerobotics, Automation, and Human Supervisory Control. Cambridge, MA: MIT Press. 1992

[26] Adriaensen A, Patriarca R, Smoker A, Bergström J. A socio-technical analysis of functional properties in a joint cognitive system: A case study in an aircraft cockpit. Ergonomics. 9 Sep 2019;**62**(12): 1598-1616

[27] Hollnagel E, Woods DD. Joint Cognitive Systems. Boca Raton, Florida: CRC Press; 2005

[28] Rauffet P, Chauvin C, Morel G, Berruet P. Designing sociotechnical systems: A CWA-based method for dynamic function allocation. In: ACM International Conference Proceeding Series, 01–03 July, 2015

[29] Erik Hollnagel FRAM. The Functional Resonance Analysis Method: Modelling Complex Socio-Technical systems. Boca Raton, Florida: CRC Press; 2017

[30] Haslgrubler M, Gollan B, Ferscha A. A cognitive assistance framework for supporting human workers in industrial tasks. IT Professional. 2018;**20**(5):48-56

Section 3

IIoT and Data Analytics

Chapter 8

Current Transducer for IoT Applications

Erik Leandro Bonaldi, Levy Ely de Lacerda de Oliveira, Germano Lambert-Torres, Luiz Eduardo Borges da Silva and Vitor Almeida Bernardes

Abstract

The evolution of communication technology and the reduction of its costs have driven several advances in measurement systems. Points that could not be measured before can now be monitored. Points with difficulty to reach or with major security restrictions can begin to have their quantities measured and informed to control centers. This chapter presents one of these evolutions showing a current transducer (CT), which can measure this magnitude, make an initial treatment of the signal, and transmit it to a panel or control center. Besides, this current transducer does not require an energy source to operate, being self-powered by the current it is measuring. Because it is inexpensive, it can be spread through the facilities, supplying the current at various points of the observed electrical network. With signal treatment, useful information can be inserted in this device so that it informs already preprocessed elements to reading devices, becoming part of the world of IoT. This article presents its use in motor condition monitoring at the Pimental hydroelectric power plant.

Keywords: measurement, current transducer, IoT, IIoT, energy monitoring, condition-based maintenance

1. Introduction

In recent times, new scenarios, many of them futuristic and revolutionary, have emerged based on technological advances in two areas, the development of processors with high processing power and high energy efficiency [1] and the development of communication protocols with high transfer rates and low consumption [2].

On the one hand, these advances have stimulated a revolution in the world of sensors that has been called the "Industrial Internet of Things" (IIOT) [3–5], where it is seen that all devices will present, shortly, some kind of intelligence and interconnection through the Internet. On the other hand, in the industrial environment, another revolution related to these technological advances has been establishing, the so-called fourth Industrial Revolution, or Industry 4.0 [6, 7], where the physical systems of the factory floor will have their parameters monitored and digital models of your operative and maintenance condition will be updated for decision-making and optimization purposes.

And more, another equally strong trend, due to concerns about the environmental impact generated by all this diffusion of consumer electronics and industrial electronics, is the energy collection from the environment, named "energy harvesting." This tendency is based on the energy collection from the environment to drive highly efficient electronics, avoiding the dependence of the electrical system and eliminating the use of batteries or significantly reducing it. Another advantageous aspect of devices with power collection is related to the ease of installation, since power sources and cables connected to power outlets are not required, configuring a wireless power supply.

In accordance with those recent trends, this chapter proposes a wireless self-supplied current transducer (CT) as an IIOT application for induction motor monitoring. Section 2 presents an overview of the proposed current transducer and the modeling considerations about the measurement and power extraction CTs. In Section 3, the basic components used in the implementation of the proposed current transducer are presented. Section 4 considers the available wireless interface standards and details the chosen one. The final assembly of the resulting prototype is presented in Section 5. In Section 6, test results are presented attesting the prototype performance. And Section 7 presents the conclusions.

2. Overview of the current transducer

Figure 1 presents the general overview of the developed current transducer, where there are two current transducers, one for measurement and the other for energy extraction. The system is complete with a wireless communication module, IEEE 802.11 Standard (Wi-Fi) [8]. The device presented in this chapter can be applied widely throughout the industrial sector, regardless of its specificity, since the need of current measurement for energy monitoring or monitoring of the condition of machinery is widespread enough.

2.1 Measuring CT modeling

For monitoring large-scale equipment, the measurement units can be considered ideal transformers in the frequency range of interest between ~ 5 and ~ 3 kHz. The only concern is the input impedance of the AD converter which is in parallel with the "shunt" resistor in a direct connection or the input impedance of the amplifier making the buffer function to protect the AD converter in an indirect connection. However, in both cases, the input impedance tends to be much higher than 50 Ω. For a direct connection to the AD converter, the input impedance for the high-resolution mode is 16.4 kΩ. For a connection through a buffer, for example, the suggested configuration on the ADS1271EVM rating board, the 50 Ω shunt will

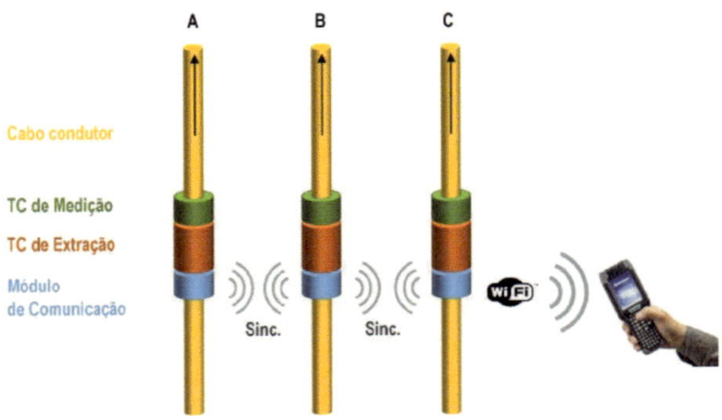

Figure 1.
Concept of application of the wireless and self-powered current transducer.

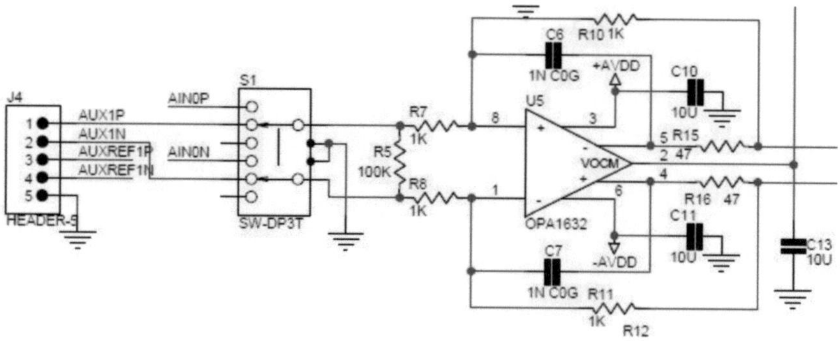

Figure 2.
ADS1271EVM evaluation board input buffer.

be in parallel with the 100 kΩ/2 kΩ arrangement which is about 40 times greater. **Figure 2** presents this arrangement. There are arrangements with a better input impedance, but it is worth remembering that any minor transformation relationship errors arising from the interaction between shunt resistor and input impedance can be compensated by a software in the microcontroller.

2.2 Modeling and simulation of the power extraction CT

An extraction CT can be modeled by the scheme and equation shown in **Figure 3**. As can be perceived, the power in the load, RL, depends on the current in the secondary of the CT, I_s, and the current splitter formed by the inductance of magnetization, L_m, and the own load, RL. The higher the L_m, the higher is the portion of the current of the secondary that will pass through the load, I_L, and the higher is the power extracted.

In **Figure 3**, by the equation of the magnetization inductance referred to the secondary, $L_{m,s}$, it is perceived that it is proportional to the effective area of its section, A_e, and is inversely proportional to its average length, D. On the other hand, the magnetization inductance is also proportional to the square of the number of turns of the secondary, N_2. However, the increase in N causes the decrease of the current of the secondary and therefore of the power in the load so that there is an optimum value of N for a given configuration. For modeling, a common CT with a bipartite

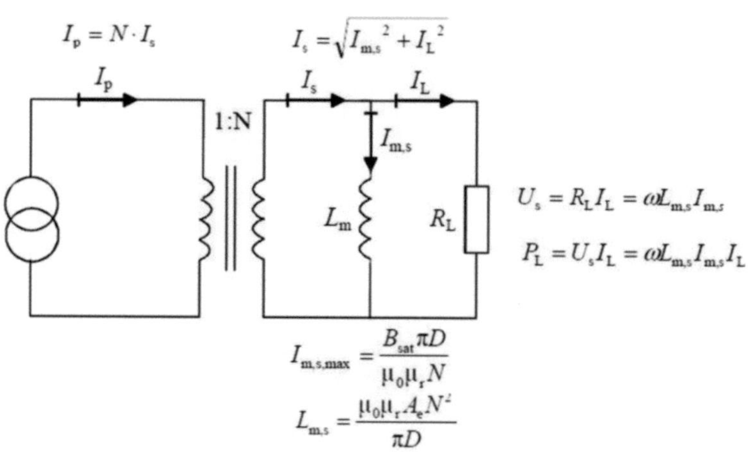

Figure 3.
CT modeling of power extraction, schematic, and equations (toroidal core).

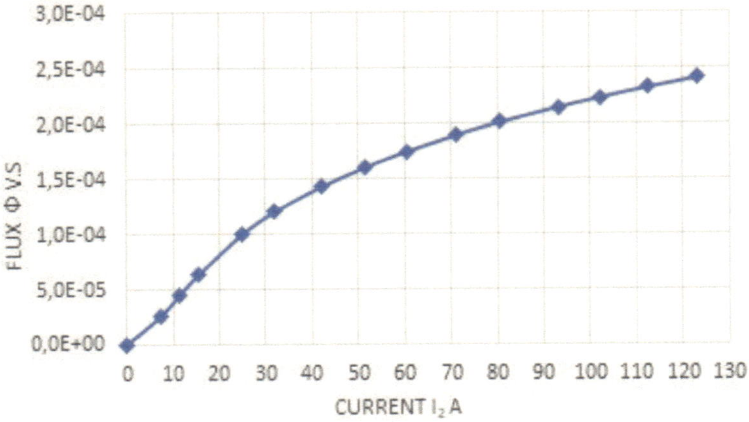

Figure 4.
CT magnetization curve.

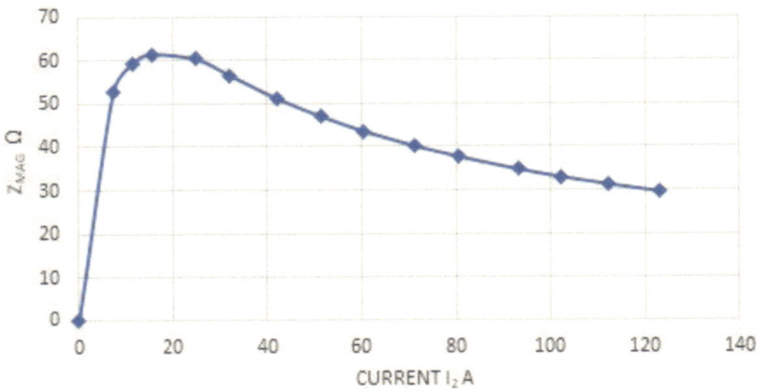

Figure 5.
Behavior of CT magnetization impedance.

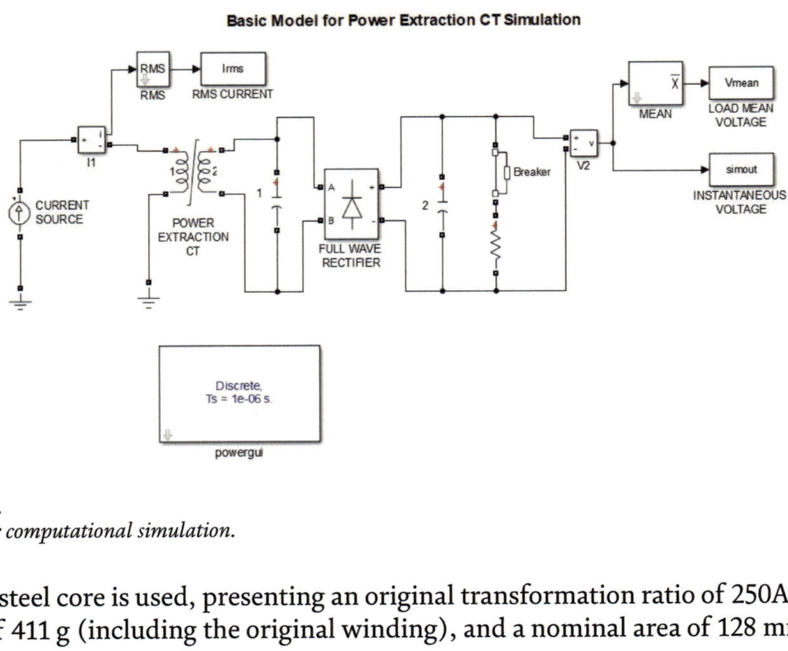

Figure 6.
Model for computational simulation.

silicon steel core is used, presenting an original transformation ratio of 250A:1A, a mass of 411 g (including the original winding), and a nominal area of 128 mm^2.

Figure 4 presents the magnetization curve of the core, separately and together. The tendency of CT with double core saturated with a higher current in the primary is perceived. In any case, according to the estimated currents and measurements in the cable, the CT works far from the core saturation point. It should also be noted that the saturation of the core plays an important role in the aid to the protection of the extractor electronics. **Figure 5** presents the behavior of the magnetization impedance of the test core.

Figure 6 presents the model for computational simulation of the power extraction CT. The transformer block uses the magnetization curve shown above. In this model a CT self-inductance compensation capacitor, a complete wave rectifier to produce a continuous voltage in the load, and a capacitor for voltage "ripple" filtration are included. The resistor has been chosen to be equivalent to the load of the application. It was estimated, previously, that the final prototype would be equivalent to a maximum load of 1.1 W, operating at 5 VDC. This power equates to a resistive load of 22.72 Ω, which was approximated to a load of 25 Ω, for availability, with three 75 Ω resistors in parallel being used.

3. Implementation of the current measurement module

The current measuring module digitalizes the output of the measuring CT and makes it available for processing and transmission. The digital-to-analog conversion is performed by the ADS1271 converter, and its control is performed by the CC3200 microcontroller. The interconnection of the two modules, ADS1271 and CC3200, is presented in the figure below. The set is powered by 5 VDC, and communication between modules is done by the serial peripheral interface (SPI) communication interface.

The CC3200 microcontroller is the master device, and the ADS1271 is the slave device in the SPI communication scheme. The master device provides the clock signal for the SPI interface of the slave device, which sends the data signal (PIN slave out-master in) to the master device. The slave device also sends the data-ready signal to an interrupt line of the master device, interrupting the microcontroller and stating that a valid data is ready for reading and processing.

The power metering module is composed of the magnetic field power extraction CT and the power conditioning circuit. The extraction CT is composed of the core and the winding of the secondary, whose main parameter is the number of turns, which is determined, to extract the estimated power for the application with the minimum current in the primary.

The power conditioning circuit consists of compensating capacitors, a full-wave rectifying bridge, and a DC-DC converter with buck topology, whose main parameter is the output voltage, defined by the power supply voltage of the electronics of the application, in this case 5 VDC. In the buck topology, the output voltage is

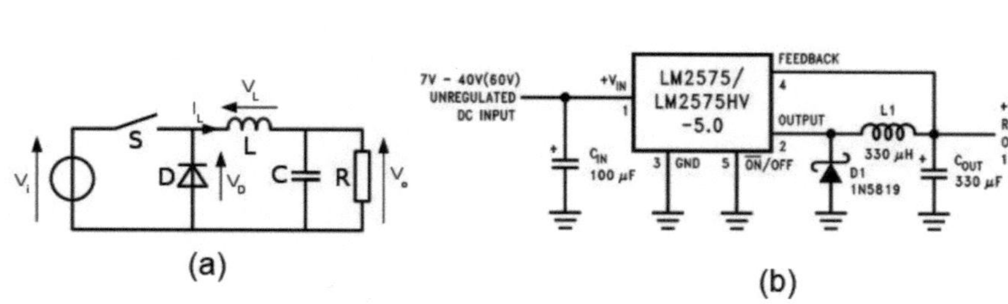

Figure 7.
DC-CC converter with buck topology: (a) overall topology scheme and (b) real circuit with integrated circuit LM2575-5.0.

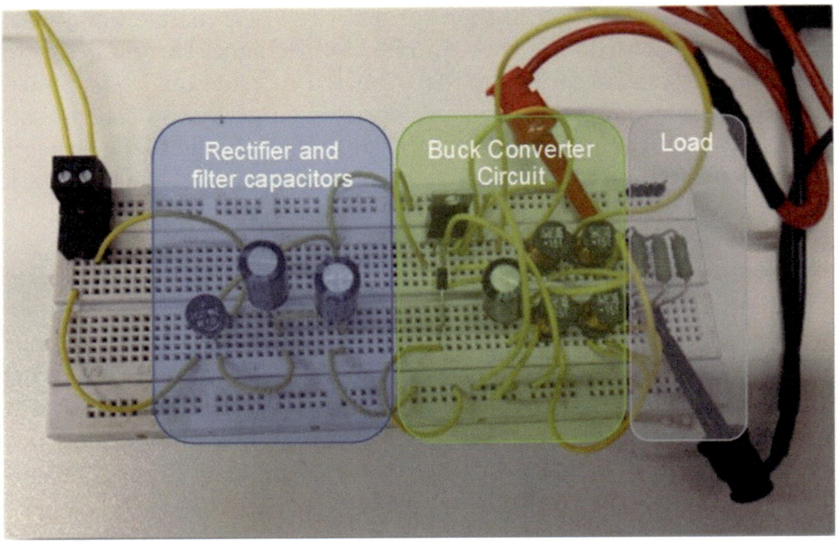

Figure 8.
Protoboard assembly of the buck CC-CC converter circuit, including the rectifier and equivalent resistive load.

less than the input voltage and was chosen according to the voltages obtained at the output of the extraction CT in the range of possible currents for the application.

Figure 7 presents the general schematic of the topology and the schematic of the actual circuit implemented with integrated circuit LM2575-5.0.

Figure 8 introduces the protoboard implementation of the buck converter. In this figure, the rectifier with the ripple filtering capacitors, the buck converter itself, and a resistive load equivalent to the estimated load of the application are shown.

4. Wireless interface specifications

There are a large number of wireless communication technologies for the most diverse purposes. Among these, we can cite three well-known: IEEE 802.15.4 known as Zigbee [9], IEEE 802.11 known as Wi-Fi [8], and IEEE 802.15.1 known as Bluetooth [10].

The IEEE 802.15.4 Standard, Zigbee, is an open standard designed exclusively for use in device networks. It is a technology that does not require much processing or power, being suitable for devices with batteries. The standardization is not yet total so that a device with interface said Zigbee would not necessarily be able to communicate with another device with interface. Since the standard is oriented to device networks, "streaming" applications, which require the continuous submission of data at relatively high rates, are not well attended because the maximum baud rate is 250 Kbps. The range can also be a limiting factor for applications based on this standard.

The IEEE 802.11 Standard, Wi-Fi, is best known and commonly used for connecting devices such as notebooks, tablets, and smartphones to Internet routers. The standard uses radio bands in the range of 2, 4, and 5GHz. It is possible to obtain a "Wi-Fi Certified" certification for a device to ensure its full compatibility with the standard and ensure its interoperability with other devices as well as certificates. This standard is quite suitable for "streaming" applications, being used commonly for audio and video streaming applications, much more demanding, in terms of speed, than the transducer proposed in this project. Data transmission rates of 10 Mbps or larger are common. Another positive point is the long range usually obtained with interfaces of this standard, which can reach 100 m or more.

The IEEE 802.15.1 Standard, Bluetooth and Bluetooth Low Energy (BLE), establishes an interface geared to the transmission of data in short distance, 2–10 m. Streaming applications are serviced very well as long as the distance limitation does not adversely affect the application. The data throughput is between 1 and 3 Mbps. Another limiting factor is the limit of seven devices on a Bluetooth network. The Bluetooth standard is well controlled, and every device needs to be certified to use the name.

Thus, considering the general characteristics of these three wireless interface standards, the IEEE 802.11 Standard, Wi-Fi, shows the most indicated, taking into account the general requirements of this application, which are range, greater than 10 m; data transmission rate, in the order of Mbps; and practicality and integration facilitated with the communication network of the plant.

The two most common and known transport layer protocols are transmission control protocol (TCP) and user datagram protocol (UDP). The CTP is one of the main protocols of the Internet protocol set. It enables reliable, orderly, and error-checking packet transmission. The UDP uses a simpler, connectionless communication model. UDP checks the integrity of the data with "checksum" and uses a system of several ports for different functions, both in the target and in the source. There are no handshake dialogs between the source and the destination because there is no established connection. Therefore, there is no guarantee of delivery of packages. Thus, the UDP is suitable for applications where the integrity and correctness of the data are not necessary or can be done in the application itself, avoiding the cost of this processing in the protocol stack. In general, real-time applications that privilege speed use UDP, as it is preferable to lose a package waiting for a delayed package. In the "streaming" data-type applications, the first transport protocol option is UDP.

The application of this device is related to the monitoring of engine condition, and the condition of a motor changes slowly, at least in the parameters of interest. Therefore, if there is a loss of a package compromising a measurement, another measurement can be requested without prejudice to the monitoring. Besides, it is more appropriate for data integrity checking to be done on the target computer, which probably has more processing capacity than the application microcontroller.

The hardware of the prototype Wi-Fi communication interface module consists of the CC3200-LaunchXL card. This board is composed of circuits for the use of external peripherals of the CC3200 microcontroller, circuits for debugging functionalities, and the antenna of the wireless communication system itself.

The CC3200 is a single-chip microcontroller with integrated Wi-Fi connectivity for the Internet of Things applications. Its core consists of an ARM Cortex-M4 processor that allows the implementation of applications with processing and wireless communication interface with a single integrated circuit.

Provisioning on Wi-Fi-type wireless networks is the process of connecting a new Wi-Fi device (called a station) to a Wi-Fi network (called a hotspot). The provisioning process involves loading the station with the network name (called SSID) and the security credentials. The Wi-Fi security standard distinguishes between personal security, for home and business use, and business security, for use in large offices and large networks. In the case of the enterprise security standard, certificates are installed that are used to verify the health of the station and the network by interacting with a secure server managed by the IT department. In the case of the personal security standard, only the use of a password is required.

In the case of CC3200 devices with the SimpleLink application programming interface (API), there are three provisioning methods: SmarConfig, AP mode, and Wi-Fi protected setup (WPS).

The SmarConfig Technology owns the Texas Instruments and consists of a provisioning method for non-peripheral input/output devices (keyboards, mice,

```c
long WlanConnect()
{
    SlSecParams_t secParams = {0};
    long lRetVal = 0;

    secParams.Key = (signed char*)SECURITY_KEY;
    secParams.KeyLen = strlen(SECURITY_KEY);
    secParams.Type = SECURITY_TYPE;

    lRetVal = sl_WlanConnect((signed char*)SSID_NAME, strlen(SSID_NAME), 0, &secParams, 0);
    ASSERT_ON_ERROR(lRetVal);

    // Wait for WLAN Event
    while((!IS_CONNECTED(g_ulStatus)) || (!IS_IP_ACQUIRED(g_ulStatus)))
    {
        // Toggle LEDs to Indicate Connection Progress
        GPIO_IF_LedOff(MCU_IP_ALLOC_IND);
        MAP_UtilsDelay(800000);
        GPIO_IF_LedOn(MCU_IP_ALLOC_IND);
        MAP_UtilsDelay(800000);
    }

    return SUCCESS;

}
```

Figure 9.
C code using the SimpleLinkK API to connect to the provisioned Wi-Fi network.

monitors, and CT), as is the case with the application of this project. This method uses an application to broadcast network credentials through a smartphone, tablet, or PC to a Wi-Fi device that has not yet been provisioned.

When the unprovisioned device uses the SmartConfig mode, it enters a special scanning mode, hoping to collect the network information being broadcast by the SmartConfig application on a smartphone, for example. The smartphone needs to be connected to a Wi-Fi network to broadcast its credentials.

The access point (AP) method is the most widespread method for provisioning non-peripheral input/output devices over Wi-Fi networks. In this method, the unprovisioned device starts in access point mode, creating its network with SSIDs and credentials set by the application's manufacturer, so a smartphone or PC can connect directly to the unprovisioned device and configure your provisioning on the desired network. These elements are the provisioning method adopted in the final version of the CT.

The Wi-Fi protected setup (WPS) method is the only industry standard available for provisioning non-peripheral input/output devices. It was introduced by the Wi-Fi Alliance in 2006 and is a safe and easy method of provisioning devices without knowing the SSID of the network or long typing passwords. The default defines two mandatory methods for access points with WPS: using personal identification number (PIN) and using a push-button-connect (PBC).

Once the SSID and the access credentials have been established, the code, shown in **Figure 9**, makes the connection to the chosen network using the SimpleLink application programming interface (API) in C code.

The basic flow of connecting, transmitting, and receiving data with a UDP socket from the SimpleLink application programming interface (API) of the CC3200 microcontroller in C language is presented next to the client and server side.

On the client side, you first create a socket of the IPv4 type and select a UDP connection, as follows:

```c
int SockID;
SockID = sl_Socket(SL_AF_INET, SL_SOCK_DGRAM, 0);
```

In the code above, the first parameter, SL_AF_INET, indicates the selection of an IPv4 socket; the second parameter, SL_SOCK_DGRAM, selects the UDP protocol; the third parameter, 0, selects the protocol default mode; and the SockID variable is the handler for the socket that will be used in all subsequent operations. The parameters used above and others are established in the header file "socket. h."

Because UDP is a connectionless protocol, the client can begin sending data to a specific address without verifying that the device is active or not. The following code is an example of how to do this:

```
#define IP_ADDR         0xc0a80164
#define PORT_NUM        5001

Addr.sin_family      = SL_AF_INET;
Addr.sin_port        = sl_Htons((UINT16)PORT_NUM);
Addr.sin_addr.s_addr = sl_Htonl((UINT32)IP_ADDR);

Status = sl_SendTo(SockID, uBuf.BsdBuf, BUF_SIZE, 0,   (SlSockAddr_t *) &Addr,
sizeof(SlSockAddrIn_t));
```

In the code above, IP_ADDR is the IP address in hexadecimal format, PORT_NUM is the port number used, and Addr is a structure that gathers all the necessary information (user-specified information and other standard information) to the operation.

Finally, to close the socket, you use the following function:

```
sl_Close(SockID);
```

On the server side, the creation of the socket is identical to the client side:

```
SockID = sl_Socket(SL_AF_INET,SL_SOCK_DGRAM, 0);
```

The socket then needs to be bound to the local IP address through the sl_Bind function:

```
#define PORT_NUM        5001

SlSockAddrIn_t  LocalAddr;
AddrSize = sizeof(SlSockAddrIn_t);

TestBufLen  = BUF_SIZE;

LocalAddr.sin_family      = SL_AF_INET;
LocalAddr.sin_port        = sl_Htons((UINT16) PORT_NUM);
LocalAddr.sin_addr.s_addr = 0;
Status = sl_Bind(SockID,  (SlSockAddr_t *) &LocalAddr, AddrSize);
```

From this point, you can try to receive data by the socket of the source specified by Addr, the fifth parameter of sl_RecvFrom:

```
#define BUF_SIZE 1400
SlSockAddrIn_t  Addr;
char            RecvBuf[BUF_SIZE];

Status = sl_RecvFrom(SockID, RecvBuf, BUF_SIZE, 0, (SlSockAddr_t *) &Addr, (SlSocklen_t*)
&AddrSize );
```

If the "nonblocking" option was not specified, the command is locked until the amount of data specified in BUF_SIZE is received.

To close the socket, use the sl_Close function as before:

```
sl_Close(SockID);
```

5. Assembly of the current transducer

The produced prototype boards are presented in **Figures 10** and **11**.

An enclosure was designed with a more rounded and nicer shape visually. The 3D design can be seen in **Figure 12**.

The enclosure design was executed in Delrin® Resin, conferring resistance and robustness to the prototype. **Figures 13–15** show the prototype in its final enclosure.

Figure 16 below presents the operation flow chart for the prototype device. Once the wireless self-supplied module is installed around the motor cable and there is enough current to drive the power conditioning circuit, a timer starts to count. After a stabilization time, the available power is supplied to the main application modules: microprocessor, wireless interface, and analog-to-digital converter. After that, a Wi-Fi network is created for provisioning, as described in Section 4, or direct connection, if desired. Once the device is connected to the desired Wi-Fi network, it can receive commands from the main software or execute operations according to a setup schedule.

(a) (b)

Figure 10.
Device board: (a) top view and (b) bottom view.

(a) (b)

Figure 11.
Board of the device mounted with the SBC and ADS1271-EVM board: (a) front view and (b) rear view.

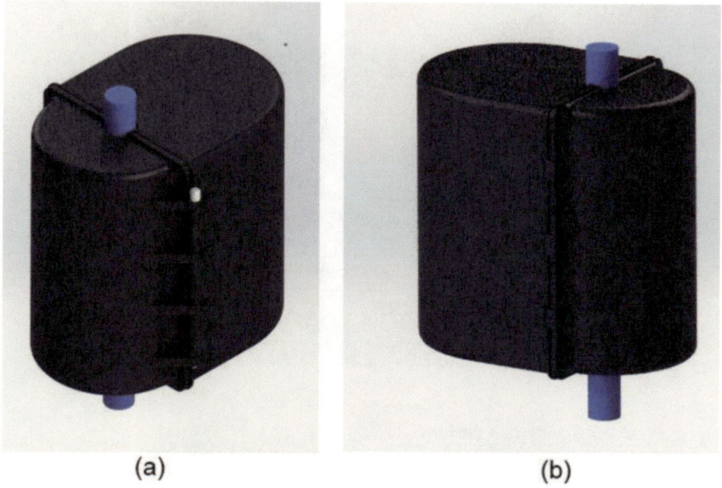

Figure 12.
3D design of the device enclosure.

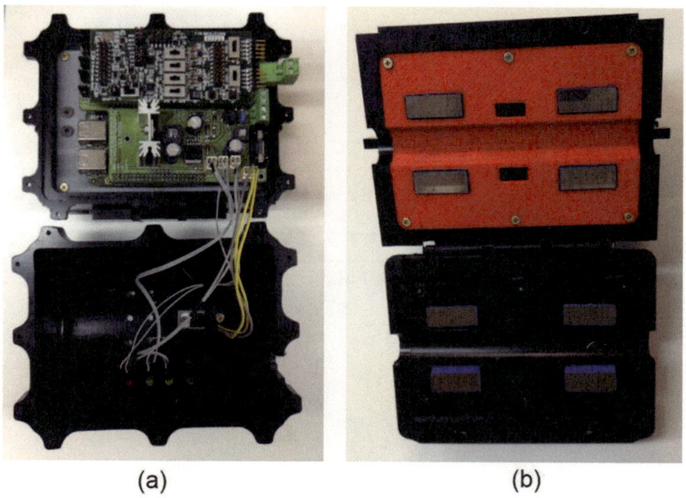

Figure 13.
The open device enclosure exposing (a) the electronics and (b) the CTs for measuring and extracting power.

Figure 14.
Front view of the device.

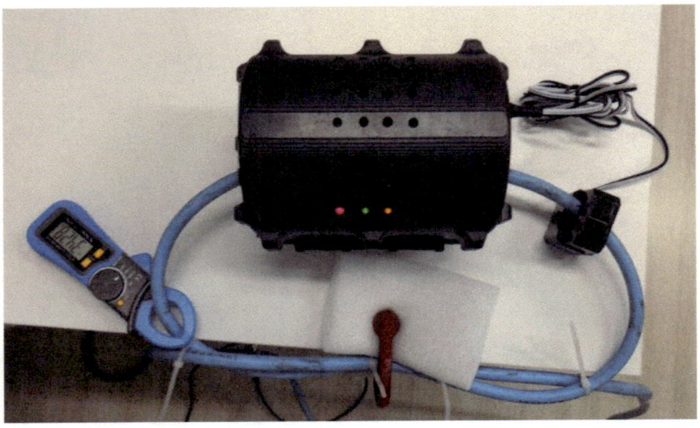

Figure 15.
Device operating in a test setup with 34 a current.

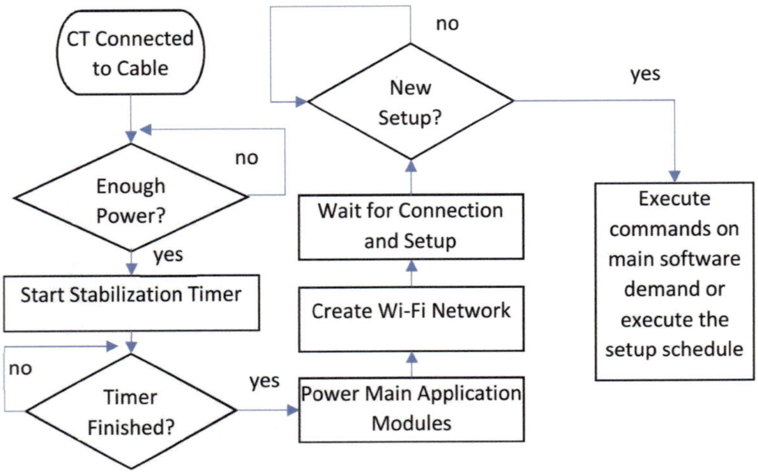

Figure 16.
Operation flowchart for the wireless self-supplied current transducer.

6. Results of tests

6.1 Tests in the laboratory

The objective of these tests was to simulate the actual operating conditions that the device will face when installing on the electric motors in the field. For example, in the case of off-road vehicle (ORV) motors (speed regulator), the prototype must:

- Support the starting condition offered by the "soft-starter" system.
- Work, most of the time, with the current in "no load" (30–60 A).
- Withstand the operating current of the motor (about 162 A), which lasts about 1 min.

Also, for the case of motors without soft starter, the condition of direct starting with currents of the order of six times the nominal current has been tested. For this, a motor of 2.1 A was used, and the cable was passed through one of the phases by the prototype 18 times, producing a motive magnet force of about 36 At in normal

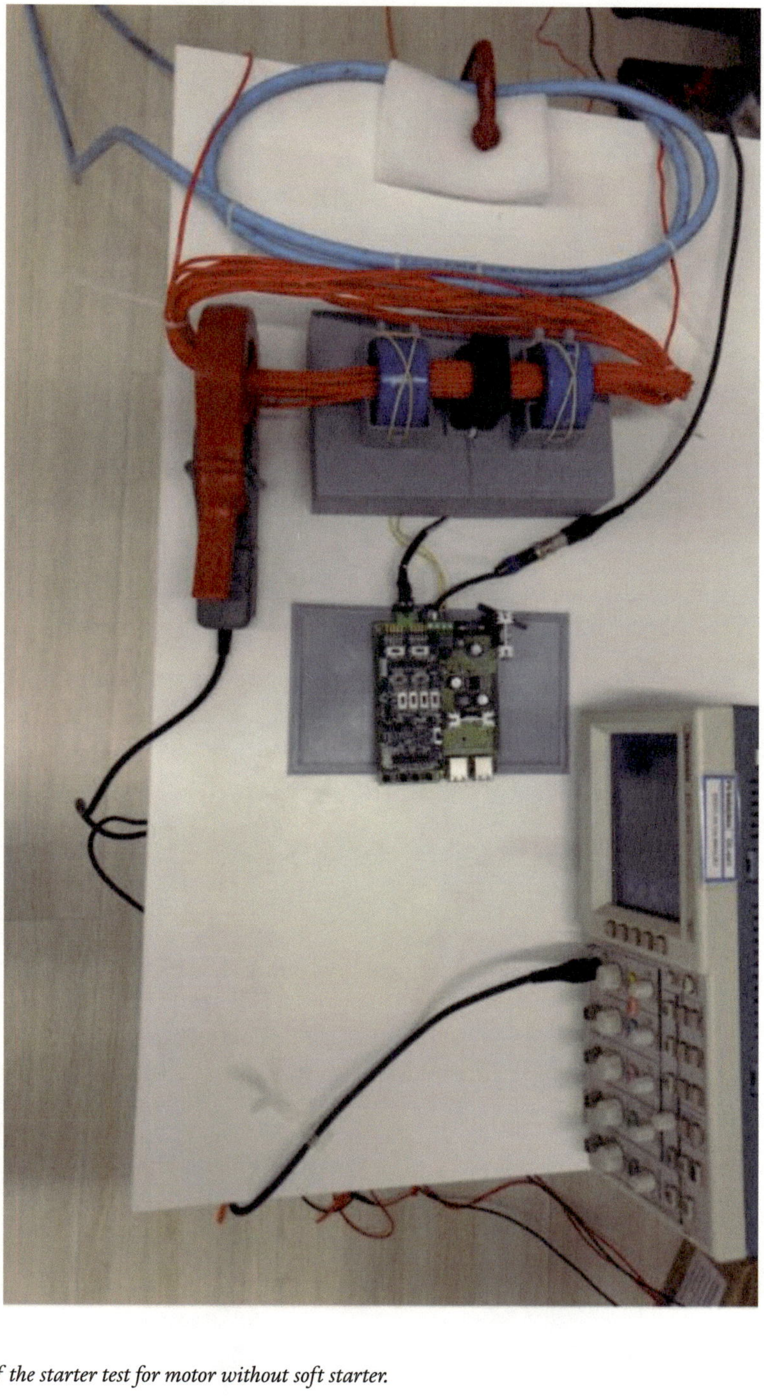

Figure 17.
Assembly of the starter test for motor without soft starter.

condition and 243 At in the starting condition. The assembly for the simulation of the starting situation is presented in **Figure 17**; meanwhile, the starting curve of the motor is displayed in **Figure 18**.

The main points verified were:

- Prototype stability for operation and communication in the presence of available minimum currents

- Stability of overvoltage protection in the presence of maximum available currents

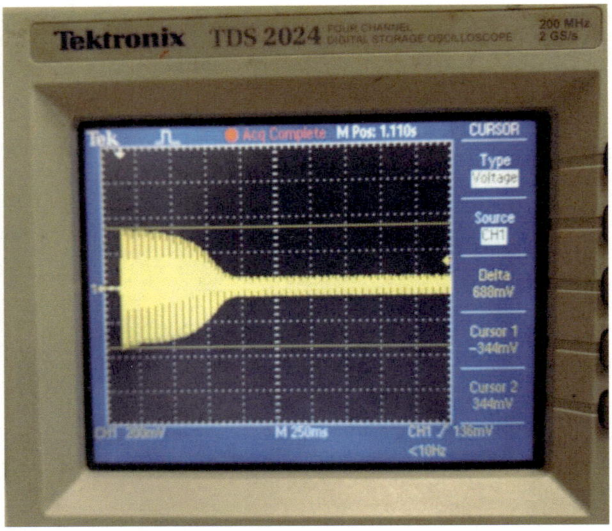

Figure 18.
Engine starting test indicating that the starting current reached about 344 to peak (243 Arms)—the ratio of the current transducer equal to 1 MV/a.

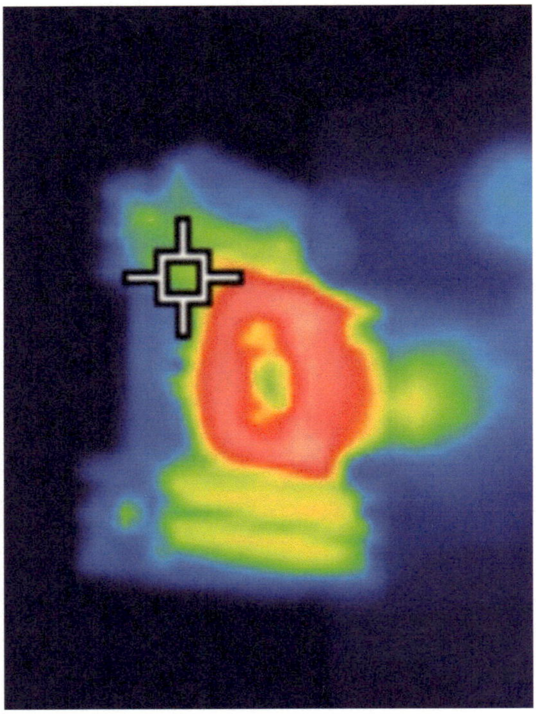

Figure 19.
About 79°C at the hottest point (set operating above the nominal for 4 min).

During the tests, the main subsystem verified was the protection circuit of the buck converter, which prevents the input voltage from being greater than the allowable limit, 40 VDC. In this case, the protection is specified to reap the voltage at about 36 Vcc, keeping the application running and dissipating surplus energy in the protection transistor buffer. The temperature of the transistor/heat sink assembly was monitored with the extractor operating with a current of 170 A (greater than the operation of about 162 A) over 4 min that is four times longer than the operating period reported in this condition, as shown in **Figure 19**. The system operated normally, and the maximum temperature in the set reached 79°C.

6.2 Operation at the Pimental hydraulic power plant

Figure 20 presents the device installed and operating in the motor BB-ORV101, at Pimental hydraulic power plant, in Altamira, north of Brazil.

The prototype proved to be stable from a minimum current of about 34 A, as presented in **Figure 21**.

According to field measurements, the BB-ORV motors operate for about 1 min in current slightly higher than the nominal board. This condition was measured and presented in **Figure 22**.

Figure 20.
Device installed at Pimental hydraulic power plant in Brazil.

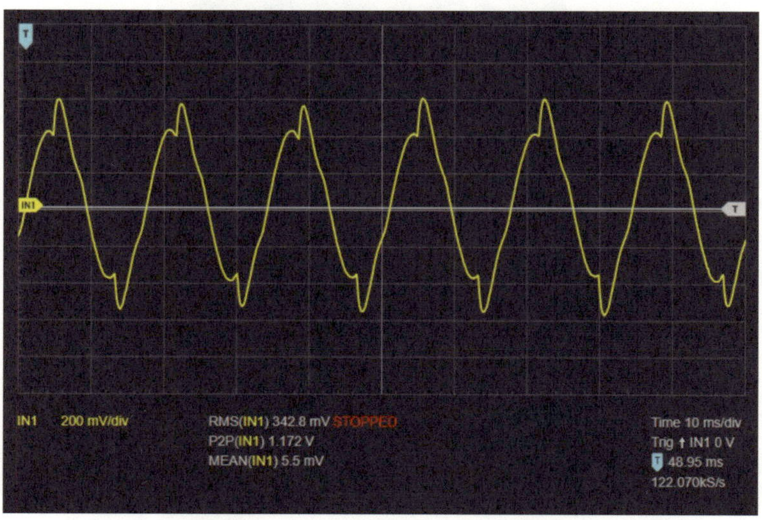

Figure 21.
Waveform presented by the oscilloscope in the current condition of minimum, 34 A.

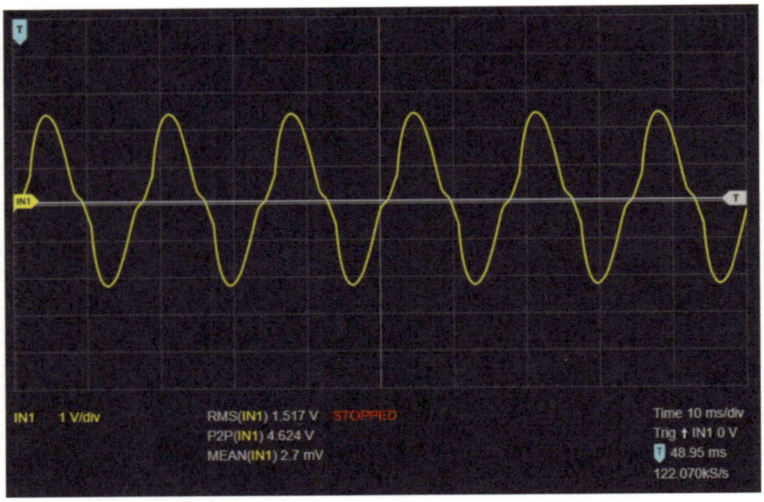

Figure 22.
Waveform presented by the oscilloscope in the current condition near the nominal, 149 A.

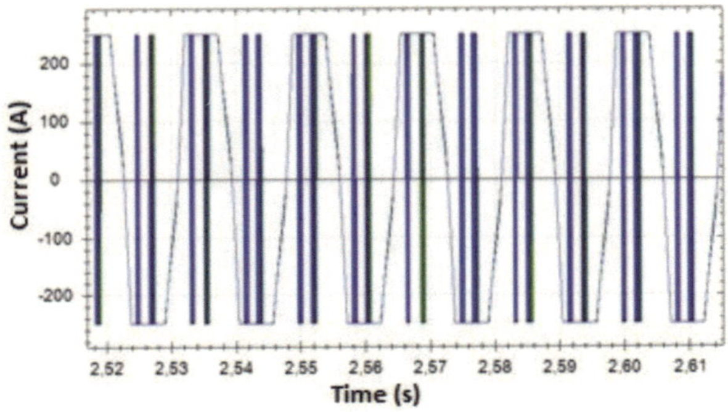

Figure 23.
Saturated and distorted waveform presented by the prototype in the condition of starting current, 602 A.

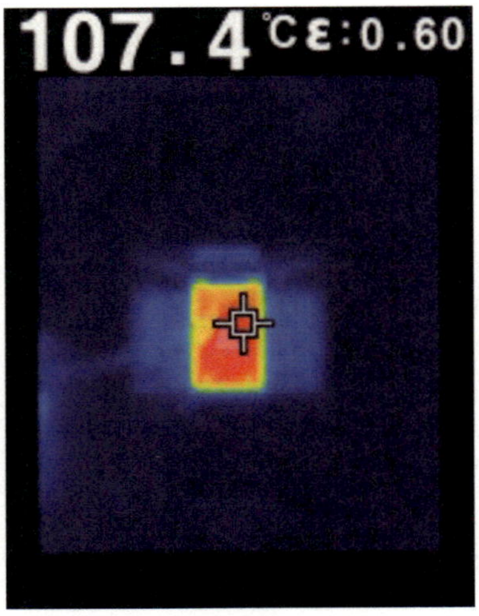

Figure 24.
Thermal image of the transistor/protection sink of the buck converter, in the condition of starting current, 602 A, after about 60 s of operation.

In the field measurements, it was found that in the BB-ORV motors, which have a soft-starter device, the starting condition takes about 4 s and reaches a current of 400 A. To introduce a safety factor, the prototype was subjected to currents of 600 A for more than 60 s. The objective is not that the prototype can measure these currents, as they are far above the nominal CT, which is 200 A but can withstand them without fail. Therefore, it is normal, in this condition, that the prototype displays saturated or distorted currents, as shown in **Figure 23**. **Figure 24** shows the thermal image of the transistor/protection sink of the buck converter, in the condition of starting current, 602 A, after about 60 s of operation.

6.3 Considerations about the power harvesting capability of the prototype

The power harvesting capability of the prototype reaches 2.5 W in the condition of a minimum current of 34 A in the measured cable. This power suffices to drive a single-board computer based on an ARM microprocessor with 64 bit architecture, 1 GHz clock, 512 Mb RAM, Linux operating system, and many peripherals. Such a system is able to perform many digital signal processing (DSP) techniques in the electric current signals acquired from the monitored electric motor, for motor monitoring applications do not require a real-time processing, since a few signals a day suffice for a condition diagnostics of the slow developing faults that can be monitored by the current spectral analysis technique.

7. Conclusions

This chapter aims to show the development and implementation of an innovative current transducer inserted in the context exposed above, i.e., dynamic current measurement (waveform) or its RMS value, for the purpose of monitoring the energy and/or monitoring the condition of assets; wireless interface with remote viewing and/or recording device, self-powered by the magnetic field of the current measure, without connection to the electrical system through external sources and power cords; and ability to synchronize with other gauges or use a real-time base, allowing the correlation of the measurements of various transducers in the same time base.

The main objective of this chapter was to present the development of a current transducer with wireless data transmission self-supplied by the magnetic field of the transduced current. The proposed measuring device involves the cable, whose current is intended to be measured, extracting power from the magnetic field around the conductor to feed the current transducer itself and the data flow generator circuit of the measured current ("streaming") through a wireless transmission protocol. The measured current can be viewed on a handheld device such as a "smartphone" or data collector, for example. The extracted signal was used to monitor the condition of the cooling system motors of the Pimental hydraulic power plant through the analysis of the electrical signature analysis.

The main advantages of the proposed system are:

- Ease of installation: the device involves the cable whose current is to be measured.

- Easy access to data: wireless and remote interface with data collectors or "smartphones."

- Nonintrusive: the only interface with the system to be measured is the magnetic field, and there will be no sources or cables interfering with the electrical panels of the plant.
- Record of the data in the "cloud" if desirable.
- Ease of implementation of energy monitoring and condition-based maintenance applications.

Acknowledgements

The academic authors would like to express their thanks to the ANEEL Research and Development, CNPq, CAPES, FINEP, and FAPEMIG for supporting this work.

Author details

Erik Leandro Bonaldi[1], Levy Ely de Lacerda de Oliveira[1], Germano Lambert-Torres[1*], Luiz Eduardo Borges da Silva[2] and Vitor Almeida Bernardes[3]

1 Itajuba Federal University, Brazil

2 Gnarus Institute, Brazil

3 Norte Energia, Altamira, Brazil

*Address all correspondence to: germanoltorres@gmail.com

References

[1] Haj-Yahya J, Mendelson A, Ben Asher Y, Chattopadhyay A. Power modeling at high-performance computing processors. In: Haj-Yahya J, Mendelson A, Ben Asher Y, Chattopadhyay A, editors. Energy Efficient High Performance Processors. 1st ed. Singapore: Springer Singapore; 2018. pp. 73-105. DOI: 10.1007/978-981-10-8554-3_3

[2] Salman T, Networking Protocols JR. Standards for Internet of Things. In: Geng H, editor. Internet of Things and Data Analytics Handbook. 1st ed. Indianapolis (IN): John Wiley & Sons; 2017. pp. 215-238. DOI: 10.1002/9781119173601.ch13

[3] Chou T. Precision: Principles, Practices and Solutions for the Internet of Things. 1st ed. Birmingham(UK): Lulu.com; 2016. 312p

[4] Kellmereit D, Obodovski D. The Silent Intelligence: The Internet of Things. 1st ed. DnD Ventures: Warwick (NY); 2013. 156p

[5] Lea P. Internet of Things for Architects: Architecting IoT Solutions by Implementing Sensors, Communication Infrastructure, Edge Computing, Analytics, and Security. 1st ed. Morrisville (NC): Packt Publishing; 2018. 524p

[6] Gilchrist A. Industry 4.0: The Industrial Internet of Things. 1st ed. New York City: Apress; 2016. 250p

[7] Ustundag A, Cevikcan E. Industry 4.0: Managing the Digital Transformation. 1st ed. Chan (Switzerland): Springer International Publishing; 2016. 286p. DOI: 10.1007/978-3-319-57870-5

[8] IEEE Standard. IEEE 802.11. 2019. Available from: https://ieeexplore.ieee.org/browse/standards/get-program/page/series?id=68

[9] IEEE Standard. IEEE 802.15.4. 2018. Available from: https://ieeexplore.ieee.org/document/8410916

[10] IEEE Standard. IEEE 802.15.1. 2005. Available from: https://ieeexplore.ieee.org/document/1490827

Chapter 9

How the Data Provided by IIoT Are Utilized in Enterprise Resource Planning: A Multiple-Case Study of Three Change Projects

Jyri Rajamäki and Petra Tuppela

Abstract

An extreme increase in data production has taken place over the past few decades with a large number of sensor and smart devices acquired from distributed data sources. Industrial Internet of Things (IIoT) enables seamless processing of information by integrating physical and digital world devices that can be used ubiquitously. This multiple-case study analyzes how the data generated by the IIoT benefit enterprise resource planning. In the analyzed cases, IIoT has been produced using and integrating various digital services and software in the enterprise. Data produced by IIoT might be raw data or pre-analyzed by the IIoT service provider according to the enterprise's needs. Services based on IIoT solutions ensure competitiveness within the enterprise since IIoT is flexible and easy to apply on future demands. IIoT generates increased amount of data and enterprises can utilize it to provide significant benefits to their operations. The cross-case conclusions emphasize that improving operational processes with data does not provide maximal benefit to the enterprise. Data-driven procedure and the entire change project (digital transformation) together with new procedures will provide most benefits to the enterprise.

Keywords: multiple-case study, digital transformations, change project, industrial internet of things, enterprise resource planning

1. Introduction

An emergent number of enterprises are deploying new solutions utilizing Industrial Internet of Things (IIoT). IIoT solutions provide many benefits to an enterprise, but they also drive the enterprise to redesign its operations to data-driven processes. On the other hand, the solution adjusts the enterprise's services to make them more profitable and precise. This requires the enterprise to make strategic but also organizational changes in order to succeed in the change [1]. During the development process, enterprises brainstorm, generate ideas, compare and test IIoT solutions for later changing the business model. The services provided by IIoT require not only an IT competence developer but also competence in business activity insight and expertise. IIoT solutions also affect sales, marketing, and mostly development of service concepts. In some cases, IIoT can be the base of a new service concept or a total digital transformation process.

Change, derived from IIoT solution, requires time in every organization. Change includes planning, deployment, and implementation of current solution. In some cases, the Industrial Internet can affect the enterprise's whole strategy by remodeling or modifying its operations. IIoT solution may even influence value proposition since data drive the operations and accurate data provide new possibilities in daily business. Due to technical solution that collects data, new information is created. Therefore data can even have an impact on enterprise management tools; using of data driven management tools to assess processes [1].

This chapter presents a multiple-case study research (MCSR) of three change projects in which new IIoT solutions have been put into operations in three different Finnish enterprises. The research questions are:

- How and when the enterprise recognizes the changes required by applying the new IIoT solution?
- How the enterprise applies the new data provided by the IIoT solution?
- Why the change is crucial, and how the whole organization succeeded in implementing the change?

The chapter follows a linear-analytic structure of the sequence of subtopics involving the issue being studied, the methods used, a review of the relevant literature, the findings from the collected and analyzed data, and conclusions and implications from the findings. After the introduction, Section 2 proposes a used methodology of the deliverable. Section 3 handles the theory and how it has been built. Section 4 presents the individual case study analysis. Section 5 includes cross-case study conclusions and concludes the chapter.

2. Research approach

Figure 1 shows how the MCSR approach is applied in this research. The initial step in designing a MCSR consists of theory development (see Section 3), and the next steps are case selection and definition of specific measures in the design and data collection process. Each individual case study consists of a whole study, and

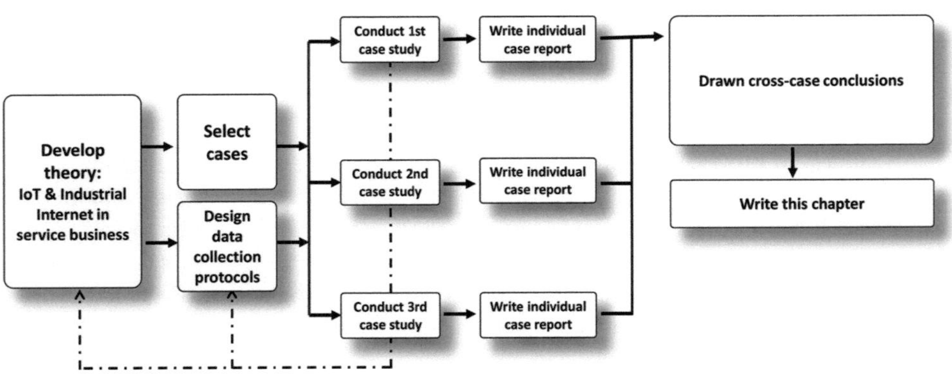

Figure 1.
Applied multiple-case study approach.

then conclusions of each case are considered to be the replication by other individual cases. Both the individual case and the multiple result should be the focus of a summary report. For each individual case, the report should indicate how and why a particular result is demonstrated. Across cases, the report should present the extent of replication logic, including certain and contrasting results [2].

Any use of multiple-case design should follow a replication, not a sampling logic, and choosing of each case should be made carefully [2]. In **Figure 1**, the dashed-line feedback represents a discovery situation, where one of the cases does not suit the original multiple-case study design. Such a discovery implies a need to reconsider the original theoretical propositions. At this point, redesign should take place before proceeding further, and in this view, the replication approach represents a way of generalizing that uses a type of test called falsification or refutation, which is the possibility that a theory or hypothesis may be proven wrong or falsified [3]. This MCSR consists of three individual case studies presented in Section 4. The sources of evidence used in the individual case studies consist of documentation, archival records, interviews of enterprises' top management and IIoT solutions suppliers, direct observations, participant-observation, and physical artifacts. The data are retrieved in a specific time period (cross-sectional), the largest part of the data is qualitative (empirical) and involves purposive sampling and a specific selection of a phenomenon (case studies). Every individual case study was reported separately to the top management of the enterprise in question. Cross-case conclusions were carried out via a document analysis exercise.

3. Industrial Internet of Things in service business

The Internet of Things (IoT) refers to a system of smart devices connected to each other through the Internet [4]. These things include technology that enables them to communicate, sense and interaction with internal space as well as external environment. In other words, physical things can collect data, be connected to other things, and share data. These things can be sensors, smartphones, smartwatches, computers, and home and industrial appliances—anything that can collect, handle, and send data for forward treatment and analyses. First, IoT systems were consumer-centric, but the disruptive nature of this technology has enabled the adoption of IoT technology in a gamut of industrial settings, thus leading to the development of Industrial Internet of Things (IIoT) technology [5]. Technology enables new success stories in every business industry. The true success factors, in order to succeed in IIoT solution implementations, are people in enterprises, processes, and context.

Data alone that are provided by IIoT solutions are not of any value. The collected data connected to business unit's context or other sources of data provide the valuable benefits. Data can be used to understand challenges better or to enhance processes. Collected data may even support management in decision-making process.

By purchasing IIoT solutions, enterprises maintain their competitive advantage. The solution would respond quickly for future spontaneous and accurate demands since things are connected to network and therefore can be updated online. Services can be adjusted both due to competition, commercial, and also to legislation requirements. IIoT solutions mostly include technology, network, and software. In addition, they are always designed for enterprises' needs and desires. IIoT solutions are custom-made and they are to be integrated into the enterprise's existing systems. Data can be provided as raw data, pre-analyzed, or expressed in visual dashboards.

Since the experimental period of IIoT solutions has been exceeded in the past few years, companies are today seeking sustainable solutions to support their operational processes and bringing real value to the company. The technology behind the solution has been proved to operate as it should which means that the expected data can be provided by it and it is accurate. The price of sensors and detectors has been decreasing, which means that enterprises' investment of the technology solutions covers only project and implementation costs. In addition, data storage and several cloud services are available at reasonable price. Low maintenance costs encourage companies to store data for further need.

There are several data strategies that companies can apply data provided by IIoT solutions. Companies can collect data in order to use it to support and enhance their own operational process and business activity. Data can be used not only to guide operations but also show real-time data. These are valuable in enterprises' daily operations. Data can be used to prevent unnecessary actions, the so-called fire situations. In optimal conditions, the data are used to forecast and control actions before they turn into these fire tasks.

For creating business model around Industrial Internet fundamental, there are five key elements:

1. Value creation in service network

2. Building and developing global service network

3. Customer-centric and cost-efficient service process planning

4. Creating positive customer experience

5. Inventing profitable revenue generation logic

When designing a new business model that is based on IIoT, enterprises can use these elements to base it on. This encourages enterprises to place customers and services in the center in order to not only gain higher customer satisfaction but also increase sales in service. These elements can also be applied to develop business activities and generate profitable core or supporting functions.

Because the amount of data grows at an unprecedented scale and depth with the proliferation of smart and sensor devices, big data analytics has emerged as a key initiative in the IIoT field [6–8]. Recently, artificial intelligence (AI) has become a key factor in big data analytics in industrial applications [9].

4. Empirical cases

This section briefly describes the three empirical cases that belong to this multiple-case study analysis. The individual case reports were published earlier, but this section summarizes their main research results with regard to this MCSR.

4.1 Case I: OnniBus.com

OnniBus.com (later OnniBus) started their transportation business at 2012. Within few years, they have managed to grow their business to one of the largest brands in Finland. OnniBus has disrupted mass transportation with competitive, rather low, pricing. Today, they move customers frequently in the most popular routes and also daily all around Finland with their 128 buses. About 28 million kilometers are bring customers from one city to another. With Telia Connected Vehicle solution, OnniBus primarily seeks savings in costs.

OnniBus among others is the first transportation company that applied the Telia Connected Vehicle solution. This solution monitors ground vehicles in action and it optimizes the operation of hardware by using real-time data installed in the vehicles. In addition, the solution enables combining different services that beforehand were provided to OnniBus from different service providers. When considering the bus driver, it also takes much less effort to follow only one screen rather than several.

In the early phase, Telia's solution was installed in all 68 double-decker buses and later in the 60 single-storey buses. The service requires that the driver of the bus logs into the vehicle system with an identifying digital card, which is a very secure way to log in. In the past, drivers did not always remember to sign in and no data could be obtained at that time. OnniBus uses Telia's solution to remotely read digital plotters and cards. They are able to monitor remotely that driving times are being realized and digital cards are always being used by drivers. This kind of data is a very powerful management tool. The CEO of OnniBus Lauri Helke sums up "what you don't measure, you can't lead." In order to motivate drivers to drive more ecologically, OnniBus started to publish driver-specific results to the staff every month. Such transparent information encourages everyone in the company to see what kind of data can be achieved with financial driving.

In order for OnniBus to achieve savings in costs, the most important thing about implementing this service is to report about OnniBus driver habits and fuel consumption per driver. Only the fuel savings from the data generated by Connected Vehicle-solution will be 1–5% annually. In double-decker buses alone, OnniBus consumes approximately 5.5 million liters of fuel per year, which means a fuel cost of EUR 6 million. This saving as such is significant. Since Telia's solution also monitors the vehicles, there are savings directly on tire costs and other vehicle operating costs. In addition, it provides an ecofriendly approach to bus transportation business.

4.2 Case II: Pohjolan liikenne

Transportation industries are under critical inspection since the environmental cause. In order to utilize different sources of data and manage with data, companies can achieve massive advancements by how they optimize their actions. Focusing on fuel economy and improving effective fuel consumption are significant ecologically friendly approaches in the transportation industry and furthermore companies reserve in costs.

Oy Pohjolan Liikenne Ab (later Pohjolan Liikenne) has been serving in the transportation industry since 1949. They offer transportation services in commuter traffic, country traffic, local transportation, metropolitan area, order and contract driving as well as Finnair CityBus traffic driving.

Telia's solution means that bus vehicle's actions are being monitored and optimized according to real-time data. Cost-efficient driving and measurement have been challenging before but since the new solution provides data real time, information can be used proactively. Despite that, the savings in fuel are concrete. With that said, data from consumption of fuel are precise and therefore the company has been able to seek the best-practice driving mode for drivers. With Telia's solution, Pohjolan Liikenne can react to drivers' driving habits in real time. Along with the service, Pohjolan Liikenne is able to measure driver's driving index and thereby develop better driving performances. In addition, the company can get an insight into drivers' driving period, breaks, and working hours. In addition, the solution saves data from certain periods and uses data to analyze it according to critical aspects that are relevant for the company. Data can be analyzed for instance with weather.

The other remarkable feature is that Telia's solution monitors the coach vehicles' condition real time. The solution is integrated to the CAN bus which all the coaches include and from there data is collected real time and the output in a readable way. No extra sensors are needed to be installed. The information that already exists can be now used to resolve problems. By adding weather information or how people move, solution can bring data bases together and analyze big data.

4.3 Case III: Delete

Delete Finland Oy (later Delete) is one of the leading providers of full-service environmental services in the Nordic countries. The company was established in 2010. Delete provides business-critical services that require specialized expertise and specialized equipment in three business areas: cleaning services, demolition services, and recycling services.

Delete's priority is to optimize maintenance processes and furthermore to improve their customers' business. Unpredictable demand of maintenance or drainage are usually unpleasant and rarely expensive for customers. Customers' daily actions are being paused during the time needed to manage these kinds of sudden drainages. Delete tested Narrow Band IoT (NB-IoT) solution as a pilot in order to obtain how NB-IoT will help to anticipate maintenance. Delete wants to experiment with technology on how to avoid unexpected service disruption in restaurants and car wash lines and enable proactive maintenance and planning. Today, Delete drains hundreds of wells monthly and most of them at short notice. With the experiment, they aim to create new stable processes that decrease unnecessary visits, develop processes according to better planning, save in costs, and, due to all these, enhance customers' daily business. "The wastewater from restaurants and service stations carries sediment that accumulates in sewer wells built for this purpose. The sensors installed in the wells allow us to monitor the amount of grease and sand accumulated in the wells in real time, while also anticipating the need for emptying the," says Markku Salminen, Director of Development and HSEQ.

Telia generates the pilot with a NB-IoT communications network, cloud data solution and a service interface. For the first time in Finland, NB-IoT remotely read sensors that are used to determine the drainage needs of a restaurant's grease separator wells and a service station's car wash line. NB-IoT technology can be used to track up to thousands of IoT devices. In the pilot, NB-IoT sensors are being installed to anticipate the maintenance and drainage needs of the sand separator wells at Stockmann's restaurant in Helsinki and the Neste K Hatanpää and Neste K Kekkosentie car wash line in Tampere. Pilot's NB-IoT takes advantage of existing 4G networks, but is also compatible with future 5G networks.

Narrowband IoT (NB-IoT) is a global standardized network technology that leverages existing 4G and 5G networks. With NB-IoT, one can connect many devices to network cheaply and reliably. The data sent by the devices can be used to monitor real-time operational and production processes. The battery of the NB-IoT sensor that collects and transmits data can last up to 10 years. It is activated and transmits data only when the programmed measurement limit is exceeded. Hundreds of thousands of devices can be connected to a single access point.

5. Cross-case conclusions

When an enterprise acquires an IIoT solution as a part of the business operations, a change in the organization is always required. The change has a direct impact on the operational process, resource planning, and people that are operating within the solution in the context. The change also affects employees who are working to provide the service. Every IIoT project with its implementation and accustoming phase in the organization requires time in which the enterprise should be prepared. In order to succeed, the change always requires identifying the change objects early enough and defining the relevant process points. However, the essential prerequisite for the success is the commitment of the uppermost management.

In one analyzed case, the enterprise outlines its new operating process by completely redesigning it based on digitalization and data. In another case, the enterprise adapts new operating processes to apply its own operating environment. Using data to streamline business processes does not bring all the potential benefits to the enterprise. The case study result reveals that when the project as a whole is successful, it will provide the company with benefits in terms of productivity, efficiency, and competitiveness. The change project itself includes, among other things, a clear definition of the cause and goals of the change, communication, staff engagement, and evaluation.

The data provided by IIoT are a valuable asset compared to the competitors of the case enterprises. By analyzing data properly and applying it to the enterprise's own business environment and processes, one is possible to gain business benefits in financial as well as international market aspects.

The study cases showed that enterprises that have strong support and contribution from management team are able to implement IIoT solution within the enterprise. The management team or the CEO of the company drives change projects other than this and they are open-minded of new technical possibilities in their industry. They believe that if they do not take advantage of technical innovation solutions, someone else in the same industry will.

In addition, the individual case studies showed that motivation for each organization level is essential in order to succeed in the implementation of the change project. The new IIoT solution needs to serve motivation for each department: CEO, financial, resource planning, logistics, service and driver's perspective.

In the future, AI will be a fundamental part of business in most sectors. The data-driven digital transformation creates new and modifies existing business processes, culture, and customer experiences to meet changing business and market requirements. Today, the lack of good-quality data in enterprises is the biggest barrier for fully exploiting AI. With good planning, new IIoT solutions can bring good-quality data, but they should be integrated into existing systems not always containing good-quality data. When the amount of good-quality data grows, possibilities to exploit AI improve. However, the success factor of data-driven digital transformation depends on the business strategy and the commitment of the top management, who should put the business strategy into practice.

Author details

Jyri Rajamäki[1*] and Petra Tuppela[2]

1 Laurea University of Applied Sciences, Espoo, Finland

2 Division X – Telia Company, Helsinki, Finland

*Address all correspondence to: jyri.rajamaki@laurea.fi

References

[1] Martinsuo M, Kärri T. Teollinen internet uudistaa palveluliiketoimintaa ja kunnossapitoa. Helsinki: Kunnossapitoyhdistys Promaint ry; 2017

[2] Yin RK. Case Study Research Design and Methods. Thousand Oaks: Sage Publications; 2009

[3] Popper K. Conjectures and Refutations: The Growth of Scientific Knowledge. London: Routledge Classics; 2009

[4] Gubbi J, Buyya R, Marusic S, Palaniswami M. Internet of Things (IoT): A vision, architectural elements, and future directions. Future Generation Computer Systems. 2013;**29**(7):1645-1660

[5] Sisinni E, Saifullah A, Han S, Jennehag U, Gidlund M. Industrial Internet of Things: Challenges, opportunities, and directions. IEEE Transactions on Industrial Informatics. 2018;**14**(11):4724-4734

[6] Williams S, Hardy C, Nitschke P. Configuring the Internet of Things (IoT): A review and implications for big data analytics. In: Proceedings of the 52nd Hawaii International Conference on System Sciences; 2019. pp. 5848-5857

[7] Dey N, Hassanien A, Bhatt C, Ashour A, Satapathy S. Internet of Things and Big Data Analytics Toward Next-Generation Intelligence. Cham: Springer International Publishing; 2018

[8] Minteer A. Analytics for the Internet of Things (IoT): Intelligent Analytics for Your Intelligent Devices. Birmingham: Packt Publishing; 2017

[9] Nguyen H, Tran K, Zeng X, Koehl L, Castagliola P, Bruniaux P. Industrial Internet of Things, big data, and artificial intelligence in the smart factory: A survey and perspective. In: ISSAT International Conference on Data Science in Business, Finance and Industry; Da Nang, Vietnam; 2019

Chapter 10

Big Data Analytics and Its Applications in Supply Chain Management

Saeid Sadeghi Darvazeh, Iman Raeesi Vanani and Farzaneh Mansouri Musolu

Abstract

In today's competitive marketplace, development of information technology, rising customer expectations, economic globalization, and the other modern competitive priorities have forced organizations to change. Therefore, competition among enterprises is replaced by competition among enterprises and their supply chains. In current competitive environment, supply chain professionals are struggling in handling the huge data in order to reach integrated, efficient, effective, and agile supply chain. Hence, explosive growth in volume and different types of data throughout the supply chain has created the need to develop technologies that can intelligently and rapidly analyze large volume of data. Big data analytics capability (BDA) is one of the best techniques, which can help organizations to overcome their problem. BDA provides a tool for extracting valuable patterns and information in large volume of data. So, the main purpose of this book chapter is to explore the application of BDA in supply chain management (SCM).

Keywords: big data, analytics, supply chain analytics, manufacturing, finance, healthcare, demand planning, procurement management, customized production, inventory management

1. Introduction

Big data are characterized as the gigantic or complex sets of data, which usually encompass extend of more than exabyte. It outstrips the traditional systems with limited capability in storing, handling, overseeing, deciphering, and visualizing [1]. Nowadays, data are expanding exponentially and are anticipated to reach zettabyte per year [2]. The scholarly world and professionals concur that this surge of data makes modern opportunities; subsequently, numerous organization attempted to create and upgrade its big data analytics capabilities (BDA) to reveal and gain a higher and deeper understanding from their big data values. The study of big data is persistently advanced and extended, and the most properties of big data are presently extended into "5 V" concept containing variety, verification/veracity, velocity, volume, and value [3, 4]. Akter et al. recommended BDA as one of the most important factors affecting organizational performance [5]. By progressing BDA, organizations could make better understanding from their customer's needs, provide suitable service to satisfy their needs, improve sales and income, and penetrate into new markets. Several research studies indicated the big data applications in various sectors such as financial services sector, marketing, bank industry, insurance industry, logistics, and manufacturing [6]. However, the present book chapter indicates the benefits of big data application in extracting new insights and creating new forms of value in ways that have influenced supply chain relationships. Regarding this purpose, first, the authors defined the key concepts of BDA and its role in predicting the future. Second, the authors paid to the role of statistical analysis, simulation, and optimization in supply chain analytics. Third, the authors had a review on application of BDA in supply chain management areas. Forth, the authors provided a brief information about application of BDA in different types of supply chain. Fifth, the authors presented some insight into future application of BDA in supply chain, and lastly, the book chapter ends with the conclusion, some managerial implications, and recommendations for future research.

2. BDA capabilities

To fully understand the impact and application of BDA, we first need to have a clear understanding of what it actually is. As a simple definition, big data refer to large quantity of data. Big data specifically refer to large data sets whose size is so large that the quantity can no longer fit into the memory. These data can be captured, stored, communicated, aggregated, and analyzed. As the volume of data has grown, the need to revamp the tools has used for analyzing it. These data do not ought to be set in neat columns and rows as traditional data sets to be analyzed by today's technology, not at all like within the past. Big data appear completely in different kinds of data. They incorporate all types of data from every possible source. They can be structured, semi-structured, or fully unstructured. As another categorization, big data consist of numerical data, image data, voice, text, and discourse. They can come in the form of radio-frequency identification (RFID), global positioning system (GPS), point-of-sale (POS), or they can be in the frame of Twitter feeds, Instagram, Facebook, call centers, or customer blogs. Today's progressed analytical technologies empower us to extract knowledge from all kinds of data. Analytics is a mix of math and statistics to large quantities of data. BDA mean using statistics and math in order to analyze big data. Big data without analytics are just lots of data. The authors have been accumulating a lot of data for years. Analytics without big data is simply mathematical and statistical tools and applications. Companies can extract intelligence out of these huge amounts of data. This is made possible through today's massive computing power available at a lower cost than ever before. However, combining the big data and analytics makes the different tools that help decision makers to get valuable meaningful insights and turn information into business intelligence.

3. Supply chain analytics

The supply chain is the number of firms from raw material suppliers to producer/central organization, wholesalers, retailers, customers, and end users. The supply chain not only includes physical flows involving the transfer of materials and products but also consists of information and financial flows. Supply chain analytics (SCA) means using BDA techniques in order to extracting hidden valuable knowledge from supply chain [7]. This analytics can be categorized into descriptive, predictive, and prescriptive analytics [7, 8]. Well-planned and implemented decisions contribute directly to the bottom line by lowering sourcing, transportation, storage, stock out, and disposal costs. Hence, using BDA techniques in order

Category	Features
Descriptive Analytics What happened and	• Foundational • Filters big data into useful nuggets and interpretable information • Provides a historical summary of what happened in the past • Focus on minimizing bias Example: providing historical insights regarding the company's production, financials, operations, sales, finance, inventory, and customers.
Predictive Analytics What might happen?	• Insightful • What-if analysis • Forecasting supply chain requirements • Focus on minimizing the combined bias and variance Example: Analyzing past trends to estimate future needs, supply and demand, set accurate delivery time and etc.
Prescriptive Analytics What should we do?	• Strategic • Scenario and knowledge based • Optimization and automation of decisions Example: optimizing production, scheduling and inventory.

Table 1.
Features of descriptive, predictive and prescriptive analytics.

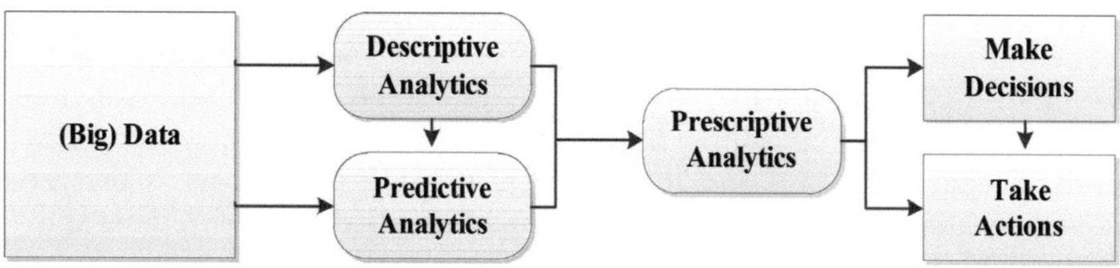

Figure 1.
Using descriptive, predictive and prescriptive analytics to make decisions and take actions.

to solve supply chain management problems has a positive and significant effect on supply chain performance. For a long time, managers and researchers have used statistical and operational research techniques in order to solving supply and demand balancing problems [8, 9]. However, recent progress in the use of analytics has opened new horizons for managers and researchers. The summary of the challenges and features of the three types of analytics is shown in **Table 1**. Also, the relationships among descriptive, predictive, and prescriptive analytics to make decisions or take actions are shown in **Figure 1**.

The different potential advantages that can be achieved utilizing data-supported decision making have incited academicians and researchers to pay attention to the possible integration of big data in SCM. This has resulted in the number of scholarly articles on this topic, which has risen precipitously in recent years. The importance of using BDA techniques in SCM is true to an extent that organizations will not stand a chance of success in today's competitive markets. Since 2010, numerous articles have been published, which emphasized on the application of BDA in SCM and their major achievements [2, 3, 10–13]. Since 2011 to 2015, Mishra et al. identify the influential and prominent researchers and articles with most citations carried out a bibliographic analysis of big data. The results indicated that the number of articles in the field of BDA has increased [14]. Barbosa et al. conducted a systematic literature review to investigate the application of BDA in SCM areas. The results indicated that BDA techniques usually use the predictive and prescriptive approaches rather than descriptive approach [10]. Dubey et al. carried out a research in order to identify the effects of big data and predictive analysis on two aspects of sustainability, including environmental and social aspects. Data were collected from 205 manufacturing companies, and using structural equation modeling based on partial least square was analyzed. The results indicated that big data have a positive and significant effect on social and environmental components of sustainability [15]. Gupta et al. carried out a systematic literature review based on 28 journal articles to investigate the impact of using BDA techniques on humanitarian SCM [16]. Gupta et al. investigated the applications of big data in the context of humanitarian SCM based on 28 journal articles. They proposed some important future research directions based on key organization theories such as complexity theory, transaction cost economics, resource dependence theory, resource-based view, social network theory, institutional theory stakeholder theory, and ecological modernization theory. Zhao et al. proposed a multiobjective optimization model for green SCM using BDA approach. They considered three different scenarios for optimizing the inherent risk associated with hazardous materials, carbon emission, and overall costs. They utilized a big data approach to acquire data and manage their quality [17]. Song et al. studied the problems and challenges arising due to big data in the context of environmental performance evaluation along with summarizing latest developments in environmental management based on big data technologies [18].

- In descriptive analysis, the following questions are answered:

What has happened, What is happening, and Why, In this process, visualization tools and online analytical processing (OLAP) system are used and supported by reporting technology (e.g. RFID, GPS, and transaction bar-code) and real-time information to identify new opportunities and problems. Descriptive statistics are used to collect, describe, and analyze the raw data of past events. It analyzes and describes the past events and makes it something that is interpretable and understandable by humans. Descriptive analytics enables organizations to learn from their past and understand the relationship between variables and how it can influence future outcomes. For example, it can be used to illustrate average money, stock in inventory, and annual sale changes. Descriptive analytics is also useful to an organization's financials, sales, operations, and production reports.

- Predictive analytics techniques are used to answer the question of what will happen in the future or likely to happen, by examining past data trends using statistical, programming and simulation techniques. These techniques seek to discover the causes of events and phenomena as well as to predict the future accurately or to fill in the data or information that already does not exist. Statistical techniques cannot be used to predict the future with 100% accuracy. Predictive analytics is used to predict purchasing patterns, customer behavior and purchase patterns to identifying and predicting the future trend of sales activities. These techniques are also used to predict customer demands, inventory records and operations.

- Prescriptive analytics deals with the question of what should be happening and how to influence it. Prescriptive analytics guides alternative decision based on predictive and descriptive analytics using descriptive and predictive analytics, simulation, mathematical optimization, or multicriteria decision-making techniques. The application of prescriptive analytics is relatively complex in practice, and most companies are still unable to apply it in their daily activities of business. Correct application of prescriptive analytics techniques can lead to optimal and efficient decision making. A number of large companies have used data analytics to optimize production and inventory. Some of the crucial scenarios that prescriptive analytics allows companies to answer include in the following:

a. What kind of an offer should make to each end-user?

b. What should be the shipment strategy for each retail location?

c. Which product should launch and when?

Statistical analysis, simulation, optimization, and techniques are used to supply chain decision making [19].

3.1 Statistical analysis

Statistical analysis basically consists of two types of analysis: descriptive and inferential. In descriptive statistics, past data are used to describe or summarize the feature of a phenomenon; it uses either graphs or tables or numerical calculations. Inferential statistics are used to deduce the properties of phenomena and predict their behavior based on a sample of past data. **Table 2** shows differences between descriptive and inferential analyses. Both quantitative and qualitative methods can be used simultaneously to take the advantage of both the methods and the right decisions. Statistical analysis is used when faced with uncertainty, such as in distribution, inventory, and risk analysis. Statistical multivariate techniques are also used for supply chain monitoring to effectively manage the flow of materials and minimize the risk of unintended situation [20]. Given the volume, variety, veracity, and velocity of big data, the supply chain needs robust and easy techniques for analysis. Traditional statistical methods are no longer responsive because the massive data lead to noise accumulation, heterogeneity, and so on. Therefore, proposing and applying effective statistical methods are very important, and major attention has been paid to this issue recently. For example, in a research, a parallel statistical algorithm is presented to do a sophisticated statistical analysis of big data. This algorithm uses specific methods such as Mann-Whitney *U* testing, conjugate gradient, and ordinary least squares to model and compare the densities and big data distribution squares [2].

3.2 Simulation

Manufacturers need simulation tools to optimize the product development process and increase the creativity, speed the time-to-market product, reduce the production costs, and create the innovation. Simulation provides many proven benefits for

Basis for comparison	Descriptive statistics	Inferential statistics
What it does?	Organizing, analyzing, and presenting data in meaningful way	Comparing, testing, and predicting data
Form of final result	Charts, Graphs, and Tables	Probability
Usage	To describe the current situation	To explain the chances of occurrence of an event
Function	It explains the data that are already known to summarize	It attempts to reach the conclusion to learn about the population that extends beyond the data availability

Table 2.
Comparing descriptive and inferential analyses.

each stage of the product design and manufacturing process, for example, producing more innovative products with greater efficiency for the customer and creating a better experience for them [21]. For example, when consumer goods giant Proctor & Gamble develops new dishwashing liquids, they use predictive analytics and modeling to predict how moisture will excite certain fragrance molecules, so that the right scents are released at the right time during the dishwashing process. Modeling and simulation techniques should be used to develop the application of large data, for example, simulation-driven product design. In today's competitive environment, the use of simulators to produce innovative products is considered a challenge. Because manufacturers have to continually drive their operational efficiencies, meet the cost, require the time-to-market product, and predict the customer preferences.

Modeling and simulation help developer to run the "what-if" analysis under different system configuration and complexity [22]. Shao et al. developed a simulation model to analyze the huge data collected from the surrounding and shop floor environment of a smart manufacturing system. This model improved the decision making in this production system [23]. For example, as a predictive tool, simulation can help the manufacturers to predict the need for machines and additional equipment based on customer order forecast and learning from other historical data such as cycle time, throughput, and delivery performance. LLamasoft [24] outlined some examples of where supply chain simulation can be used as follows: predicting the service, testing the inventory policy, analyzing the production capacity, determining the asset utilization, and validating the optimization result. SCA provides new methods for the simulation problem with a large amount of data. Nowadays, there are several simulation software that allow to evaluate the performance of a system before its creation. Enterprise dynamics (ED) is one of the strongest and most used software that researchers and practitioners use it to simulate SCM issues.

3.3 Optimization

The optimization technique is a powerful tool for supply chain data analytics [25]. Optimization techniques by extracting the insights and knowledge of the enormous data generated by complex systems that include multiple factors and constraints such as capacity and route can analyze multiple objectives such as demand fulfillment and cost reduction. Finally, using supply chain optimization techniques along with multiuser collaboration, performance tracker, and scenario management enables organizations to achieve their different goals. The use of optimization techniques supports supply chain planning and also increases the accuracy of planning but presents the large-scale optimization challenge [7]. Slavakis et al. [26] have used several signal processing and statistical learning techniques to analytic optimization, principal component analysis, dictionary learning, compressive sampling, and subspace clustering. Based on SCOR supply chain model, Souza explored the opportunities for applying BDA in SCM [8]. BDA play a critical role at all operational, tactical, and strategic levels of the supply chain; for example, in the strategic level, SCA is used for product design, network design, and sourcing; in the tactical and operational levels, SCA can also be used for procurement, demand planning, logistics, and inventory.

4. Application of BDA in SCM areas

In the production department, a large amount of data is generated by external channels and also by internal networks that contain sensor networks or instrumentation on the production floor. Using big data to tighter analysis and integration of these databases, it can improve the efficiency of the distribution and sales process and the continuous monitoring of process and devices. Manufacturing companies need to use big data and analytics techniques to grow their manufacturing sector. Predictive maintenance of equipment is an immediate segment in this sector ripe for growth. Due to the large number of vendors, as well as the variety of their evaluation and selection indicators, the process of selecting the right and optimal vendor for the supply chain is difficult. Applying Cloud Technologies to selecting vendors is making a big impact. With new systems, access and exposure to data are more intuitive and customer focused with the power of APIs and integration to modern big data applications and analytic packages. A review in the literature indicates that BDA can be used in several areas of SCM. In the following sections, an overview of BDA applications in different areas of supply chain is provided [27].

4.1 BDA and supplier relationship management

Supplier relationship management involves establishing discipline in strategic planning and managing all interactions with organizations' suppliers in order to reduce the risk of failure and maximize the value of these interactions. Establishing close relationships with key suppliers and enhancing collaboration with them are an important factor in discovering and creating new value and reducing the risk of failure in SRM. Strategic resources and supplier relationship management (SRM) are the success factors of organizations, which focus on relationship management and collaboration. Using BDA techniques can provide accurate information on organizational spending patterns that help manage supplier relationships [28]. For example, big data can provide accurate information on the return on investment (ROI) of any investment and in-depth analysis of potential supplier. In a study, fuzzy synthetic evaluation and analytical hierarchy process (AHP) were used to supplier evaluation and selection, given the high capacity of big data processing as one of the evaluated factors has been used [29]. The objective is to select supply partner that can adapt to the future challenges from big data.

4.2 BDA and supply chain network design

Supply chain design is a strategic decision, which includes all decisions regarding the selection of partners of the supply chain and defines company policies and programs to achieve long-term strategic targets. Supply chain network design project involves determining supply chain physical configuration that affects most business units or functional areas within a company. In designing the supply chain network, it is important to determine the customer satisfaction and supply chain efficiency. The purpose of supply chain design is to design a network of members that can meet the long-term strategic targets of the company. When designing a supply chain, the following steps must be followed: (1) define the long-term strategic targets; (2) define the project scope; (3) determine the form of analyses to be done; (4) the tools that will be used must be determined; and (5) finally, project completion, the best design.

Selecting the optimal supply chain design and appropriate planning, the company will achieve a significant competitive advantage. Wang et al. (2016b) proposed a mixed-integer nonlinear model for locating the distribution centers, utilized big data in this model, and randomly generated big datasets applied for warehouse operation, customer demand, and transportation. They assumed that the behavioral dataset has been analyzed using marketing intelligence tools. Their findings show that big data could provide all the necessary information about penalty cost data and service level; therefore, it is a very powerful tool for complex distribution network design [30]. A study investigates the application of BDA in design intervention such as healthcare, disaster relief, and education in supply chain [31]. Since humanitarian data have the characteristics of high volume, high diversity, accuracy, and speed, BDA can be used in the humanitarian supply chain.

4.3 BDA and product design and development

One of the major concerns of adaptable product manufacturers is ensuring that these products conform to their customers' preferences. As customers' preferences and expectations change throughout the product lifetime, designers need tools to predict and measure those preferences and expectations. Lack of enough information about customers' preferences and expectations is an important issue in the product design process. If designers continuously monitor customer behavior and access up-to-date information on customer preferences, they can design products that meet customer preferences and expectations. Continuous monitoring of customer behavior, product design, and manufacturing process generated huge data that are considered as big data. Collecting, managing such huge data, and applying new analytical methods to gain insights and useful information and then apply them to decisions can reduce uncertainty [32]. Engineering design is defined as a process of transforming customer needs into design specifications [33]. Data science (DS) is defined as a process of transforming observed world reality data into comprehensible information for decision making [34]. Although different approaches are available for product design [35, 36], all of these methods are common in DS perspective. A schematic view of the design process is shown in **Figure 2**.

Big data are going to impact many industries, and product design is no exception. That is in part because engineers will increasingly design sensors and communication technology into their products. Therefore, in the process of supply chain design, the product specificities of the company must be considered, and all partners and constraints of the supply chain must be integrated at the design stage [37]. Supply chain design according to product design creates competitive advantage and flexibility in the supply chain [38]. Recently, BDA techniques have been used for product design and development, which lead to the production of new products according to customer preferences. Applying BDA to product design enables the designer to be constantly aware of customer preferences and expectations that lead to produce a product according to their needs and preferences [32]. Designers can use online behavior and customer purchase record data to predict and understand the customer needs [39]. Designers can identify product features and predict future product trends by continually monitoring the customer behavior and informing the customers' opinions and needs. In the automotive industry, the importance of big data is derived from the vehicle that shows huge performance data and customer needs [40]. The ultimate goal of companies producing consumer durables is to maintain their competitiveness over the longest possible period [41]. Nowadays, this is facilitated the implementation

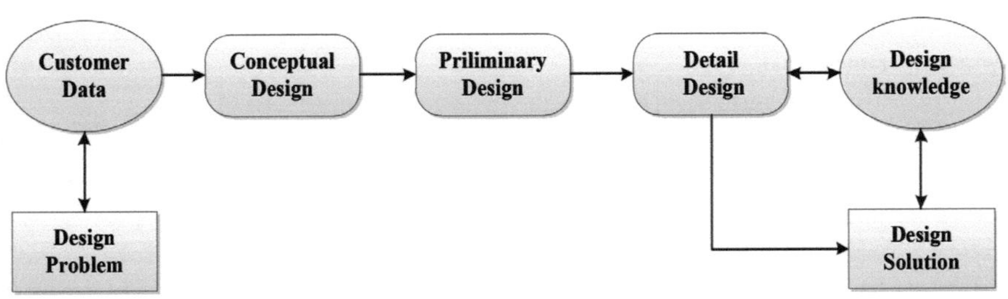

Figure 2.
Design process from data science view [32].

of the concept of (run-time) data-driven design. The recent developments of data analytics and application of data analytics tools have opened up a new path for generating knowledge for product enhancement and achieving their objectives [42]. As one doctrine, product developers can achieve a perpetual enhancement of their products and services based on real-life use, work, and failure data. Though numerous data analytic (software) tools and packages have been developed for extracting product-associated data, exploiting data analytic methods and tools in product enhancement is still in a rather premature stage [43]. Designers still face many challenges and should consider many limitations. Reportedly, choosing the most relevant data analytic tools (DATs) and using them in design projects are not trivial for designers [44].

Here are some other ways the design engineering might change as a result of big data it enables:

- Better-informed product development: How would the way organizations design product's change if they could learn not only how customers are using them, but also where they are having trouble with them and what features they are ignoring altogether? That information is going to be available to organizations soon. Mechanical engineers have the opportunity for product insights that were never possible before. With an Internet of Things (IoT)-enabled device, products can stream usage data back to engineers. Imagine, for example, a bike fork that captures force measurements or a utility cabinet that transmits internal temperature readings.

- More empowered engineering: Traditionally, engineers rely on marketers, customer visits, or their own best guesses to design the competitive products. However, big data could provide volumes of reliable feedback that none of those channels offer. Products are generating a lot of information during their lifecycle, and new trends for Internet of Things will bring even more information to manufacturing companies. A tremendous amount of data will be collected from connected devices, and this can be transformed into consumable information assets. Because products will be able to talk back to engineers, engineers will be empowered like never before to have a direct impact on the competitiveness of their products.

- Faster product development: As much more data reside on the cloud, more people can securely reach information faster (and at a lower cost) compared to working within corporate networks and specific platforms. That may lead to more participants and disciplines involved in the product development cycle early on. The IT infrastructure of cloud computing will enable new approaches for concurrent CAD design and system engineering principles combining mechanical, electrical, and software in product development.

Concluding with all these different disciplines in product design connected and accessing the big data throughout the various phases of the design cycle, the engineers will be confronted with many surprises and few unpleasant shocks as well. The real challenge will lie in solving these minute hassles and in developing better products reaching a new level in the product design as a whole.

4.4 BDA and demand planning

Many supply chain executives are keen to improve demand forecasting and production planning with big data [45]. Accurate demand forecast has always been a major puzzle in SCM [46]. Trace consumer loyalty, demand signal, and optimal price data can be determined by BDA. However, one of the challenges the organizations face is the ability to apply advanced hardware and software and algorithm architecture [47]. BDA allow to identify new market trends and determine root causes of issues, failures, and defects. Data analytics can predict customers' preferences and needs by examining customer behavior, which can drive creativity and innovation in business services [48]. In one study, a model was presented to predict the electric vehicle charging demand that used weather data and historical real-world traffic data. This model enables operators to plan the generation profiles and operation by determining the charging demand [49]. Another study presents a model for predicting demand for air passenger demand, which uses big data to estimate air passenger demand. The results of this study show a 5.3% prediction error [50].

4.5 BDA and procurement management

As tactical and operational decisions, procurement consists of a series of action mechanism and contracting [8]. Logistic organizations, given the high volume of widely dispersed data generated across different operations, systems, and geographic regions, need advanced systems to manage these enormous data, as well as skilled professionals who can analyze these data, and extract valuable insights and knowledge into them in order to apply them in their planning and decisions. In the past, organizations faced laborious processes that took several weeks to gather internal and structural data from the operations and transactions of the company and its partners. But today, at a significant speed, in real time, in many cases, all of the diverse structural, nonstructural, internal, and external data generated from automated processes are made available to these organizations. SCA can be used to manage suppliers' performance and supply chain risk [7]. In one study, external and internal big data have been used to quickly identify and manage the supply chain risk [51]. For example, informing the social media and news about exchange rate movement and disasters affects the supply chain. Applying this framework to identify supply chain risk enables real-time risk management monitoring, decision support, and emergency planning. Schlegel [52] also provided a big data predictive analytic framework to identify, evaluate, mitigate, and manage the supply chain risk.

4.6 BDA and customized production

With BDA, manufacturers can discover new information and identify patterns that enable them to improve processes, increase supply chain efficiency, and identify variables that affect production.

In today's global and interconnected environment, the supply chains and manufacturing processes involve long and complex processes; it should be possible to examine all components of each process and link supply chain in granular detail to simplify the processes and optimize the supply chain. Data analytics enables manufacturers to accurately determine each person's activities and tasks through timely and accurate data analysis of each part of the production process and examine entire supply chain in detail. This ability enables manufacturers to identify bottlenecks and reveal poorly performing processes and components. In the past, centralized production and production at scale were not rational because they focused only on the ordering of a small group of customers, while today's BDA have made it possible to accurately predict customer demands and tastes for customized products. Some studies have investigated the applied techniques of BDA in the production area. For example, Zhong et al. applied RFID-enabled big data to support shop floor logistic planning and scheduling [53]. He then implemented the Physical Internet concept by using the Internet of Things, wireless technology, and BDA to create an RFID-enabled intelligent shop floor environment [54]. Stich et al. have used BDA techniques to predict demand and production levels in manufacturing companies [55]. On the other hand, early additive manufacturing (also called 3D printing) was developed in the 1980s. This new technologies and trends are emerging that will change the rules of supply chain design and management [56]. 3D printing is any of various processes in which material is joined or solidified under computer control to create a three-dimensional object [57]. 3D printing is an innovative technology that makes possible to create a physical object from a digital model. Understanding the uses and implications of big data and predictive analytics will be urgent as additive manufacturing makes traditional models of production, distribution, and demand obsolete in some product areas [58].

4.7 BDA and inventory management

Inventory control is the system that involves requisition process, inventory management, purchase, and physical inventory reconciliation. The following key objectives define the design of inventory control:

- informing the quantity of goods in warehouse and also the amount of goods needed in the warehouse;
- facilitating the requisition process to finish in time;
- automatic recording and backorder serving;
- minimizing the inventory by analyzing previous purchasing and consumption patterns of the organization;
- using the automated tools to facilitate management of the inventory, servicing, and purchasing; and
- improving the financial control of the inventory through a timely and regular checkup of the inventory balances with the physical counts.

Big data by integrating business systems in distribution of nonperishable products improve operational efficiency on a broad scale while also delivering greater profitability. The benefits of using BDA in supply chains are listed below. Below are some ways the big data are changing the way companies manage inventory. Following are a few examples of ways big data manage inventory.

Improved operational efficiency: Due to the possibility of continuous monitoring and analysis of operational data by operational managers and better access to metrics, efficiency has improved, and bottlenecks have been removed. Big data increase efficiency and performance in whole supply chain.

Maximized sales and profits: Using the real-time data, financial managers can continuously monitor and analyze these data and manage the profit margins with greater insights to ensure maximum profitability from their investment.

Increased customer service satisfaction: The access to real-time data and the ability to timely analyze these data provide operational managers with the ability to match their inventory levels with customer orders and tastes, which will increase customer satisfaction. Data analysis techniques can also be used to predict spikes or depressions in customer demand and seasonal trends to accurately inventory planning at different times.

Reduced costs by migrating to the cloud: A Software-as-a-Service (SaaS) approach to IT management means that the cloud-based nature of big data reduces hardware and maintenance costs. It can also be seamlessly integrated to existing systems with a minimum of expense.

There are only two publications in the field of BDA applications in the inventory management in Perish or Publish Software. Big data create significant competitive advantage by connecting and integrating internal production system with external partners (customers and suppliers) in inventory management [59]. With the help of big data, an automated inventory control system can be designed [60]. Data analysis techniques can be used to analyze the data, extract the relationships between them, and predict the optimal rate of inventory ordering [7].

4.8 BDA and logistics

The logistic industry has undergone a fundamental transformation due to the emergence of large volumes of data and devices, emission concerns, complex regulatory laws, changing industry models, talent limitations, infrastructure, and rise of new technology. In this industry, the standardization of structure and the content of data interchanges must be given great importance to improve and facilitate communication and collaboration between different sectors, including shippers, manufacturers, logistic companies, distributors, and retailers, as well as to the creation of new common business processes. However, reducing costs by driving down excessive inventory, both staged and in-transit, proactively responding to inbound and outbound events and sharing assets has become critical in today's supply chain environment.

Today, due to the high volume of data generated from various sources such as sensors, scanners, GPS, and RFID tags, as well as due to integrating business judgment and fusing multiple data sources, powerful techniques are needed to quickly and timely analyze these data and provide real-time insights for a timely and accurate decision making. Given the high volume of orders and massive flow, huge data sets and methods for timely analysis are needed to manage and maintain them. Since high volumes of data such as size, weight, origin, and destination are being generated daily for millions of shipments, there is a huge potential for new business creation and operational efficiency and customer experience improvement. Organizations need data platforms and data analytic processes to pervade their insights into organizations, which are not easy, and it is a new challenge for organizations. Infosys offerings are designed to help logistic companies rethink, evolve, and achieve their vision through a three-pronged strategy:

- Boundary-less information: A strategic alliance has been created among customers, logistics enterprises, and suppliers in the logistic industry, and the huge data set produced by the industry is placed on logistic technologies such as Warehouse Management Solutions (WMS), Transport Management System (TMS), supply chain execution systems, and IOT devices to share and access all members. A platform in the supply chain manages and integrates a huge variety of data created from different internal and external systems and provides the right validations and governance to improve the trustworthiness of the data and make right data available to business users in a self-service manner for exploratory analysis and insight generation.

- Pervasive analytics: An open and adaptive framework is needed to integrate seamlessly the different insights into an organization and to apply them effectively.

- Progressive organization: The dynamic changes in markets and the emergence of advanced data management and analysis technologies as well as "boundary-less" paradigm make organizations to abandon traditional BI analytic methods and governance structures and use new advanced techniques. Organizations will become knowledge-based organizations that utilize powerful horizontal platform and supportive tools that are in line with associated security, next-gen data sets, and business semantic policies.

Many research studies pointed to the application of BDA in the areas of transportation, and logistics. BDA have been used to gain competitive advantage and provide new services in logistics [61]. Maritime companies have also used prescriptive and predictive BDA to solve their planning problems [62]. In another study, we have used big data to share transportation capacity in order to improve the efficiency of urban healthcare services [63]. It is an obvious fact that BDA can support all supply chain activities and processes and create a supply chain strategies/agiler logistics.

4.9 BDA and agile supply chain

The most successful organizations create supply chains that can respond to unexpected changes in the market [64]. Choi et al. argue that big data have significant effects on operation management practices [65]. Gunasekaran et al. further argue that supply chain disruptions have negative effects, and agile supply chain enablers were progressively used with the aid of big data and business analytics to achieve better competitive results [66, 67]. Srinivasan and Swink further argue that although BDA have been using to understand customer intentions/behaviors, the use of analytics for supply chain operational decisions is less understood [68]. Gunasekaran et al. [66] and [67] argue that big data and predictive analytics have positive effects on supply chain performance and organizational performance [67, 68]. Swafford et al. found that IT capability has positive effect on SCA [69]. Srinivasan and Swink noted that supply chain visibility is a prerequisite for building data analytic capability and vice versa [68]. Supply chain visibility and BDA are complementary in the sense that each supports the other [66, 67]. Supply chain visibility is a desired organizational capability to mitigate risk resulting from supply chain disruptions [70]. Following Srinivasan and Swink's arguments that organizations investing in building supply chain visibility capability are likely to invest in BDA [68], Dubey et al. found a positive impact of supply chain visibility on SCA [15]. By accurately anticipating consumer trends based on historical data, real-time data, and future predictions, organizations can put that knowledge to work to become more agile, efficient, and responsive.

Some other studies have been done to examine BDA that support the advanced supply chain agility [71]. Many parts and processes of the supply chain BDA have been widely used; however, publications regarding data analysis applications in the supply chain remain limited. Many parts and processes of the supply chain BDA have been widely used; however, publications regarding data analysis applications in strategic sourcing and inventory management are still limited. People working in this area should be able to extract knowledge and insight into the enormous data available and use it in their planning and decisions, and this is a challenge for them. Big chain analytics will help optimize decision making by aligning organization's strategy to the sourcing strategies and providing proper insights [7]. BDA also improve inventory decision through a better understanding of uncertain customer demand [72].

4.10 BDA and sustainable supply chain

Although sustainable SCM has been discussed in corporate offices for some time, actually implementing the sustainability phenomenon in the extended supply chain has proved difficult [73]. Nevertheless, large corporations perceive sustainability efforts as long-term investments aimed toward building strategic resources [74]. Corporations are increasingly interested in using BDA in their sustainable efforts, which in turn give them a strategic edge [75]. According to a Mckinsey survey report, companies using BDA are able to predict the 65% of customers that make repeated purchases through shop alerts and 75% of those customers reported that they are likely to use the service again [76].

Several scholars acknowledge sustainability (environmental, social, and financial) as an emerging area for BDA applications in business [77, 78]. Therefore, BDA techniques should be applied throughout the supply chain in order to achieve full benefits [79]. As decision making in organizations has been based on data, organizations must change their strategic capabilities, which affect sustainability. Given the growing importance of sustainability and BDA, organizations must integrate these two areas to achieve sustainable competitive advantage [78, 80]. Despite the pressing need to integrate data analysis with sustainability and supply chain measures, little progress has been made so far [81]. Few scholars have addressed this issue that to achieve strategic and competitive advantages, BDA and sustainability must be integrated [78, 80]. Today's organizations must use methods to analyze high volumes of data to gain insights and knowledge in order to achieve the three dimensions of environmental, social, and economic sustainability [82].

Some studies have used big data analysis to predict natural disasters to take preventive action against them, and simulation has been used reduce the effects of these environmental hazards [83]. Big data are also collected for melting glaciers, deforestation, and extreme weather through satellite images, weather radar, and terrestrial monitoring devices. Such data are used to comprehensively study global climate change and assign specific causality [21]. Big data have also been used for community health and welfare. For example, BDA have been used in Europe and USA to identifying and predicting prostate cancer biomarkers to take preventive measures at the right time [84, 85]. Another study applied policy-driven big data to support and improve sustainability measures in various operations. For instance, to protect the environment and take the sustainable measures, computer platforms are used to collect and share environmental data (i.e., big data), and such data have used for government-led publication of data on medical records for risk mitigation and research, among the other applications [86]. However, literature on the application of BDA for supply chain sustainability has been much less explored. Thus, scholars acknowledge the need for further exploration in this domain [75, 77, 87, 88]. Furthermore, for the supply chain to be sustainable, the potential risks disrupting operations must be identified and predicted. In the next section, the authors explore the literature related to supply chain risk management.

5. Application of BDA in different types of supply chain

In the current years, BDA practices have been extensively reported. One of the main reasons is to make full usage of the data to improve productivity, by providing "the valuable right information, for the right user, at the right time." In this section, an overview of BDA applications in different companies including manufacturing, finance, and healthcare is provided.

5.1 Application of BDA in manufacturing

Despite the importance of big data in today's world, many organizations overlook the importance of using big data for their organizational performance. Proper application of BDA techniques can be used to track, analyze, and also share employee performance metrics. BDA techniques also are used to identify employees with poor or excellent performance, as well as struggling or unhappy employees. These techniques allow organizations to monitor and analyze continuously real-time data, rather than just annual investigations based on human memory. In today's world, the manufacturing industry must use advanced data analytic technologies to gain competitive advantage and improve productivity in design, production, sales, and timely product delivery processes. Approximately, manufacturing industry stores 2 exabytes of new data in 2010 [89]. Since in production lines and factories, various electronic devices, digital machineries, and sensors are used, and a huge amount of data is generated. Therefore, BDA can be used to build intelligent shop floor logistic system in factories [54, 90]. A huge amount of data also creates from design and manufacturing engineering process in the form of CAM and CAE models, CAD, process performance data, product failure data, internet transaction, and so on. Data analysis techniques can be applied to defect tracking and product quality and to improve activities of the product manufacturing process in manufacturing [91].

Data analysis techniques can also be used to predict customer demands and tastes. Raytheon Corp manufacturing company has develop smart factories through the powerful capacity of handling huge data that collect from various sources including instruments, sensors, CAD models, Internet transactions, digital records, and simulations that enable the company in real-time control of multiple activities of the production process [92]. General electric creates innovative and efficient servicing strategies by continuous observation and analysis of huge data obtained from various sensors in manufactured products including in GE's case, jet engines, locomotives, medical imaging devices, and gas turbines [93]. Schmitz Cargobull, a German truck body and trailer maker, uses sensor data, telecommunication, and BDA to monitor cargo weight and temperatures, routes, and maintenance of its trailers to minimize their usage breakdown [94]. Toyota Motor Corporation to dramatically improve its data management capabilities launches Toyota Connected as their Big Data Business Unit. Toyota also uses vehicle big data collected from connected car platform to create new business and service such as adding security and safety service and to create mobility service, traffic information service, and feedback to design [95]. The integration of BDA into manufacturing system design should move from a descriptive to a predictive system performance model over a period of time, such as using what-if analysis, cause-effect model, and simulation [96].

5.2 Application of BDA in finance

Maintaining the sustainable competitive advantage and enhancing the efficiency are important goals of financial institutions. In order to achieve sustainable competitive advantage and stay afloat in the industry, these institutions must continually use big data and appropriate analytic techniques into their business strategy. In recent years, there has been a great deal of improvement in big data and analytic techniques, and there has been a lot of investment in them. Banks and financial service organizations using big data and analytical techniques gain valuable knowledge and insights that can be used in continuous monitoring of client behavior in real time, predict their wants and needs, and provide the exact resource and service according to customer's requests and needs. Using the findings of this real-time data analysis and evaluation result in turn, it enhances overall profitability and performance. After the 2008 global financial crisis, financial institutions need to use big data and analytic techniques to gain competitive advantage [2]. Due to the high volume of financial transactions and activities, the application of big data and analytic techniques is very necessary and important in most of the financial organizations such as asset management, insurance companies, banks, and capital market. Organizations need to be able to manage their huge data and extract the knowledge and insight contained in these data and then use them in all their business processes and decision making. Bean reported that 70% of global financial service organization thought BDA was important and 63% has applied big data in their organizations [97]. According to Technavio, costs of big data technology in the global financial industry will grow by 26% from 2015 to 2019, which suggests the importance of big data in this industry [98]. BDA techniques provide important insights through continuous monitoring of customer behaviors and data analysis, which improve customer intelligence such as customer risk analysis, customer centricity, and customer retention. BDA is applied to all transactions and activities of the financial service industry, including forecasting and creating new services and products, algorithmic trading and analytics, organizational intelligence (such as employee collaboration), and algorithmic trading and analytics. BDA is also used to support risk management and regulatory reporting activities [99]. Chief Financial Officer (CFO) should use analytic techniques to analyze data of big data and extract knowledge and insights into them and then use information and knowledge in their strategic decision making. Therefore, Chief Financial Officer (CFO) can apply a business analytics and intelligence tool to improve data accuracy, make better decisions, and provide greater value [100]. Data analysis techniques can also be used in financial markets to examine the market volatility and calculate VPIN [101]. Financial institutions can use real-time decision making and predictive modeling to gain a competitive advantage in the dynamic financial markets [102]. The Barclays Finance Company has widely used big data to support its operations and create and maintain primary competitive advantage. They apply big data in many areas such as financial crime, treasury, financial crime, risk, intelligence, and finance [103]. Deutsche Bank also has applied the big data in their businesses. Deutsche Bank has set up a Data Lab that provides internal data, analytics consultancy, test-out business idea, and technology support to other division and business function [104].

5.3 Application of BDA in healthcare

In the health industry, a large amount of data is generated to control and monitor the various processes of treatment, protection, and management of patients' medical records, regulatory requirements, and compliance. Big data in healthcare are critical due to the various types of data that have been emerging in modern biomedical including omics, electronic health records, sensor data and text, and imaging, which are complex, heterogeneous, high-dimensional, generally unstructured, and poorly annotated. Modern and strong techniques are needed to quickly manage and analyze these data. "Big data" in the healthcare industry include all data related to well-being and patient healthcare. According to the report of US Congress in August 2012, big data are defined as "large volumes of high velocity, complex, and variable data that require advanced techniques and technologies to enable the capture, storage, distribution, management, and analysis of the information." Big data in healthcare encompass such characteristics as high-dimensional, variety, heterogeneous, velocity, generally unstructured, poorly annotated, and, with respect specifically to healthcare, veracity. Big data in the healthcare industry include these characteristics of high-dimensional, variety, heterogeneous, velocity, generally unstructured, poorly annotated, and, with respect specifically to healthcare, veracity. Application of analytical techniques in Medical Healthcare System includes image detection, lesion detection, speech recognition, visual recognition, and so on. Existing analytical techniques can be applied to the vast amount of existing (but currently unanalyzed) patient-related health and medical data to reach a deeper understanding of outcomes, which then can be applied at the point of care. A large amount of diverse healthcare data from personal medical records to radiology images, laboratory instrument reading, and population data is, and human genetics currently being created, requiring robust, modern systems for protection and maintenance. Big data reduce healthcare costs and also improve the accuracy, speed, quality, and effectiveness of healthcare systems. Bort reported on combating influenza based on flu report by providing near real-time view [105]. Other big data initiatives were to monitor inhaler usage and reduce the risk of the asthma attack and cancer [106]. BDA can also help health insurance companies to identify fraud and anomaly in a claim, which is difficult to detect by the common transaction processing system [107]. Big data application has many values in healthcare including right care, right living, right innovation, right provider, and right value [108]. Big data can be used to population health management and preventive care as a new application of Huge Data in the future [106]. Despite the high potential of using massive data in healthcare, there are many challenges, for example, improving the available platform to better support the easy friendly package, a menu driven, data processing, and more real times. There are also other challenges in using big data in the healthcare industry including data acquisition continuity, ownership, standardized data, and data cleansing [109].

6. Analytics in supply chain

Big data create different capabilities in the supply chain that provides networks with greater data accuracy, insights, and clarity and also create a greater e-contextual intelligence shared across the supply chains. Big data are a powerful tool for solving supply chain issues and driving supply chains ahead. For example, currently, BDA techniques have applied in the retail supply chains to observe customer behaviors by accurately predicting the customer tastes and preferences. Supply chain decision makers to succeed in today's competitive markets must always seek ways to effectively integrate and manage big data sources to gain more values and competitive advantage. The effective and appropriate use of big data sources and techniques resulted in enormous improvements in processes of supply chain:

- Building agile or responsive supply chains through predicting and gaining a better understanding of the market trends and customer expectations and preferences. BDA can facilitate the real-time monitoring of supply chain and managing of data that enhance the speed, quality, accuracy, and flexibility of supply chain decision. Utilize a wide range of data from news, social media, weather data (SNEW), and events as well as direct data inputs from multiple static and dynamic data points provide the capability to predict and proactively plan all supply chain activities.

- Building reliable and intelligent supply chains through the application of Internet of Things (IoT), machine learning, and deep learning techniques in each supply chain activities. For instance, IoT can provide real-time telemetry data by the real-time monitoring of supply chain to reveal the details of production processes. Machine learning algorithms that are trained to analyze the data can accurately predict imminent machine failures. Deep learning techniques can also be used to accurately predict customers' demand and their preferences and expectations.

- Supporting the creation of sustainability in SCM. BDA undoubtedly will enhance social, environmental, and financial performance measures. For example, detailed planning for timely delivery of the product can be done by analyzing the real-time traffic data provided by the GPS that reduces production of carbon emission and the cost of fuel consumption.

- Enabling global supply chains to adopt a preventive rather than a reactive measures to supply chain risks (e.g., supply failures due to natural hazards or fabricated, contextual and operational disruptions). In a more complex global supply chain, BDA techniques can help supply chain managers to predict external future events and adopt a proactive against them.

BDA can also be applied across the end-to-end supply chain. For instance, the points of sales (POS) data on retailers provide real-time demand data with price information. It gives the signal for replenishment such as in the vendor managed inventory system. RFID data provide automated replenishment signal, automated receiving and storing information, and automated checkout data, which inform the real-time inventory status. Supplier data provide important data about suppliers and ordering processes that can help the supplier risk management and better coordination with supplier processes. Manufacturing sensor data provide real-time monitoring of manufacturing equipment and identify an inevitable problem. During the delivery process, GPS data provide real-time inventory location data and help in finding optimal routes and reducing inventory lead times and fulfillment [110].

Despite the potential use of big data, many supply chains are unable to harness the power of BDA techniques to generate useful knowledge and insights into available data for their businesses. The underlying reasons are due to the lack of ability to apply appropriate techniques for big data analysis, which result in significant cost reduction [110]. Therefore, the efforts to strengthen the BDA capabilities in supply chain are considered as an important factor for the success of all supply chains [2].

7. Conclusion and managerial implications

BDA have become an important practical issue in many areas such as SCM. There are many scopes for advancement in the application of appropriate analytic techniques in this area. As stated in previous literature [7–9], there are a variety of techniques and fundamental applications in the SCM (e.g., predictive, descriptive, and prescriptive). This chapter tries to demonstrate some of the most fundamental and recent applications of BDA within the SCM and also notice some of these techniques in SCM that are critical for managers. BDA have important applications across the end-to-end supply chain. BDA have many important applications across the end-to-end supply chain. For example, this is applied in various areas of SCM including the demand data at the sales department, retailer data, delivery data, manufacturing data, and until supplier data. BDA are also used in various supply chain activities and support them, including supplier relationship management, product design, development, demand planning, inventory, network design, production, procurement, until logistics and distribution, as well as the reverse. Applying big data sources and analytics techniques have led to many improvements in supply chain processes. Furthermore, BDA can support the development and improvement of responsive, reliable, and/or sustainable supply chain. BDA can able to manage and integrate huge sets of diverse data in a complex global supply chain. Many researchers have applied various techniques of BDA across different industries including the healthcare finance/banking and manufacturing. Other industries such as hospitality, technology, energy, and other service industry will also take advantage of BDA techniques. Depending on the contexts used and the strategic requirements of organizations, different techniques of BDA are applied. The culture, politics, environment, and the management team within the organization are very critical factors in decision making. Since, sufficient resources with analytic capabilities become the biggest challenges for many today's supply chain. Supply chain has to establish close and continuous links between data experts and their business function and also apply appropriate BDA techniques according to the context of their application in their decision making, processes, and activities to answer the question of how data can help drive supply chain result. Hence, mutual coordination and cooperation between different supply chain units must be established, use BDA techniques to link these units, and exist an ability to share and access data and information throughout the entire supply chain.

Author details

Saeid Sadeghi Darvazeh*, Iman Raeesi Vanani and Farzaneh Mansouri Musolu
Department of Industrial Management, Faculty of Management and Accounting, Allameh Tabataba'I University, Tehran, Iran

*Address all correspondence to: saeid.sadeghi@atu.ac.ir

References

[1] Kaisler S, Armour F, Espinosa JA, Money W. Big data: Issues and challenges moving forward. In: 2013 46th Hawaii International Conference on System Sciences. IEEE; 7 Jan 2013. pp. 995-1004

[2] Tiwari S, Wee HM, Daryanto Y. Big data analytics in supply chain management between 2010 and 2016: Insights to industries. Computers and Industrial Engineering. 2018;**115**:319-330

[3] Addo-Tenkorang R, Helo PT. Big data applications in operations/supply-chain management: A literature review. Computers and Industrial Engineering. 2016;**101**:528-543

[4] White M. Digital workplaces: Vision and reality. Business Information Review. 2012;**29**(4):205-214

[5] Akter S, Wamba SF, Gunasekaran A, Dubey R, Childe SJ. How to improve firm performance using big data analytics capability and business strategy alignment? International Journal of Production Economics. 2016;**182**:113-131

[6] Zhong RY, Newman ST, Huang GQ, Lan S. Big data for supply chain management in the service and manufacturing sectors: Challenges, opportunities, and future perspectives. Computers & Industrial Engineering. 2016;**101**:572-591

[7] Wang G, Gunasekaran A, Ngai EW, Papadopoulos T. Big data analytics in logistics and supply chain management: Certain investigations for research and applications. International Journal of Production Economics. 2016;**176**:98-110

[8] Souza GC. Supply chain analytics. Business Horizons. 2014;**57**(5):595-605

[9] Trkman P, McCormack K, De Oliveira MP, Ladeira MB. The impact of business analytics on supply chain performance. Decision Support Systems. 2010;**49**(3):318-327

[10] Barbosa MW, Vicente AD, Ladeira MB, Oliveira MP. Managing supply chain resources with big data analytics: A systematic review. International Journal of Logistics Research and Applications. 2018;**21**(3):177-200

[11] Lamba K, Singh SP. Big data in operations and supply chain management: Current trends and future perspectives. Production Planning and Control. 2017;**28**(11-12):877-890

[12] Nguyen T, Li ZH, Spiegler V, Ieromonachou P, Lin Y. Big data analytics in supply chain management: A state-of-the-art literature review. Computers and Operations Research. 2018;**98**:254-264

[13] Schoenherr T, Speier-Pero C. Data science, predictive analytics, and big data in supply chain management: Current state and future potential. Journal of Business Logistics. 2015;**36**(1):120-132

[14] Mishra D, Luo Z, Jiang S, Papadopoulos T, Dubey R. A bibliographic study on big data: Concepts, trends and challenges. Business Process Management Journal. 2017;**23**(3):555-573

[15] Dubey R, Altay N, Gunasekaran A, Blome C, Papadopoulos T, Childe SJ. Supply chain agility, adaptability and alignment: Empirical evidence from the Indian auto components industry. International Journal of Operations & Production Management. 2018;**38**(1):129-148

[16] Gupta S, Altay N, Luo Z. Big data in humanitarian supply chain management: A review and further research directions. Ann. Oper. Res. 2017:1-21

[17] Zhao R, Liu Y, Zhang N, Huang T. An optimization model for green supply chain management by using a big data analytic approach. Journal of Cleaner Production. 2017;**142**:1085-1097

[18] Song ML, Fisher R, Wang JL, Cui LB. Environmental performance evaluation with big data: Theories and methods. Ann. Oper. Res. 2018;**270**(1-2):459-472

[19] Fan Y, Heilig L, Voß S. Supply chain risk management in the era of big data. In: International Conference of Design, User Experience, and Usability. Cham: Springer; 2015. pp. 283-294

[20] Mele FD, Musulin E, Puigjaner L. Supply chain monitoring: A statistical approach. Computer Aided Chemical Engineering. 1 Jan 2005;**20**:1375-1380

[21] Kambatla K, Kollias G, Kumar V, Grama A. Trends in big data analytics. Journal of Parallel and Distributed Computing. 2014;**74**(7):2561-2573

[22] Ranjan R. Modeling and simulation in performance optimization of big data processing frameworks. IEEE Cloud Computing. 2014;**1**(4):14-19

[23] Shao G, Shin SJ, Jain S. Data analytics using simulation for smart manufacturing. In: Proceedings of the Winter Simulation Conference. IEEE; 7 Dec 2014. pp. 2192-2203

[24] LLamasoft. Supply chain simulation: why its time has come. 2016. LLamasoft white paper, 14/08/16. <http://www.llamasoft.com/supply-chain-simulation-time-come-white-paper/>

[25] Balaraj S. Optimization model for improving supply chain visibility. Infosys Labs Briefings. 2013;**11**(1):9-19

[26] Slavakis K, Giannakis GB, Mateos G. Modeling and optimization for big data analytics:(statistical) learning tools for our era of data deluge. IEEE Signal Processing Magazine. 2014;**31**(5):18-31

[27] Panchmatia M. Use Big Data to Help Procurement' Make a Real Difference. 2015

[28] Jin Y, Ji S. Partner choice of supply chain based on 3d printing and big data. Information Technology Journal. 2013;**12**(22):6822

[29] Wang G, Gunasekaran A, Ngai EW. Distribution network design with big data: Model and analysis. Annals of Operations Research. 2018;**270**(1-2):539-551

[30] Prasad S, Zakaria R, Altay N. Big data in humanitarian supply chain networks: A resource dependence perspective. Annals of Operations Research. 2018;**270**(1-2):383-413

[31] Afshari H, Peng Q. Using big data to minimize uncertainty effects in adaptable product design. In: ASME 2015 International Design Engineering Technical Conferences and Computers and Information in Engineering Conference. American Society of Mechanical Engineers; 2015. pp. V004T05A052-V004T05A052

[32] Suh NP, Suh NP. Axiomatic Design: Advances and Applications. New York: Oxford university press; 2001

[33] Mistree F, Smith WF, Bras B, Allen JK, Muster D. Decision-Based Design: A Contemporary Paradigm for Ship Design. Vol. 98. Transactions, Society of Naval Architects and Marine Engineers; 1990. pp. 565-597

[34] Dym CL, Little P. Engineering Design: A Project-Based Introduction. John Wiley and Sons; 1999

[35] Martin MV, Ishii K. Design for variety: Developing standardized and modularized product platform

architectures. Research in Engineering Design. 2002;**13**(4):213-235

[36] Labbi O, Ouzizi L, Douimi M. Simultaneous Design of a Product and its Supply Chain Integrating Reverse Logistic Operations: An Optimization Model. 2015

[37] Khan O, Christopher M, Creazza A. Aligning product design with the supply chain: A case study. Supply Chain Management: An International Journal. 2012;**17**(3):323-336

[38] Jin J, Liu Y, Ji P, Liu H. Understanding big consumer opinion data for market-driven product design. International Journal of Production Research. 2016;**54**(10):3019-3041

[39] Johanson M, Belenki S, Jalminger J, Fant M, Gjertz M. Big automotive data: Leveraging large volumes of data for knowledge-driven product development. In: 2014 IEEE International Conference on Big Data (Big Data). IEEE; 2014. pp. 736-741

[40] Shapiro N. Competition and aggregate demand. Journal of Post Keynesian Economics. 2005;**27**(3):541-549

[41] Li Y, Thomas MA, Osei-Bryson KM. A snail shell process model for knowledge discovery via data analytics. Decision Support Systems. 2016;**91**:1-2

[42] Baraka Z. Opportunities to manage big data efficiently and effectively (Doctoral dissertation, Dublin Business School). 2014

[43] Andrienko N, Andrienko G. Exploratory analysis of spatial and temporal data: A systematic approach. Springer Science & Business Media; 28 Mar 2006

[44] Chase CW Jr. Using big data to enhance demand-driven forecasting and planning. The Journal of Business Forecasting. 2013;**32**(2):27

[45] Feng Q, Shanthikumar JG. How research in production and operations management may evolve in the era of big data. Production and Operations Management. 2018;**27**(9):1670-1684

[46] Hassani H, Silva ES. Forecasting with big data: A review. Annals of Data Science. 2015;**2**(1):5-19

[47] Balar A, Malviya N, Prasad S, Gangurde A. Forecasting consumer behavior with innovative value proposition for organizations using big data analytics. In: 2013 IEEE International Conference on Computational Intelligence and Computing Research. IEEE; 2013. pp. 1-4

[48] Arias MB, Bae S. Electric vehicle charging demand forecasting model based on big data technologies. Applied Energy. 2016;**183**:327-339

[49] Kim S. Forecasting short-term air passenger demand using big data from search engine queries. Automation in Construction. 2016;**70**:98-108

[50] Fan J, Han F, Liu H. Challenges of big data analysis. National Science Review. 2014;**1**(2):293-314

[51] Leveling J, Edelbrock M, Otto B. Big data analytics for supply chain management. In: 2014 IEEE International Conference on Industrial Engineering and Engineering Management. IEEE; 9 Dec 2014. pp. 918-922

[52] Schlegel GL. Utilizing big data and predictive analytics to manage supply chain risk. The Journal of Business Forecasting. 2014;**33**(4):11

[53] Zhong RY, Huang GQ, Lan SL. Shopfloor logistics management using rfid-enabled big data under physical

internet. In: Proceeding of 1st International Physical Internet Conference. 2014. pp. 1-14

[54] Zhong RY, Huang GQ, Lan S, Dai QY, Chen X, Zhang T. A big data approach for logistics trajectory discovery from RFID-enabled production data. International Journal of Production Economics. 2015;**165**:260-272

[55] Stich V, Jordan F, Birkmeier M, Oflazgil K, Reschke J, Diews A. Big data technology for resilient failure management in production systems. In: IFIP International Conference on Advances in Production Management Systems. Cham: Springer; 2015. pp. 447-454

[56] Bird J. Exploring the 3D printing opportunity. The Financial Times. Retrieved. 2012:08-30

[57] Excell J, Nathan S. The rise of additive manufacturing. The engineer. 24 May 2010;**24**

[58] Waller MA, Fawcett SE. Data science, predictive analytics, and big data: A revolution that will transform supply chain design and management. Journal of Business Logistics. 2013;**34**(2):77-84

[59] Cohen MA. Inventory Management in the Age of Big Data. Harvard Business Review. 2015. Available from: https://hbr.org/2015/06/inventory-management-in-the-age-of-bigdata

[60] Sharma M, Garg N. Inventory control and big data. In: Optimal Inventory Control and Management Techniques. IGI Global; 2016. pp. 222-235

[61] Ayed AB, Halima MB, Alimi AM. Big data analytics for logistics and transportation. In: 2015 4th International Conference on Advanced Logistics and Transport (ICALT). IEEE; 20 May 2015. pp. 311-316

[62] Brouer BD, Karsten CV, Pisinger D. Big data optimization in maritime logistics. In: Big Data Optimization: Recent Developments and Challenges. Cham: Springer; 2016. pp. 319-344

[63] Mehmood R, Graham G. Big data logistics: A health-care transport capacity sharing model. Procedia Computer Science. 2015;**64**:1107-1114

[64] Lee HL. The triple-a supply chain. Harvard Business Review. 2004;**82**(10):102-113

[65] Choi TM, Wallace SW, Wang Y. Big data analytics in operations management. Production and Operations Management. 2018;**27**(10):1868-1883

[66] Gunasekaran A, Papadopoulos T, Dubey R, Wamba SF, Childe SJ, Hazen B, et al. Big data and predictive analytics for supply chain and organizational performance. Journal of Business Research. 2017;**70**:308-317

[67] Gunasekaran A, Yusuf YY, Adeleye EO, Papadopoulos T. Agile manufacturing practices: The role of big data and business analytics with multiple case studies. International Journal of Production Research. 2018;**56**(1-2):385-397

[68] Srinivasan R, Swink M. An investigation of visibility and flexibility as complements to supply chain analytics: An organizational information processing theory perspective. Production and Operations Management. 2018;**27**(10):1849-1867

[69] Swafford PM, Ghosh S, Murthy N. Achieving supply chain agility through IT integration and flexibility. International Journal of Production Economics. 2008;**116**(2):288-297

[70] Jüttner U, Maklan S. Supply chain resilience in the global financial crisis:

An empirical study. Supply Chain Management: An International Journal. 2011;**16**(4):246-259

[71] Giannakis M, Louis M. A multi-agent based system with big data processing for enhanced supply chain agility. Journal of Enterprise Information Management. 2016;**29**(5):706-727

[72] Bertsimas D, Kallus N, Hussain A. Inventory management in the era of big data. Production and Operations Management. 2016;**25**(12):2006-2009

[73] Brockhaus S, Kersten W, Knemeyer AM. Where do we go from here? Progressing sustainability implementation efforts across supply chains. Journal of Business Logistics. 2013;**34**(2):167-182

[74] McWilliams A, Siegel DS. Creating and capturing value: Strategic corporate social responsibility, resource-based theory, and sustainable competitive advantage. Journal of Management. 2011;**37**(5):1480-1495

[75] Jelinek M, Bergey P. Innovation as the strategic driver of sustainability: Big data knowledge for profit and survival. IEEE Engineering Management Review. 2013;**41**(2):14-22

[76] Manyika J, Sinclair J, Dobbs R, Strube G, Rassey L, Mischke J, et al. Manufacturing the Future: The Next Era of Global Growth and Innovation. McKinsey Global Institute; https://www.mckinsey.com/business-functions/operations/our-insights/the-future-of-manufacturing

[77] Hazen BT, Skipper JB, Ezell JD, Boone CA. Big data and predictive analytics for supply chain sustainability: A theory-driven research agenda. Computers and Industrial Engineering. 2016;**101**:592-598

[78] Hsu J. Big Business, Big Data, Big Sustainability. Carbontrust.com. Oct 2013

[79] Davenport TH. Competing on analytics. Harvard Business Review. 2006;**84**(1):98

[80] Hsu J. Why big data will have an impact on sustainability. The Guardian. 2014. Available online: http://www.theguardian.com/sustainable-business/big-dataimpact-sustainable-business [Accessed: 31 January 2014]

[81] Keeso A. Big data and environmental sustainability: A conversation starter. Smith School of Enterprise and the Environment. Working Paper Series. Dec 2014. (14-04)

[82] Garetti M, Taisch M. Sustainable manufacturing: Trends and research challenges. Production Planning and Control. 2012;**23**(2-3):83-104

[83] Belaud JP, Negny S, Dupros F, Michéa D, Vautrin B. Collaborative simulation and scientific big data analysis: Illustration for sustainability in natural hazards management and chemical process engineering. Computers in Industry. 2014;**65**(3):521-535

[84] Bettencourt-Silva JH, Clark J, Cooper CS, Mills R, Rayward-Smith VJ, De La Iglesia B. Building data-driven pathways from routinely collected hospital data: A case study on prostate cancer. JMIR Medical Informatics. 2015;**3**(3):e26

[85] Halamka JD. Early experiences with big data at an academic medical center. Health Affairs. 2014;**33**(7):1132-1138

[86] Baek H, Park SK. Sustainable development plan for Korea through expansion of green IT: Policy issues for the effective utilization of big data. Sustainability. 2015;**7**(2):1308-1328

[87] Dubey R, Gunasekaran A, Childe SJ, Wamba SF, Papadopoulos T. The impact of big data on world-class

sustainable manufacturing. The International Journal of Advanced Manufacturing Technology. 2016;**84**(1-4):631-645

[88] Shen B, Chan HL. Forecast information sharing for managing supply chains in the big data era: Recent development and future research. Asia-Pacific Journal of Operational Research. 2017;**34**(01):1740001

[89] Nedelcu B. About big data and its challenges and benefits in manufacturing. Database Systems Journal. 2013;**4**(3):10-19

[90] Zhong RY, Xu C, Chen C, Huang GQ. Big data analytics for physical internet-based intelligent manufacturing shop floors. International Journal of Production Research. 2017;**55**(9):2610-2621

[91] Wang L, Alexander CA. Big data in design and manufacturing engineering. American Journal of Engineering and Applied Sciences. 2015;**8**(2):223

[92] Noor A. Putting big data to work. Mechanical Engineering. 2013;**135**(10):32-37

[93] Davenport T. The Future of the Manufacturing Workforce. Report One: Technology and the Manufacturing Workforce: An Overview. Milwaukee; 2013

[94] Chick S, Netessine S, Huchzermeier A. When big data meets manufacturing. Instead Knowledge; 2014

[95] Toyota Motor Corporation. Toyota's Connected Strategy Briefing. 2016. Available from: http://newsroom.toyota.co.jp/en/detail/14129306/

[96] Cochran DS, Kinard D, Bi Z. Manufacturing system design meets big data analytics for continuous improvement. Procedia CIRP. 2016;**50**:647-652

[97] Bean R. Just using big data isn't enough anymore. Harvard Business Review. 2016;**2**:2016

[98] Technavio. Global Big Data IT Spending in Financial Sector - Market Research 2015-2019. Available from: https://www.technavio.com/report/global-big-data-it-spending-infinancial-sector-marketresearch-2015-2019

[99] Connors S, Courbe J, Waishampayan V. Where have you been all my life? How the financial services industry can unlock the value in Big Data. PwC Financial Services Viewpoint; 2013

[100] Chen H, Chiang RH, Storey VC. Business intelligence and analytics: From big data to big impact. MIS Quarterly. 2012;**36**(4)

[101] Wu K, Bethel E, Gu M, Leinweber D, Rübel O. A big data approach to analyzing market volatility. Algorithmic Finance. 2013;**2**(3-4):241-267

[102] Peat M. Big data in finance. InFinance: The Magazine for Finsia Members. 2013;**127**(1):34

[103] Barclays. Big Data: Getting to grips with a rapidly changing landscape. 2015. Available from: https://www.barclayscorporate.com/content/dam/corppublic/corporate/Documents/insight/Big-Data-report.pdf

[104] Bank D. Big Data: How it can become a differentiator. Deutsche Bank White Paper. Interactive. 2014. Available from: http://www.cib.db.com/insights-and-initiatives/flow/35187.htm

[105] Bort J. How the CDC is using Big Data to save you from the flu. Available from: http://www.businessinsider.com/the-cdc-is-using-big-data-to-combat-flu-2012-12

[106] Nambiar R, Bhardwaj R, Sethi A, Vargheese R. A look at challenges and

opportunities of big data analytics in healthcare. In: 2013 IEEE international conference on Big Data. IEEE; 6 Oct 2013. pp. 17-22

[107] Srinivasan U, Arunasalam B. Leveraging big data analytics to reduce healthcare costs. IT Professional. 2013;**15**(6):21-28

[108] Groves P, Kayyali B, Knott D, Kuiken SV. The 'Big Data' Revolution in Healthcare: Accelerating Value and Innovation

[109] Raghupathi W, Raghupathi V. Big data analytics in healthcare: Promise and potential. Health Information Science and Systems. 2014;**2**(1):3

[110] Rowe S, Pournader M. Supply Chain Big Data Series Part 1. KPMG Australia. Available from: https://assets.kpmg.com/content/dam/kpmg/au/pdf/2017/big-data-analytics-supply-chainperformance.pdf.2017